DOCTRINE
AND
EXPERIENCE

DOCTRINE AND EXPERIENCE

Essays in American Philosophy

Edited by
VINCENT G. POTTER

FORDHAM UNIVERSITY PRESS
New York
1988

Printed in the United States of America

CONTENTS

PREFACE

The publication of these essays is the outcome of a decade of collaboration and of two United States bicentennial celebrations. Their original preparation was occasioned by the bicentennial of American Independence in celebration of which Fordham University's philosophy department planned to run a special series of public lectures on American Philosophy during the Fall semester of 1976. Professor John McDermott, then at Queens College of The City University of New York, agreed to organize and coordinate the lectures, one of which he himself was to give. In conjunction with this public lecture series the department offered two graduate seminars, one on the Master's level (which I directed) and one on the Doctoral level (directed by Professor McDermott). One of the attractive features of this arrangement was that the lecturers held a session with each seminar at which they discussed the lecture topic and answered questions.

The credit for this wonderful format goes to Professor McDermott to whom the department and the participating students owe a debt of gratitude for bringing together from all over the United States such a distinguished company of experts in American Philosophy. I wish to take this opportunity to express my personal appreciation for his generous help in making the seminars and the lecture series such a success.

A second bicentennial has now been celebrated. During the intervening years Professor McDermott and I had hoped to get that series of lectures published. Finally, having overcome various obstacles (monetary and editorial), we are pleased to present these essays as the fruit of that lecture series. We think they form a splendid collection and we hope that the reader will find them both informative and entertaining.

We consider the timing fortunate. Just as the drafting of the United States Constitution in 1787 was the fruit of what had been sown in 1776, so the completion of these essays in 1987 is the fruit of what had been sown in 1976. We trust that this volume will be welcomed not only by the specialist in American Philosophy, but also by anyone interested in the intellectual and cultural history of the United States.

Fordham University   VINCENT G. POTTER
July 1987

DOCTRINE
AND
EXPERIENCE

INTRODUCTION

THE ORDER IN WHICH the materials are presented here is not that of the original lecture series, but rather one which is roughly chronological. In this way we hope to highlight the changes and developments in thought from Puritanism to Pragmatism to Process Philosophy. The period of American Philosophy frequently called "classical" has been given the most space and emphasis. Post–World War II influences on American thought are not taken up in this collection even though the present state of philosophy in the United States cannot be fully understood without them.

TITLE AND THEME

Perhaps a word should be said about the title "Doctrine and Experience." It was chosen with some care and deliberation. One of the most noticeable features of "classical" American philosophy is the prominent role given to "experience" in human knowing and doing. Of course, in itself an appeal to experience is nothing new in philosophy. Both rationalists and empiricists have done so for centuries. What the pragmatists attempted, however, was to "recover" the richness and fullness of experience lost at the hands of the empiricists and positivists. Peirce, James, and Dewey, for example, looked upon experience as the rich womb of novelty, creativity, and knowledge. It was no longer merely the barren and austere depository of sense impressions. Hence, all human conscious activity is connected with and rooted in experience in this pregnant sense.

Over against "experience" there was for the "classical" American philosophers "doctrine," that is, "what is learned" and so what is handed down. "Doctrine" in this sense comes close to "tradition" and so connotes "belief" rather than "experience," even though, of course, belief in doctrine handed down can be, and perhaps should be, supported by "experience." No doubt, too, what comes to be believed by one generation (and so becomes what they hand down to the next) is modified in appropriate ways by experience.

In this regard, let it be clearly understood that these American thinkers were very wary of anything "dogmatic." They held to "free-thinking" in the literal sense. Uncritical beliefs that frequently take the form of absolutes block the road to inquiry and so become obscurantist. Hence, the classical American philosophers wished to submit doctrine (and belief) to the test of experience (and knowledge.)

But even more than this is implied in the use of "experience" and "doctrine." More generally this distinction is meant to cover all sorts of dialectical tensions of which "what is experienced" and "what is handed down" is but one, even if, perhaps, the major one. Clearly a special case of this tension is between faith and reason, which, while not peculiar to American thinkers, was one of their great preoccupations. Again, this dialectical tension showed itself in the relation of theory and practice that was at the heart of the pragmatic movement. The strong recent interest in American pragmatism shown by German philosophers is in part due to this attempt to deal with that relation. They see it as an interesting alternative to, or at least a corrective of, the Marxist version.

The Essays

The first essay, "Jonathan Edwards and the Great Awakening" by John E. Smith, takes up the experience–doctrine tension precisely in its faith–reason form. Smith argues that although Edwards favored "experimental religion" and the "new sense of the heart" in religious matters, he, at the same time, fought the excesses and exaggerations that sometimes marked "revivalism." Edwards wished to find a middle ground between religious experience without doctrine and religious doctrine without experience.

Andrew Reck's essay "Heart and Head: The Mind of Thomas Jefferson" examines the dialectical tension between "the Heart" and "the Head," which had become such a popular theme among leaders of the (French) Enlightenment. Reck argues that Jefferson held for the primacy of the Heart in moral matters and of the Head in scientific affairs. Reck concludes that for Jefferson the significance of theory (the Head's contribution) is its practicality (the Heart's motivation), and this personal conviction made him a man of achievement.

The third essay, by the late Robert C. Pollock, "Emerson and America's Future," argues that Emerson strove to liberate human experience from the routine of custom and habit formalized in the institutionalization of human life. Pollock sees Emerson as America's conceptual pioneer who, before pragmatism was formulated, advocated that ideas be translated into experience and that experience be illuminated with a "cosmic breadth of view."

Edward Madden's chapter, "Chauncey Wright and the Pragmatists" deals with the tension between Wright's empiricism and Peirce's new "pragmatism." The dialectical tension here is between two understandings of "experience": one, narrowly sensist; the other, widely experimentalist. Madden points out that Wright was Peirce's philosophical sparring partner and that the formulation of pragmatism owes much to these interchanges. Wright remained an empiricist, agnostic, and utilitarian.

The fifth essay is mine: "Charles S. Peirce: Action Through Thought—The Ethics of Experience." In it I try to show that Peirce insisted that theoretical and practical considerations be carefully and thoroughly kept apart in any scientific inquiry after the truth. This is not to say that there is not ultimately a set of important relations that link the practical and the theoretical, but that failure to keep those concerns separate will jeopardize the search for the truth and so ultimately will thwart effective action. Action is the outcome or upshot of thought but neither its purpose nor its logical interpretant.

John McDermott's " 'Life Is in the Transitions': Radical Empiricism and Contemporary Concerns" takes up again the enriched notion of experience, which is the hallmark of the pragmatist movement. James called this rehabilitated doctrine of experience "radical empiricism." McDermott urges that James relates this doctrine to the human situation, individual and social, in order to solve human problems. On this view, ideas are evaluated not in terms of other ideas but in terms of their ability to meet actual situations. Clearly this orientation prepared the way for both Dewey and Mead. By making radical empiricism the metaphysical basis for pragmatism, James has eliminated any trans-empirical support for the solutions to "problems of men." All that the human mind can bring to bear in these situations is already contained in human experience. James "thickens relations" as found within experience. The key to successful human living is the affective experiencing of those relations.

The seventh essay, by R. W. Sleeper, is entitled "John Dewey and the Metaphysics of American Democracy." He argues that the success of American Democracy has been in its ability to adapt to changing situations. In a word, American democratic institutions are "transactional." Dewey's philosophical analysis concludes that what constitutes human life is a series of transactions between nature and human experience. Sleeper maintains that Dewey's philosophy captures the genius of American Democracy and so he deserves to be called the "Philosopher of American Democracy." Dewey's experimental temper made him distrustful of ideology and of absolutes. Hence man is in constant dynamic tension with his environment. Nature is not fixed and static but in constant interaction. There is nothing beyond this ever-changing nature. Hence philosophy needs to be reconstructed continuously as does democracy.

Thelma Z. Lavine, in "Individuation and Unification in Dewey and Sartre," compares the way in which each of these thinkers meets the dialectical opposition of the individual and the group. Each formulates a thesis (doctrine); Dewey emphasizes unification of the group, while Sartre emphasizes the individual as individual. Any theoretical interpretation must be subject to experience and is to be seen as a reaction to experience. The Deweyan and Sartrian theses might be viewed as limits on a scale of world process. Where one situates the world on this scale (hence how much of each thesis one accepts) is determined by a cultural response to one's environment.

The ninth essay, "Josiah Royce, Anticipator of European Existentialism and Phenomenology," by Jacquelyn Ann K. Kegley, argues that Royce in his belief in the practical importance of many metaphysical ideas both anticipated and went beyond the phenomenological and existentialist movements later developed in Europe. Royce too tried to handle the dialectical tension between human experience and doctrinal interpretation of that experience. He argued for the mutuality of individual and community. This mutuality provides the possibility of authentic self-development by creating new possibilities from past actuality. Community is created out of conflict and plurality precisely through the mediation of ideas interpreting experience. Hence Professor Kegley sees this classical American figure's philosophical message as still relevant today.

John Lachs, in "The Transcendence of Materialism and Idealism in American Thought," answers the often heard remark that Santayana is not in the stream of American Philosophy at all. Lachs argues that while Santayana's thought is in continuity with continental philosophy, he gives that continental thought a definite and unmistakable American "twist." At the base of Santayana's philosophy is the dialectical tension between theoretical and practical reason. Kant's theory of human experience replaced theoretical with practical reason as the central and dominating factor. Hence the resulting metaphysics is activity-centered. From this move came one of the most important features of American pragmatism: namely, the primacy of will and of the concept of activity. Pragmatists used transactional analysis to overcome the opposition between subject and object, mind and matter, individual and society, etc. Santayana is squarely in this camp of activity-centered metaphysics and therefore squarely in the American tradition of philosophizing.

The eleventh essay, "C. I. Lewis and the Pragmatic Tradition in American Philosophy" by Sandra Rosenthal, argues that Lewis is sometimes erroneously interpreted as being in the tradition of Analytic Philosophy and then severely criticized for falling short of their norms for philosophizing. While it is true that Lewis writes with technical rigor on logic and epistemology, still he is philosophically a pragmatist in the classical American tradition. Lewis makes experience central to his understanding of human knowing and doing but without falling into reductionism (whether empiricist or phenomenologist). Again the dialectical tension between thought and action is overcome in the realization that sense experience must be interpreted in order to come to the level of awareness and that to interpret man (hence hold a theory about him) as an active agent is not anti-theory but transactional and dispositional. Rosenthal traces these pragmatic characteristics through Lewis' account of meaning, of method, and of truth.

The late David Miller's paper, "The Social Philosophy of George Herbert Mead," deals with Mead's application of pragmatist insights to the psychology of human communication. While man's thinking function is irreducible to overt action, still it is related to it inasmuch as mind emerges from social behavior and in turn becomes the instrument for such behavior. Miller argues that for Mead behavioral transaction with others gives rise to meaning and that, therefore, meaning is a social phenomenon. The social has priority over the individual, and indeed the self, as Royce saw, is defined by its relations to others. Thinking is due to the dialectical tension between the individual and the group and serves as an instrument to overcome it.

The final essay, "Existence as Transaction: A Whiteheadian Study of Causality," by Elizabeth Kraus, argues that Whitehead's process philosophy is in the tradition of American pragmatism since it agrees that the foundational experience of being human is that of the organism responding to its environment. Kraus argues, however, that Whitehead's process analysis provides a metaphysical basis for this ongoing interaction insisted upon by the pragmatists. The rest of the article illustrates such metaphysical grounding by analyzing how Whitehead's understanding of genuine causal interaction solves the problem of the temporal flow as being made up of discrete and atomic events.

1

Jonathan Edwards and the
Great Awakening

JOHN E. SMITH
Yale University

SAMUEL HOPKINS, the first biographer of Jonathan Edwards, wrote
in the Foreword to his work: "In this world, so full of darkness and
delusion, it is of great importance that all should be able to distinguish between true religion and that which is false. In this,
perhaps, none has taken more pains, or labored more successfully,
than he whose life is set before the reader."[1] Hopkins' judgment is
well-founded; testing the spirits and determining the marks of genuine piety were lifelong concerns of Edwards'. Both his preaching
and his writing on this topic are crucial in the confusing task of
evaluating the complex phenomenon that is to be the focus of our
attention: the Great Awakening in eighteenth-century America.
But before considering the series of religious revivals that are
known by that name and Edwards' critical appraisal of them, it
will be helpful to present a brief sketch of the man himself and
especially of his pattern of thought. As Perry Miller has rightly
said, the authentic life of Edwards was the life of the mind, a life
which he seems to have pursued for no fewer than thirteen hours a
day! The results of this labor represent his legacy to us and have
served to establish him, both at home and abroad, as the foremost
thinker of our colonial period.

No one can undertake to speak about Edwards without men-
tioning a peculiar irony that has no parallel in the history of a major
thinker. Edwards wrote at least 650 sermons, most of which we
possess in manuscript, but one of these sermons, by no means typical, has turned out to be the only piece of his writing known to

those who know his name at all. I refer, of course, to the famous Enfield sermon, "Sinners in the Hands of an Angry God."[2] This sermon, for more than half a century, has been cited in handbooks of American literature as the very hallmark of Puritan rhetoric. In it, Edwards' angry God is depicted as suspending sinners over the fiery pit of hell on a thread no stronger than that spun by a spider and used for flying on the wind. I do not mean to underestimate either the dramatic force or the significance of this sermon—in fact, one member of the congregation slit his throat after hearing it—but it seems to me most unfortunate that Edwards, easily the greatest thinker on the American scene prior to Charles Peirce, and author of such classics as *Religious Affections, Freedom of the Will, The Nature of True Virtue*, to say anything of the "Theological Miscellanies" and the rest of the sermons, should come to be identified through the cliché of the preacher of "fire and brimstone" solely on the basis of the publicity given to but one of his writings. The first step in understanding Edwards is, in my view, to forget that sermon; later one can come back to it and see it in proper perspective. Fixing attention on the sermon at the outset establishes an image of the man which is virtually impossible to transcend.

Jonathan Edwards was born in 1703 in the little town of East Windsor, Connecticut. Stemming from the Connecticut Valley, Edwards was in a strategic position. Much of the religious history of America in the eighteenth century has to be written as the story of the tensions existing between the "experimental religion" of Edwards' region and the more rationalistic and restrained piety of Boston. As one of his contemporaries noted, "heart religion," as it was called, was much more powerful in the Connecticut Valley than it ever was in Boston. It took no less than the stunning oratory of George Whitfield to "awaken" the proper Bostonians, but, as the record shows, with no long-lasting effect. It was the destiny of Edwards to be born into a situation in which revivalism was making itself powerfully felt; he participated in, and intimately understood, this "experimental religion" and ultimately came to be its most incisive interpreter. He was prepared for the task by his early education at Yale College, where he studied the philosophy of Locke and some of the works of Newton, especially the *Optics*.[3] From that study, together with the reading of some works by the Cambridge Platonists—More, Cudworth, and Smith—Edwards acquired the basis for his philosophical theology, especially the quite original notion he called the "new sense of the heart" and the equally novel conception of "religious affections." They were to prove essential for his interpretation and appraisal of the Awakening.

After serving an apprenticeship under his grandfather, Solomon Stoddard, generally known as the "pope" of the Connecticut Valley, Edwards succeeded him in the church at Northampton, where he remained until his dismissal by the congregation in 1750. That action was the culmination of an antagonism between Edwards and the people centering on the qualifications for church membership and the reception of Communion. As we now know, the circumstances were complex and by no means confined to theological differences; those differences, nevertheless, were of great importance for our topic. In 1662 a Massachusetts church synod instituted what was known as the Half-Way Covenant, an arrangement whereby it was possible to become a church member without the right of Communion, the latter being reserved for those who by profession, evidence, and example were accepted as "visible saints."[4] Stoddard extended this arrangement, offering the Lord's Supper to all who desired church membership, and conducted several revivals—which he called "harvests of souls"—adding to the size of the congregation even if not to the company of the redeemed. These local revivals were the forerunners of those larger and more sustained religious renewals which occurred in 1734–1735 and again in the early 1740s and came to be known as the Great Awakening. Over the years it became clear that, although he severely criticized revivalism and subjected it to stringent tests, Edwards was even more opposed to Stoddard's Half-Way Covenant and aimed at reinstituting the older, more rigorous qualifications for Communion. These qualifications were to be determined in accordance with the marks of genuine piety exhibited by the new "heart" or "experimental" religion which Edwards believed was to be found in the Awakening. For this reason he was an avowed proponent of revivalism, but the main problem he faced was how to distinguish the authentic presence of the divine Spirit from counterfeit and vain imaginings in the midst of the noise and confusion generated by a return to primordial religious experience.

His resolution of this problem will be the main focus of our attention in what follows. In the meantime we may fill in the final chapter of what Miller has called Edwards' external biography. Dismissed from Northampton, Edwards was an exile with his large family in Stockbridge, where he preached to the Indians and wrote his monumental *Freedom of the Will*. It is a somber picture indeed to envisage America's major philosophical theologian ending his days in the rudest and most primitive surroundings. In 1758 he was called to be the new president of the College of New Jersey, now Princeton University. After responding to the invitation in a letter outlining numerous reasons why he was unqualified, Edwards accepted the post. The rest is well known. After arriving in Princeton in the midst of a smallpox epidemic, he died after receiving an innoculation against the disease.

In approaching the thought and mind of Jonathan Edwards, one is confronted with an enigma. On the one hand, he exhibits sophistication and a rigor in thinking thoroughly in accord with his learned background in philosophy, Biblical studies, and the new natural science. His writings are marked with unmistakable precision of thought and expression, and they show a unique combination of attention to fact and originality of conception. On the other hand, Edwards displays a childlike simplicity in the face of the Biblical material and, though in opposing simple fundamentalism, he always demanded interpretations controlled by linguistic, historical, and philosophical criteria, he could nevertheless be quite literalistic in his outlook. There is, for example, in the "Miscellanies" an account of how God's wisdom was manifest in allowing man to discover the mariner's compass and thus to promote the communication of both knowledge and faith throughout the earth. This manifestation of God's providence is related in much the same tone as one might adopt in recording some event taking place in the parish at Northampton or in the life of a member of the congregation. A similar duality, if not incongruity, is to be found in Edwards' explicitly theological writings. On the one hand, one finds in such works as *Original Sin* and *Freedom of the Will* all the familiar arguments of Biblically based Calvinism, including the defense of determinism and of predestination, and, although Edwards argues with the use of philosophical concepts and principles, the result has all the appearances of a fully orthodox theology in the tradition of Augustine. On the other hand, in such writings as the *Dissertation Concerning the End for Which God Created the World*, the "Theological Miscellanies," and the essay on "Being," Edwards appears as a speculative theologian with a somewhat mystical bent. He envisages God as a source or fountain from which all finite being flows, talks of the relation between God and creatures as the "consent of being to Being," and sees the entire creation as the communication of God's Being, an expression of the divine *gloria* that man alone among all the creatures is properly fitted to appreciate. In writings such as these, Edwards seems to be at a great distance from the rhetorically expressed orthodox theology of the Puritan tradition, and to be recovering the great tradition of philosophically oriented theology that had its beginnings in the writings of the early Fathers. The presence of seemingly incongruous elements in his thought has puzzled many interpreters. Judged in terms of his contemporaries, Edwards was far ahead of his time, especially in the rigor of his thought and the skill with which he appropriated secular knowledge for the interpretation and appraisal of religious experience. Yet, if one judges Edwards, as some recent revisionary historians have been doing, on the assumption that American thought has been a record of steady progress since the Enlightenment, he must of necessity appear as a reactionary and, in the eyes of one writer, a "medieval thinker." But that is, as Perry Miller suggested, only because the advancing tide of American optimism fostered dreams of worldly success which led people to cover up, if not deny, the reality of the darker side of human existence that Edwards knew so well. Were Edwards alive today, he might well find himself ringing a change on that famous sermon previously mentioned and preaching one entitled "God in the Hands of Angry Sinners."

Be that as it may, our task is, not to judge Edwards' thought as a whole, but to understand the Great Awakening and especially Edwards' critical appraisal of it. Revivalism and the upsurge of "heart religion" in America must be seen as part of a larger movement in Western religious life prompted by the sense that true piety cannot be identified with the holding of correct theological doctrines. It is not always understood, largely because of the popular image which identifies Protestantism with sheer evangelical fervor, that the Reformed Churches underwent their own scholastic period in the seventeenth century and, in the absence of one central authority, had to depend for unity and continuity on authoritative creeds and confessions essentially theological in character. These doctrinal statements were taken to be the authoritative content of faith, and they were expounded and applied in classical Puritan sermons that often lasted for three hours! Revivalism represented an attempt to return to experience in opposition to such rationalism, and a demand that theological concepts—faith, sin, justification, sanctification, grace, the fruits of the Spirit, salvation—be understood in terms of individual and personal experience. The widespread conviction was that there is a world of difference between, for example, the holding of the doctrine that God is love and the actual presence of the loving heart. One might profess the doctrine without possessing the love. On the other hand, in the midst of the emotional upheaval accompanying the new interest in heart religion, many came to believe that they possessed that love, or rather were possessed by it through the work of the Holy Spirit, who were not in fact transformed at all. This situation posed the central problem to which Edwards addressed himself: how to defend this new piety and at the same time develop criteria for testing it because, as he was fond of repeating, "many false prophets have gone out into the earth." His position was particularly difficult. He stood opposed to the rationalist critics of revivalism such as Charles Chauncy of Boston, who described it as "the late religious commotion in New England,"[5] on the ground that true piety must show itself in the form of the new self of which the New Testament speaks and therefore cannot be identical with doctrine alone. But he also stood opposed to uncontrolled, uncritical revivalism and its consequent enthusiasm, private revelations, etc., because he believed that piety cannot be all heat and no light. Moreover, the renewing presence of the Spirit is not to be confused with external symptoms of a heightened imagination, hearing voices, and having visions. Edwards' critical interpretation and appraisal of the Great Awakening were thus aimed at accomplishing the difficult task of defending revivalism and at the same time demanding that it be subject to rigorous tests.

Edwards' views are expressed in five principal documents: two sermons and three treatises, which, I am happy to say, are all now available in reliable texts. The sermons are: "God Glorified in

Man's Dependence" (1731) and "A Divine and Supernatural Light" (1734).[6] These sermons contain Edwards' conception of the new piety, which he was prepared to defend on Biblical grounds. The treatises are: *The Distinguishing Marks of a Work of the Spirit* (1741), *The Treatise Concerning Religious Affections* (1746), the most important of the three, and *Some Thoughts Concerning the Present Revival of Religion in New England* (1742).[7] These works express the heart of his conception of the activity of the Holy Spirit, and his criteria or signs of the religious affections whereby the new piety was to be judged. Naturally, I cannot hope to communicate all that is in these writings; I shall attempt to select the crucial points.

In "God Glorified in Man's Dependence" we find an idea expressed which is absolutely fundamental to Edwards' entire outlook, and one which was to find its ultimate expression in the concept of religious affections. That idea can be expressed initially as "the fusion of thought and experience." For Edwards it is not enough to think and believe that man is dependent on God; one must *feel* this dependence as a living force which serves to overcome the self-righteousness stemming from belief in one's own self-sufficiency. Not merely must an idea in religion be thought of or understood; it must be experienced or felt. I shall return to this point further on. Edwards' aim in this sermon was to establish the thesis that God's purpose in redemption is for man to glory, not in himself, but in God alone. And man must be *sensible* of this fact, along with the difference between God and man manifest in his dependence on the divine grace. The redeemed have all their excellency and pleasure in God Who communicates to them His excellence via the divine Spirit. It is important to notice that Edwards distinguished between the Spirit as *acting upon* the person and the Spirit as *dwelling within* the person. As became apparent later, this distinction enabled him to claim that the Spirit had *caused* many phenomena to take place in the Awakening—powerful images coming to the mind, premonitions, voices, etc.—which are unconnected with true piety since that is exclusively a matter of the *indwelling* of the Spirit. In short, not all those who participated in the "religious commotions" are to be numbered among the saints.

In "A Divine and Supernatural Light," Edwards came much

closer to characterizing the light by which the redeemed know and sense the divine presence. The sermon is on the text of Mt 16:17, which records Peter's confession that Jesus is the Christ. According to Edwards, God, and God alone, revealed this truth to Peter, and his possession of it is "evidence" of his being blessed. The question is: How might we know when other people stand in the same relation to God as Peter did? Edwards offers here some indications of a sort he was to develop in later writings. In accordance with his method, he begins with a statement of what the light is *not*; one can see at once the relevance of what he says to revivalism. The light is not convictions of sin and misery; it is not impressions made on the imagination; it is not the suggestion of new truths or propositions not in the divine Word (*Enthusiasm*); and it is not "every affecting view" which someone happens to take of the things of religion. The light is something quite different, and in this positive identification we see the influence both of Locke's empirical philosophy and of some ideas to be found in the Cambridge Platonists. One possessing the light has "a real sense and apprehension" of the Excellency (presence of God) in the Word. This sense is not a matter of speculative judgment but is described as a sense of the heart. To make his position clearer, Edwards distinguishes two forms of knowledge—*speculative* or "notional" (Locke) and *sense of the heart*. The former is exhibited in judgments that something is the case and represents understanding proper—that is, apart from will and disposition. Sense of the heart is delight and pleasure in the *presence* of the *idea* of the thing. Will and inclination are involved, and the person is no longer merely a neutral spectator. Notice that the sense of which he speaks is always accompanied by an *idea*. In genuine piety the two go together, and any attempt to separate them or to oppose them to each other must result in a distortion of his view. There is, however, a difference between having an *opinion* and having a *sense of*: a man may say that honey is sweet without having tasted it, but only he who has the sense as well as the idea can know what is meant when the honey is so described. True faith in the things of religion is the spiritual conviction of the togetherness of idea and having-a-sense-of, which enabled Edwards to defend and to criticize the revival at the same time.

In *Distinguishing Marks*, which is a direct foreshadowing of the

Affections, Edwards concentrates on showing that many of the external features of heart religion—"occasional causes," in his view—must be discounted because they form no certain basis for determining whether the redeeming Spirit is present or not. In this analysis, Edwards declared himself to be under the "rule of the Word," which takes seriously the *qualitative* character of spiritual experience against the prevalent psychological and even physiological tendency of the time to emphasize what was called "the motions of the blood and animal spirits," as if genetic accounts of such phenomena could adequately determine their character and validity. One can see at once from Edwards' list of negatives that he was explicitly rejecting the frenzy, mindlessness, and uncontrolled emotionalism that have always impressed the popular imagination as sure evidence of a person's "having the Spirit." Consider Edwards' list. That something happens in an *extraordinary* way, he claims, counts neither for nor against its validity (especially since man cannot plumb the mystery of the Spirit's way of acting); weeping, trembling, groaning, and other bodily expressions and affects are likewise inconclusive because, by themselves, they bear no essential relation to the ideas, the perceptions, and especially the spiritual light of those who manifest these phenomena. The existence of great passions provides no secure evidence because they are totally different from the affections that are genuine fruits of the Spirit. Heightened imagination and the having of visions are by no means the same as the sense of Excellency which is genuine. Imprudence and irregular conduct, like errors of judgment and delusions, are insufficient as criteria because, Edwards says, the wiles of Satan have always accompanied the works of the Spirit—the tares among the wheat. All the occasional causes and aberrations which, according to Edwards, the critics regarded as essential and which they used as grounds for condemning the revival, represent the work of Satan and thus provide no basis for judgment. Implicit in this claim is another: namely, that Edwards' support of the revival was at the same time a clear rejection of aberrations and excesses.

On the positive side, Edwards cites five marks of true piety for which he claimed Scriptural authority. At this point I shall merely list these criteria because the central idea behind them is the subject of our next text, *Religious Affections.* Those in whom the

Spirit resides, he says, have a raised esteem of Christ whom they do not hesitate to confess. But, he adds, with the Quakers obviously in mind, this confession is of Christ and not the testimony to the presence of a "light within." The true saints fight against Satan's kingdom. They have a great concern for Scripture accompanied by a sense of its truth. They do not substitute any rule of their "inner light" for the canonical written Word; they manifest a spirit of truth, which means being sensible of man's actual condition; and, finally, they show forth the divine love from which follows love for men, a spirit totally different from the counterfeit love which is really self-love on the part of those who pride themselves on being different from other, presumably unregenerate, men. In a spirit typical of his confidence in the trustworthiness of the Scriptures, Edwards concludes: "These marks, that the apostle has given us, are sufficient to stand alone, and support themselves. . . . they plainly show *the finger of God.* . . ." [8] Equally typical is Edwards' appeal to rational argument in support of the Scriptural view. There are, he says, certain things that Satan *would* not do, such as awaking consciousness, confirming belief in Christ and in the truth of the Scriptures, and leading people from deception. More important, there are things which Satan neither *can* nor will do: namely, bestow a spirit of divine love because he has none to bestow. Hence, according to the argument, if we find happening what Satan *cannot* do, we are safe in holding that God is the cause, since we already know that the Spirit does not come from man.

So much for the *Distinguishing Marks.* I turn now to the most important of Edwards' writings about revivalism, the *Religious Affections,* and here again I must be selective. To begin with, by "affections" Edwards means the Biblical "fruits of the Spirit"—love, joy, faith, hope, peace—which he takes to be hallmarks of genuine piety. One cannot understand "affections" on the assumption of an uncritical distinction and dichotomy between the "head" and the "heart." Edwards' contemporaries, for the most part, made this assumption in one form or another, and thus missed the force of his position. An affection is not a passion; a passion overwhelms a person to the exclusion of understanding, whereas all affections involve ideas and perceptions. An affection is a *response* of the person accompanied by understanding. More precisely, an affection is a special class of vigorous and sensible exercises of the will and inclination. Affections are always accompanied by ideas, but they pass beyond what Edwards called a merely "notional understanding" in that the individual *feels, senses, sees* the divine truth, beauty, and excellence in the idea, and is thus inclined toward the divine presence. By itself, the understanding is neutral and devoid of that inclination which is called the *will* in the case of overt action and *heart* when we are considering the orientation of the self as a whole. The affections are thus a synthesis of the two—idea and inclination as will and heart. It is a fundamental error and misunderstanding to equate affections with "emotions," especially if the latter are understood as opposed to understanding. Most of Edwards' critics made this mistake and, as a consequence, they failed to grasp his basis for interpreting and appraising the Awakening.

Love, according to Edwards, is the chief of the affections and is, at the same time, the fountain from which all others flow.[9] The foundation of that love which is manifest not merely in a single act but in the whole "propensity of the soul" is the indwelling Spirit, enlightening the understanding and inclining the will. From that undivided love for God come the other affections which are the fruits of the Spirit. By "spiritual understanding" Edwards means what he calls the "sense of the heart."[10] where the mind is sensible of the "sweet beauty and amiableness" of the divine excellence, as he says, "in the presence of the idea of it." The sense of the heart is the new foundation in the nature of the soul which the Spirit alone can establish. It is at this point that the influence of Locke's thought can be seen as crucial. Locke described the ideas of sense as *simple* and as beyond the power of the human will, which is to say that they are presented to us and can in no way be created by us. Simple ideas can be combined and compared, but we cannot originate any one of them. The new sense of the heart, Edwards declared, is a new simple idea which no man can create; its presence is the principal sign of the indwelling of the Spirit. This sense has nothing to do with the emotional accompaniments of revivalism—voices, visions, imaginings, fainting spells, etc.—but is the medium whereby the men of true faith apprehend the beauty, the excellence, and the glory of God. Edwards views the fruits of the Spirit as the outward manifestation of the new sense, and his twelve signs of gracious affections are the indicators of its presence. Experimental or heart religion is thus authentic when it meets the tests; in the absence of these signs revivalistic fervor is mere heat without light.

I cannot undertake here a detailed treatment of each of the twelve signs Edwards cites as criteria for judgment. It is highly significant, however, that after extensive discussion of the new sense of the heart,[11] and the characteristics of the transformed person, Edwards concludes the list with the sign of holy *practice*. To this sign he devotes slightly less than half the space he gave to all the other signs combined. Since, he insists, our capacity to *talk* like saints is far greater than our capacity to act like saints, an *external* evidence is required as a test. Here Edwards distinguishes between particular acts and a "whole course of life." It is the latter which counts because it is the best index of an enduring character. Through this distinction he is able to question the authenticity of particular, spectacular, and largely sporadic revival experiences. Edwards likens the evanescent experience to meteors, which appear in a brilliant stream of light and then spend themselves in a shower of sparks falling finally to earth as dark and lifeless matter. The true saints, by contrast, shine as the fixed stars, shedding their light over the infinite spaces without ceasing. The emphasis, it should be noted, on the need for an external manifestation as evidence of faith points in the direction of later American pragmatism and away from the philosophy of Locke with its emphasis on internal states of mind.[12]

The third document, *Some Thoughts*[13] (1742), preceded the *Affections* by four years; in it Edwards gives his appraisal of both the Awakening and its critics, viewing it in the broadest terms as a social phenomenon, or what he calls the "revival in the general." He criticizes both the revivalists and their critics. Against the opponents of heart religion he insists that they judged the movement *a priori* without understanding either its causes or its aims. He attacks them for not using Scripture as a rule for judgment, and for failing to see the good features of the new piety while concentrating on the evil. Edwards is no less critical of revivalism, especially as popularly understood. One of these criticisms merits special attention. On its social side, the Awakening posed a powerful threat to the peace and harmony of the American settlements, both social and religious. Those who regarded themselves as "saved" through conversion experiences, or at least many of them, stood in judgment of others whom they saw as unregenerate. A favorite practice of "redeemed" itinerant preachers was to invade an established parish and attempt to persuade the congregation that their minister was unconverted and therefore that they should abandon him and follow them to found a new communion of saints. I cannot attempt to describe the disruption this practice caused, but it was extensive and threatened the entire fabric of social life.[14] Edwards is *absolutely* opposed to this practice, in at least three respects.[15] First, he declares that those who set themselves up as judges *ipso facto* condemn themselves as hypocrites filled with spiritual pride. Secondly, he repeatedly insists that no man can judge another and that, as was invariably overlooked, the signs are meant chiefly for self-examination and provide no occasion for the display of a "pharasaic righteousness." Thirdly, he rejects those who flout the denominational authority of the Ministers' Association in usurping the power to dismiss ministers and to form new congregations. These features of the Awakening, however, Edwards regards as aberrations, Satan's tares, and he cites superstition, enthusiasm, and intemperate zeal as corruptions inevitable in any spiritual awakening. They belong, however, not to the divine Spirit, but to the domain of corruption.

The unhappy fate of Edwards, at least as regards his relation to the Great Awakening, was that he was exposed to attack not only by the opponents of revivalism but by its advocates as well. Those devoted to rational belief and decorum in religious observance found Edwards' defense of the new spirituality both uncongenial and unpersuasive. Typical of these critics was Charles Chauncy, mentioned above, who attacked Edwards in several avowedly polemical writings, charging him with aiding the cause of enthusiasm by exalting imagination and emotion at the expense of reason.[16] We have already seen that Edwards rejected these polarities and was himself a determined critic of enthusiasm. Uncritical revivalists, on the other hand, were most reluctant to acknowledge the need for the signs and tests which Edwards demanded because they were content with extravagant experiences and regarded them as authentic without question.

Edwards, as always, held firmly to the position he had taken;

genuine piety is an affair of the heart and cannot exist in a "dull and lifeless frame," but it does not follow that religion of the heart and the new sense is a mere emotionalism excluding both understanding and perception. It is of the first importance to notice that Edwards repeatedly rejected the anti-intellectualism which has often gone hand in hand with evangelical fundamentalism where it is supposed that "having the Spirit" is possible only for those who have no "book learning." Speaking of the need for an educated ministry, Edwards warns that unlearned men, "for want of an extensive knowledge," are dangerous because in times of religious revivals especially, they will not protect their congregations from "impulses, vain imaginings, superstition, indiscreet zeal" and the like, but will instead foster these unprofitable excesses.[17] Edwards attacked the sufficiency of rationalism in religion and sought to lay hold of the truth in the piety of experience, but in the end he gave no comfort to enthusiasts or to obscurantists.

NOTES

1. *The Life and Character of the Late Rev. Mr. Jonathan Edwards* (Boston, 1765), p. iv.

2. The text is available in *Jonathan Edwards: Representative Selections*, edd. C. H. Faust and T. H. Johnson (New York: American, 1935), pp. 155ff.

3. Perry Miller, *Jonathan Edwards* (New York: Sloane, 1949), pp. 35ff.

4. See Sidney E. Ahlstrom, *A Religious History of the American People*, 2 vols. (New Haven: Yale University Press, 1972), II 375.

5. *Religious Affections*, ed. John E. Smith, The Works of Jonathan Edwards 2 (New Haven: Yale University Press, 1959), p. 4n; Charles Chauncy, *Seasonable Thoughts on the State of Religion in New England* (Boston, 1743), p. 111. Edwards' and Chauncy's views about revivalism were so divergent as not to allow for any common ground on which they could discuss. Chauncy ignored Edwards' careful and subtle analysis of the affections and of the intricate relations between understanding and will. Instead he assumed a rather simple distinction between "passion" and "reason" and was content with the following, in his view decisive, formula: "Satan works upon the reason by the passion; the Spirit on the passion by reason." Moreover, Chauncy thought of heart religion as the result of uncontrolled imagination, which he regarded, in turn, as Satan's medium; he thus failed to appreciate Edwards' rejection of "vain imaginings" as merely occasional causes that are virtually without value for testing experiences.

6. Both sermons were published in Edwards' lifetime. The most available

text for most readers will be that in *Edwards: Representative Selections,* edd. Faust & Johnson.

7. See *Religious Affections,* ed. Smith, and *The Great Awakening,* ed. C. C. Goen, The Works of Jonathan Edwards 4 (New Haven: Yale University Press, 1972).

8. *Great Awakening,* ed. Goen, p. 258.

9. *Religious Affections,* ed. Smith, pp. 106–108.

10. Ibid., pp. 272ff.

11. Ibid., pp. 383ff.

12. Ibid., pp. 373–74.

13. See *Great Awakening,* ed. Goen, pp. 289ff.

14. See Richard Hofstadter, *America at 1750: A Social Portrait* (New York: Knopf, 1973), chap. 7.

15. See *Great Awakening,* ed. Goen, pp. 283–88.

16. Ibid., pp. 62–64.

17. Ibid., pp. 282–83.

2

Heart and Head:
The Mind of Thomas Jefferson

ANDREW J. RECK
Tulane University

I

DURING THE FALL OF 1786, while he was serving as American minister to France, Thomas Jefferson fell in love. He was forty-four years old and had been widowed four years earlier. The object of his affection was a twenty-seven-year-old, blue-eyed blonde, whose lips even the staid Dumas Malone, Jefferson's magisterial biographer, has described as "kissable."[1] Maria Cosway was her name; she was an accomplished artist and the wife of Richard Cosway, a man of Jefferson's age and a highly successful miniaturist then on a brief visit to Paris. However imaginations may embellish Maria Cosway's alliance with Jefferson, the record is innocent. Jefferson spent much time in her company for several weeks, dining, sightseeing, and attending social and cultural events. And sometime in September or early October, probably on an outing with Maria, Jefferson suffered an unknown injury which disabled his right hand and wrist. What happened we do not know, since the most explicit reference to it in one of his letters mentions it as simply "one of those follies from which good cannot come, but ill may."[2]

Jefferson's flirtation with Mrs. Cosway would have been swallowed up by oblivion had it not been for a remarkable twelve-page letter, written awkwardly with his left hand, and sent to her shortly after her departure in October. Although the letter conforms to the literary conventions of the period and is stilted, it remains a poignant human document. As usual in his correspondence with Maria, Jefferson addressed her as "madam," and he never mentioned her without friendly references also to Mr. Cosway. Except for its opening and closing paragraphs, the letter consists of a dialogue which Jefferson reported as taking place between his Head and his Heart when, after returning home from bidding her farewell, he was seated by his fireside, "solitary and sad."[3] Much of the letter recapitulates the innocent occasions that Jefferson and Maria enjoyed together; indeed, it furnishes the most reliable record of their association. The theme that threads the dialogue is whether it is good to enter into a friendship (or love relation) that cannot endure, inasmuch as the consequences entailed by separation are painful. The development of this theme by means of the adversary statements of the Head and the Heart illuminates the moral foundations of Jefferson's thought.

The Head represents the position of undiluted egoistic Epicureanism. It declares: "Everything in this world is matter of calculation. Advance then with caution, the balance in your hand. Put into one scale the pleasures which any object may offer; but put fairly into the other the pains which are to follow, and see which preponderates" (p. 448). The Head characterizes the art of life as "the art of avoiding pain," and contending that friendships or attachments to others afford pleasures that are laden with potentials for pain, it recommends withdrawal from society and concentration on intellectual pursuits.

> The most effectual means of being secure against pain is to retire within ourselves, and to suffice for our own happiness. Those, which depend on ourselves, are the only pleasures a wise man can count on: for nothing is ours which another may deprive us of. Hence the inestimable value of intellectual pleasures. Ever in our power, always leading us to something new, never cloying, we ride, serene and sublime, above the concerns of this mortal world, contemplating truth and nature, matter and motion, the laws which bind up their existence, and that eternal being who made and bound them by these laws. Let this be our employ [p. 449].

To judge from Maria's response, she made little sense of Jefferson's dialogue. But considered in its broadest aspect, this dialogue between the Head and the Heart illuminates the complex, perhaps divided, mind of Thomas Jefferson. The philosophical sources

from which Jefferson derived this dichotomy of the Heart and the
Head, a familiar one in eighteenth-century thought, are numerous;
and they have been well exposed by Gilbert Chinard and Adrienne
Koch.[4] The doctrine of the Head is clearly that of Epicurus, whose
philosophy, along with the Stoics and other Greek and Roman
thinkers, including Socrates, Plato, Aristotle, Epictetus, Cicero,
and Seneca, Jefferson had studied. In the case of Epicurus, however, he was inclined on occasion to esteem him the author of the
best moral system the world provided before Christianity. The
doctrine of the Heart, on the other hand, was espoused by a host
of eighteenth-century thinkers, among whom Jefferson favored
Shaftesbury, Hutcheson, Hume, and Henry Home (Lord Kames).
In the 1786 letter to Maria Cosway the Heart prevails; but its triumph is clearly circumscribed by a reason that is motivated by
more than intellectual pleasures of the Head. Jefferson was never
destined to be a gloomy monk, and in personal matters he displayed discretion and self-control, which furthered his public
career.

II

A philosopher Jefferson might well have become, provided the
term is used (as it was in the eighteenth century) to refer to a
scientist, or to one who pursues all branches of learning. In the
case of Jefferson, the terms "philosophy" and "philosopher" were
often applied to him with derision by his political enemies. Thus
the vituperative Federalist publisher William Cobbett, who ran a
quotation in his magazine to the effect that "'of all beings, a philosopher makes the worst politician,'" asserted that "'if one circumstance more than another could disqualify Mr. Jefferson from
the Presidency, it would be the charge of his being a philosopher.'"[5] Nevertheless, Jefferson was, without concealment, a
veritable polymath. A master of ancient and modern foreign languages, he was an indefatigable reader and book collector. He was
also an architect, an inventor, and a pioneer in such sciences as
linguistics, anthropology, economics, palaeontology, meteorology,
zoology, botany, and geology. His investigations, which bore fruit
as learned and scientific articles, place him after Franklin as an
American *philosophe*. To call Jefferson by this word drawn from
the French Enlightenment is to suggest not only the range of his

speculative and empirical curiosity but also the intended utilitarian bias. His philosophical heroes from the past were the favored trinity of the Age of Reason: Bacon, Newton, and Locke. From Bacon, for example, he derived generally his empirical and utilitarian conception of science, and specifically the system of classification for his library, which, of course, became the basis for the Library of Congress.

Jefferson's entitlement to the title *philosophe* was best earned by his authorship of *Notes on the State of Virginia*, which William Peden, in the Introduction to the now standard critical edition of this work, has called, "an American classic" and "[p]robably the most important scientific and political book written by an American before 1785."[6] In search of information, François Barbé Marbois, the secretary of the French delegation at Philadelphia, circulated questionnaires among members of the Continental Congress, one of which was transmitted to Jefferson. Generalizing his responses to Marbois' twenty-three queries, Jefferson furnished an astonishing record of data about American geography, geology, flora, fauna, climate, ethnology, palaeontology, agriculture, laws, religion, and other institutions. He collected detailed data on his own and gathered reports from others; and he cited twenty-eight foreign authorities and quoted from four languages.

In the pages of *Notes on Virginia*, for example, Jefferson examined and rejected the theory of petrified shells offered by the most famous of all *philosophes*, Voltaire. Shells found in elevated regions were, before the advent of evolutionary palaeontology, puzzling phenomena, explained as the deposits from a universal deluge, or the consequence of natural convulsions that raised the ocean floors. The diluvian explanation, despite its Biblical warrant, Jefferson refuted as contrary to "the laws of nature" (NV 31); and he rejected the cataclysmic theory on the grounds that it lacked evidence. Now, Voltaire had speculated that such shells, without being attached to animal bodies, are produced by natural processes, as crystals are, and Jefferson rejected this explanation, too, on the grounds that the French *philosophe* had "not established it. . . . We must be contented to acknowledge, that this great phenomenon is as yet unresolved. Ignorance is preferable to error; and he is less remote from the truth who believes nothing, than he who believes what is wrong" (NV 33).

The Baconian model of natural science, to which Jefferson subscribed, promoted scientific accuracy; it also supported his typical eighteenth-century preoccupation with natural history. In his defense of American life-forms against the charge that they were inferior to those found in the Old World, patriotism mingled with science. Buffon, of whom Jefferson said, "I take him for my ground work, because I think him the best informed of any Naturalist who has ever written" (NV 55), was his major target. For the celebrated French naturalist had disparaged the New World when he contended that its indigenous life-forms were neither as various nor as large and strong as those of the Old World, and that those forms that were transplanted from the Old invariably degenerated here. Buffon justified his derogation of American flora and fauna not so much by empirical studies as by the general theory that America has a colder and moister climate than the Old World, and that these climatic factors are injurious to life. Jefferson challenged both the alleged facts of climate with his own meteorological data and the thesis connecting such facts with life-forms. "The truth of this [hypothesis connecting climatic factors and life-forms] is inscrutable to us by reasoning a priori. Nature has hidden from us her modus agendi. Our only appeal on such questions is to experience . . ." (NV 48).

On the empirical side of the argument Jefferson compiled lists of American flora and fauna, both indigenous and transplanted, and compared them with European life-forms, to disprove Buffon's theory. He also used palaeontological data—in this instance, the remains of the mammoth—to illustrate that America could boast of animals of great size and strength. Later to his argument he added the megalonyx, which he reconstructed incorrectly from the great claw and other remains of a prehistoric ground sloth. What is pertinent, for Jefferson, these things were not prehistoric. According to eighteenth-century theory of a great chain of being, to which he adhered, there is in nature a living kind corresponding to every link in a chain of plenitude, and further, every kind, or species, is fixed and indestructible, the entire hierarchy of types having been created once for all by God. Jefferson firmly believed, therefore, that somewhere in the unexplored American wilderness the carnivorous mammoth, as reported by Indian legend, still roamed, shaming by its existence the smaller and weaker Old World elephant.

In *Notes on Virginia* Jefferson devoted pages to American ethnology and anthropology. Buffon's description of the American Indian was, he said, "[a]n afflicting picture indeed, which, for the honor of human nature, I am glad to believe has no original . . . [and is] . . . just as true as the fables of Aesop" (NV 59). Instead, Jefferson maintained the view, unpopular for an American, that the Indian is the natural equal of the white man, and that the observable differences between the two races stem from diet, exercise, and level of culture. As Jefferson declared, "This belief is founded on what I have seen of man, white, red, and black, and what has been written of him by authors, enlightened themselves, and writing amidst an enlightened people" (NV 59). The noble savage came into his own in Jefferson's pages, climaxing with the story of Logan, the Mingo chieftain whose family had been murdered by whites. Jefferson closed with Logan's oration, which he esteemed to be superior to those of Demosthenes and Cicero, and inadvertently became embroiled in a heated dispute with one of the descendants of the man whom Logan accused. While Jefferson's conception of blacks will be considered later, his defense of American whites is germane here since it illustrates his patriotic fervor in the field of science. Elaborating the implications of Buffon's theory that life-forms transmitted from the Old World to the New degenerate, Abbé Raynal had treated American whites aspersively. Jefferson naturally attacked Raynal's theory, arguing that in all likelihood when America has grown and matured her cultural and political history will surpass that of the Old World and that, for the present, with special regard for Washington, Franklin, and Rittenhouse, "of the geniuses which adorn the present age, America contributes its full share" (NV 65).

As a *philosophe* Jefferson read philosophy and pursued science throughout his long and busy life. His association with English thinkers, like Tom Paine, Richard Price, and Joseph Priestley, began during the American Revolution, which many Lockeans took up as their own cause. During his ministry in France, he befriended the Scottish philosopher Dugald Stewart, whose work he later recommended, and he established associations and friendships with a long line of distinguished French thinkers. Through John Adams and Benjamin Franklin, Jefferson was introduced to the leading intellectuals in France. Voltaire, Diderot, Rousseau—*philosophes* of an earlier generation—had passed from the scene before Jefferson's arrival. But Lafayette (whom he had met in America), La Rochefoucauld, and Condorcet, liberal aristocrats as well as intellectuals, were among those to whom he had easy access. He also met Samuel du Pont de Nemours, a distinguished physiocrat, then an economist in the French government, and destined to become one of his leading correspondents as well as an American immigrant who founded a multinational industrial enterprise. Jefferson attended the salons of Madame d'Houtetot and Madame Helvetius where he probably met the young De Stutt de Tracy, the founder of ideology, and such future ideologues as Cabanis. Indeed, beginning as a *philosophe*, Jefferson followed the development of French thought and became an *idéologue*.

Jefferson's career as an ideologue is a unique episode in the history of Franco-American cultural relations. When he sent John Adams a set of De Stutt de Tracy's works, the New Englander responded with playful skepticism.

> " '3 vols. of Ideology' Pray explain to me this Neological title! What does it mean? When Bonaparte used it, I was delighted with it, upon the common principle of delight in everything we cannot understand. Does it mean Idiotism? The science of *non compos mentuism?* The Science of Lunacy? The Theory of Delirium? Or does it mean the Science of Self Love? of *amour propre?* or the elements of vanity?" [7]

Soberly Jefferson replied:

> "Tracy comprehends, under the word 'Ideology' all the subjects which the French term *Morale*, as the correlative to *Physique*. His work on Logic, Government, Political Economy and Morality, he considers as making up the circle of ideological subjects, or of those which are within the scope of the understanding, and not of the senses. His Logic occupies exactly the ground of Locke's work on the Understanding." [8]

In respect to De Stutt de Tracy, Jefferson, a past president of the United States, performed the services of a disciple. He arranged for the translation and anonymous publication of Tracy's *Commentary and Review of Montesquieu's Spirit of the Laws* (1811). Montesquieu had been carefully studied by Jefferson, whose ex-

tracts from the *Esprit des Lois*, punctuated with occasional eluci-
dations and comments, number twenty-seven in the *Commonplace
Book*, occupying nearly forty pages of printed text. Yet next to
Hume, Montesquieu is perhaps the philosophical author whom
Jefferson both admired and condemned most. According to Jefferson, Hume had written the best available history of England,
marred unfortunately by Tory prejudices that seduced its readers;
so at one point Jefferson even suggested publication of a bowdler-
ized edition of Hume's history. Jefferson's relation to Montesquieu
is more complex. Although he leaned heavily on the French
thinker for some of his most cherished ideas and values, he also
criticized Montesquieu for presenting a compilation of common-
places and data within a conceptual framework ridden with par-
adoxes. He charged Montesquieu not only for failing to envisage
the possibility of a republic extending over a vast territory, as the
American federal system subsequently did, but also for admiring
the British constitution and hence monarchy *too* much. Thus Jefferson welcomed Tracy's tract on Montesquieu, and, in translating
and publishing the work, he was so successful in concealing the
identity of its author, who in fact feared political reprisals in
France, that Du Pont mistook Jefferson as the author and endeav-
ored to promote a French translation and publication. Furthermore, Jefferson practically translated and, in spite of numerous
obstacles, arranged for the publication of Tracy's *Treatise of Political Economy* (1817). No doubt, his adherence to ideology was
stimulated by the fact that he and Tracy shared the same views,
having arrived at them independently from common sources in
French physiocratic thought, which advocated a laissez-faire economy with agriculture as its base. Yet Jefferson, who was as chary of
metaphysics as Adams, recommended in his prospectus to the *Treatise* that readers, unless habituated to abstract speculation, skip
over the opening pages on ideology and the doctrines of the personality and the self, which comprise over one-third of the printed
volume, and begin with the section on society. Nevertheless, unlike Adams, Jefferson privately believed the positivist, materialist
metaphysics of ideology. In one letter to Adams, Jefferson mentioned Dugald Stewart, whom he reported as having met after the
New Englander had left Europe and with whom he had almost
daily converse for several months.

"Stewart is a great man. . . . I consider him and Tracy as the ablest
metaphysicians living; by which I mean investigators of the thinking
faculty of man. Stewart seems to have given its natural history from
facts and observations; Tracy its modes of action and deduction,
which he calls Logic and Ideology; and Cabanis, in his Physique et
Morale de l'homme, has investigated anatomically, and most in-
geniously, the particular organs in the human structure which may
most probably exercise that faculty. And they ask why may not the
mode of action called thought, have been given to a material organ of
peculiar structure. . . . These, however, are speculations and subtleties
in which, for my own part, I have little indulged myself. When I meet
a proposition beyond finite comprehension I abandon it as I do a
weight which human strength cannot lift, and I think ignorance, in
these cases, is truly the softest pillow on which I can lay my head.
Were it necessary, however, to form an opinion, I confess I should,
with Mr. Locke, prefer swallowing one incomprehensible rather than
two. It requires one effort only to admit the single incomprehensibil-
ity of matter endowed with thought, and two to believe, first that
of an existence called spirit, of which we have neither evidence nor
idea, and then secondly how that spirit, which has neither extension
nor solidity, can put material organs into motion."[9]

Many years later, when a young American correspondent requested
that Jefferson review his work, the aged statesman replied:

"I revolt against all metaphysical readings. . . . Some acquaintance
with the operations of the mind is worth acquiring. But any one of
the writers suffices for that: Locke, Kaims, Hartley, Reid, Stewart,
Brown, Tracy, etc. These dreams of the day, like those of the night,
vanish in vapour, leaving a wreck behind. The business of life is with
matter. That gives us tangible results. Handling that, we arrive at the
Knoledge of the axe, the plough, the steam-boat and everything useful in life; but from metaphysical speculations I have never seen one
useful result."[10]

Jefferson's career, then, even in philosophy, was dominated by the
Heart—but by the Heart in alliance with the Head. The significance of theory consisted in its practicality, not as an escape from
life as it must be lived in actual nature and society. In summary,
Jefferson was the Enlightenment concept of the statesman incar-
nate, a philosopher-president, a sage, and a man of action. With a
perfect sense of his own personal identity and historic *persona*, he
chose for his epitaph three accomplishments: Author of the Declaration of American Independence; Author of the Statute of Vir-

ginia for religious freedom; and Father of the University of Virginia. I shall consider each of these accomplishments in turn.

III

The Declaration of Independence is the culmination of fifteen years of revolutionary struggle. As an "expression of the American mind," to use Jefferson's words, it is the logical conclusion of the philosophy expressed by the patriot pamphleteers,[11] and contains both an explicit general philosophy of government and an implicit theory of the British Empire. In regard to the specific theory of the British Empire, although parts are manifest in the statements and the organization of the document, the crux of it is adumbrated. It pictures the British Empire "as a confederation of free peoples submitting themselves to the same king by an original compact voluntarily entered into, and terminable, in the case of any member, at the will of the people concerned."[12] It is an original, though gradually wrought, product of the American revolutionaries as they wrestled, under the pressure of events, with the status of colonies. The general philosophy of government is presented in the widely memorized second paragraph, in which the self-evident truths are proclaimed: that men are created equal; that they have inherent, unalienable rights; that primary among these rights are life, liberty, and the pursuit of happiness; that governments are instituted to secure these rights; that governments derive their just powers from the consent of the governed; that the people have the right to resist oppression and to revolt against a government which does not respect these rights—to quote the words of the Declaration, "to alter or to abolish it, and to institute new government, laying its foundation on such principles and organizing its power in such form, as to them shall seem most likely to effect their safety and happiness." It is a consummate expression of Enlightenment thought. This general philosophy of government belongs to every American's permanent heritage of political ideals. It is a philosophy which esteems the rights of individuals to be paramount, and as such, it poses for every establishment the challenge of justifying itself in human terms or run the risk of being disestablished.

The Declaration holds that the truths about human rights and government which it states are "self-evident," a word which replaces Jefferson's adjectival phrase in his rough draft: "sacred & undeniable." Other revisions are notable, as Jefferson in the rough draft wrote "that all men are created equal & independent; that from that equal creation they derive rights inherent and inalienable among which are the preservation of life, & liberty, & the pursuit of happiness; that to secure these ends," etc.[13] Such truths, for Jefferson at least, are apprehended not by reason, as Locke would have maintained, but by the moral sense, as the already quoted dialogue between the Head and the Heart made plain.[14] Democratic bias and a measure of anti-intellectualism influenced Jefferson in his doctrine of the moral sense, as in the advice he gave his nephew concerning studies at college reveals:

> Moral Philosophy. I think it lost time to attend lectures in this branch. He who made us would have been a pitiful bungler if he had made the rules of our moral conduct a matter of science. For one man of science, there are thousands who are not. What would have become of them? Man was destined for society. His morality therefore was to be formed to this object. He was endowed with a sense of right and wrong merely relative to this. This sense is as much a part of his nature as the sense of hearing, seeing, feeling; it is the true foundation of morality. . . . The moral sense, or conscience, is as much a part of man as his leg or arm. It is given to all human beings in a greater or less degree. It may be strengthened by exercise, as may any particular limb of the body. This sense is submitted indeed in some degree to the guidance of reason; but it is a small stock which is required for this; even a less one than what we call Common Sense. State a moral case to a ploughman and a professor. The former will decide it as well, and often better than the latter. . . .[15]

The Declaration of Independence grounds human rights in "the Laws of Nature and of Nature's God."[16] Basic human rights are natural rights, embracing existential and moral meanings. Regardless of the actual social conditions of men, natural rights are inalienable, not in the sense that no individual or government can violate them, but in the sense that they are imprescriptible human capacities that ought to be exercised, or organic human needs that ought to be satisfied. In the Declaration, life, liberty, and the pursuit of happiness are the fundamental natural rights; they appertain to men as individuals prior to the institution of government and thereafter as well. All other rights are presumably derived from the three basic rights. What surprises many students of American thought is that the phrase "pursuit of happiness" replaces the term "property," especially since the right to property, central in the writings of the philosophers who influenced the American patriots—e.g., Locke—was also crucial in the political argumentation leading up to the American Revolution. It has been tempting to suppose that in substituting "happiness" for "property" the Founding Fathers favored human rights over property rights. It is difficult to maintain, however, that they could have imagined a man happy who did not enjoy the right to property, although Benjamin Franklin and Thomas Jefferson apparently did hold that the right to property is subordinate to and definable by the laws established by the political society in which it exists. Still, years before 1776, legal philosophers like Beccaria and Jean Jacques Burlamaqui and American patriots such as John Dickinson, Josiah Quincy, and James Wilson had elevated happiness over property as the chief end of government.

The Declaration of Independence links life, liberty, and the pursuit of happiness as the basic natural rights of individuals with a fourth right, called "the Right of the People." This right has two dimensions. The first, and better known, dimension of "the Right of the People" consists in the right to resist oppression and to revolt. Unlike the natural rights to life, liberty, and the pursuit of happiness, the right to resist oppression, or the right of revolution, is, in the Declaration of Independence itself, not attributed to the individual man as such. Rather it is attributed to the people, and so pertains to the individual only insofar as he is a member of the people. It is a right to be exercised conditionally only. Consequently, there is in the Declaration of Independence no justification whatsoever for anarchy, or of radical cabals that resort immediately to violence. An individual can, of course, protest against action by the established government when he regards it to be a violation of natural law and natural rights. He can exercise the natural liberty to remonstrate with established authorities; failing in this regard, he can go further in the exercise of his natural liberty—to think, and to speak, and to write in protest against the established government. As a single individual, however, he cannot revolt or resist, although he may emigrate. By natural right, moreover, he can associate with other like-minded individuals who, forming a body, exercise their right of speech and press to arouse the people. Such a course of joint action, climaxing in popular resistance and revolution against the British government, had in fact occurred from 1761 to 1776. Not only was this course successful; it was, according to theory, *right*.

A dimension of the Right of the People more positive than the right of revolution is their right to institute new government in order to secure their basic rights. Enunciated in the Declaration of Independence, where perhaps it is overshadowed by the basic rights of individuals and the right of the people to revolt, the Right of the People to institute new government is understood in the Preamble to the Constitution of the United States, summed up with the opening words "We the People." Historically the exercise of this right preceded the Declaration of Independence. Not only had individual colonies—such as Virginia—moved to establish governments under new constitutions prior to the actual fact of American independence, but also the Continental Congress itself in May 1776, on a motion introduced by John Adams, directed the colonies to erect new governments and everywhere to suppress royal authority. In this way resistance against British authority could be pressed; the revolution could occur without the total collapse of American civil society into a state of nature with all the lawless violence and anarchy that would entail.

The Right of the People to institute new government is, in American revolutionary theory and in the prevalent political philosophy of the Enlightenment, exercised within the framework of "the Laws of Nature and of Nature's God." Americans inherited these ideas and their related values from Europe. But the Yale historian R. R. Palmer correctly recognizes that "the most distinctive work" of the American Revolution was in finding a method, and furnishing a model, for putting the ideas of liberty and equality and popular sovereignty into practical effect.[17] Thus the Right of the People to institute new government was, in the American Revolution, implemented by the innovative device of the constitutional convention. It was first exercised at the level of individual states—most memorably in Massachusetts; but its historically most conspicuous and influential exercise was at Philadelphia in 1787 when the Constitution of the United States was framed.

The recognition that the Declaration of Independence includes the Right of the People to institute government not only establishes the continuity from the revolution to the founding of the federal republic; it also illuminates Jefferson's own attitudes toward constitutions. His opposition to the Virginia constitution was prompted by several considerations, chief among which was the fact that, since it was enacted by the Assembly without ratification by the people, it was on the same footing as ordinary law, subject to repeal or amendment by ordinary legislative acts. What Jefferson sought in the case of Virginia, then, was a constitutional convention consisting of delegates elected by the people for the express purpose of drawing up a constitution to be submitted to the people for ratification. In regard to the federal constitution, it seems that in his correspondence with James Madison at the time of its ratification and at the beginning of the French Revolution, he questioned the validity of the fundamental laws and debts contracted by one generation to bind a later, stating it to be self-evident "that the earth belongs in usufruct to the living."[18] Yet with the proposal of the Bill of Rights, his opposition to the Constitution faded, and he welcomed its adoption.[19]

IV

As a monument of the Enlightenment, Jefferson's Statute for Religious Freedom ranks next to the Declaration of Independence. Proposed as early as 1776, and re-introduced in 1779 as part of the general revision of the laws of Virginia, the statute became embroiled in political debate and was not passed until 1786, when Jefferson was in France. The 1786 statute amended his 1779 draft, retaining the legal essentials but deleting some magnificent lines representative of the Age of Reason. Jefferson himself immediately published in France a version which is a hybrid of both his 1779 draft and the 1786 law. Nevertheless, it was hailed in enlightened circles throughout Europe, inasmuch as the legislature of the new state of Virginia was the first in the civilized world to protect religious freedom by law. Jefferson's 1779 draft is a remarkable document. To Shaftesbury and to Locke it owes much. Like Locke, Jefferson restricted civil government to public behavior and assigned religion to the sphere of private concern; and like Locke, he contended that to make civil right hinge upon religious belief was to corrupt religion itself. But as Jefferson recorded in his notes on Locke's *Letter Concerning Toleration,* "It was a great thing to go so far as he himself sais of the parl. who framed the act of tolern. but where he stopped short, we may go on."[20] The Virginia statute did go on; it extended religious toleration to all, including Baptists, Roman Catholics, and atheists, who would henceforth lose no civil and political rights as a result of their beliefs, and it totally separated church and state, so that no church would be established, nor would any church receive public funds. Jefferson's 1779 draft went even further; in the Age of Reason it declared total intellectual freedom. It opens:

> *Well aware that the opinions and belief of men depend not on their own will, but follow involuntarily the evidence proposed to their minds: that* Almighty God hath created the mind free, *and manifested his supreme will that free it shall remain by making it altogether insusceptible of restraint;* that all attempts to influence it by temporal punishments, or burthens, or by civil incapacitations, tend only to beget habits of hypocrisy and meanness, and are a departure from the plan of the holy author of our religion, who being lord both of body and mind, yet chose not to propagate it by coercions on either, as was in his Almighty power to do, but *to extend it by its influence on reason alone. . . .*[21]

And it later affirms *"that the opinions of men are not the object of civil government, nor under its jurisdiction"* (p. 546). Acknowledging that no act of a legislative assembly can bind another, which possesses powers equal to its own, the statute nevertheless declares that "the rights hereby asserted are of the natural rights of mankind, and that if any act shall be hereafter passed to repeal the present or to narrow its operation, such act will be an infringement of natural right" (pp. 546–47).

Although today Jefferson is almost universally praised for his advocacy of religious freedom,[22] in his own day he was often excoriated. Furthermore he attracted hostility because of the highly sophisticated content of his own religious beliefs, sometimes misrepresented as paganism and even atheism. Perhaps none of Jefferson's statements triggered more opposition to his person and his religion than his candid assertions: "[I]t does me no injury for my neighbor to say there are twenty gods, or no god. It neither picks my pocket nor breaks my leg" (NV 159). Ironically, Jefferson himself was a deeply religious man who generally eschewed theology and who, except in letters to friends and fellow-inquirers, elected reticence in matters of religion. As his statute on religious freedom makes plain, he firmly believed that reason alone could adjudicate, by reference to truth and evidence, between the conflicting creeds of various sects, and, further, that the competition of the sects operated as a kind of censor on the opinions professed. He himself never doubted the existence of God, Who as Creator, in his judgment, guaranteed the equality of men. As he explained in a letter to John Adams, the evidence of design and causal order in nature is so overwhelming that "it is impossible . . . for the human mind not to believe, that there is in all this, design, cause and effect, up to an ultimate cause, a Fabricator of all things from matter and motion, their Preserver and Regulator."[23]

Taking off from an already mentioned interpretation of Locke, Jefferson leaned toward a materialistic conception of the soul. Paradoxically, he extended materialism to Divinity itself. Thus he wrote Thomas Cooper, "The fathers of the church of the three first centuries generally, if not universally, were materialists, extending it even to the Creator Himself; nor indeed do I know exactly in what age of the Christian church the heresy of spiritualism was introduced."[24] And the next day in a letter to John Adams he amplified:

> When once we quit the basis of sensation, all is in the wind. To talk of *immaterial* existences, is to talk of *nothings*. To say that the human soul, angels, God, are immaterial, is to say, they are *nothings*, or that there is no God, no angels, no soul. I cannot reason otherwise: but I believe I am supported in my creed of materialism by the Lockes, the Tracys and the Stewarts. At what age of the Christian Church this heresy of *immaterialism*, or masked atheism, crept in, I do not exactly know. But a heresy it certainly is. Jesus taught nothing of it. He told us, indeed, that "God is a Spirit," but He has not defined what a spirit is, nor said that it is not *matter*. And the ancient fathers generally, of the three first centuries, held it to be matter, light and thin indeed, an etherial gas; but still matter.[25]

Hence Jefferson was a materialistic deist, and he cherished the historical Jesus not as a divine being but as the greatest human moral teacher. In a noteworthy letter to Benjamin Rush, written during his first term as president, Jefferson unfolded his view of

Jesus Christ. "I am a Christian," Jefferson confessed, "in the only sense in which he wished any one to be; sincerely attached to his doctrines, in preference to all others; and believing he never claimed any other."[26] Influenced by the English Unitarian Joseph Priestley, Jefferson compared the doctrines of Jesus with those of the ancient moral philosophers and of the Jews, weighing their advantages and disadvantages. On the side of Christianity's disadvantages Jefferson listed the considerations that Jesus wrote nothing, that his life was so brief that his teachings were neither comprehensive nor mature, that these teachings were recorded by uneducated men who had to rely solely upon their faulty memories, and finally that they were corrupted and disfigured by erroneous theological conceptions. Nevertheless, Jefferson esteemed Jesus to be, though wholly human, the greatest of moral teachers. Among the advantages of Jesus' teachings Jefferson recorded the following considerations: that Jesus was a deist like the Jews, but surpassed them in providing a more just conception of the one God; that he excelled all prior ethical systems "in inculcating universal philanthropy, not only to kindred and friends, to neighbors and countrymen, but to all mankind, gathering all into one family, under the bonds of love, charity, peace, common wants and common aids"; that, whereas the philosophers and the Jews laid hold of actions only in their moral precepts, Jesus "pushed his scrutinies into the heart of man; erected his tribunal in the region of his thoughts, and purified the waters at the fountain head"; and, finally, that "[h]e taught, emphatically, the doctrine of a future state, which was either doubted, or disbelieved by the Jews; and wielded it with efficacy, as an important incentive, supplementary to the other motives to moral conduct."[27] Indefatigable, Jefferson carried his quest for the historical Jesus beyond this brief but penetrating syllabus. While president, he compiled a set of Biblical texts in parallel columns of Greek, Latin, French, and English on which he later worked during retirement. It came to be known as *The Jefferson Bible*, and is today recognized as a singular presentation of the historical Jesus, consisting exclusively of extracts from the Gospels of Matthew, Mark, Luke, and John. Jefferson's title reveals the contents of his work: *The Life and Morals of Jesus of Nazareth*.[28]

V

The emphasis Enlightenment thought placed on reason and liberty is as conspicuous in Jefferson's historic role in the development of American education as in his statute on religious freedom. On his epitaph, at his own wish, he is identified as "the Father of the University of Virginia." As an historian of Jefferson's educational work has written:

> He bought the site for the university and surveyed it. He planned the buildings and superintended their construction. He wrung funds from a niggardly legislature while he sought even the smallest economy in the cost of bricks. The course of study, the plan of organization, the rules for admission, graduation, and government—all were his work. He set standards of democracy for the faculty and of manly self-reliance for the students. Nearly every detail of material construction, of organization, or of method was his. He was more than a founder. He was the Father of the University of Virginia.[29]

Historically, the establishment of the University of Virginia in 1818 was the terminus of a long train of efforts devoted to public education, harking back to Jefferson's "Bill for the More General Diffusion of Knowledge" and his "Bill for the Amending of the Constitution of the College of William and Mary" submitted in the general revival of laws to the Virginia Assembly on June 18, 1779. Out of the astonishing number and variety of Jefferson's statements on and activities in behalf of public education, it is germane, in surveying and assessing his mind, to focus on a few salient concepts and ideals. Perhaps the first principle of his educational theory is best formulated in a Baconian sentence which, although buried in an otherwise undistinguished letter, and despite his habitual misspelling, affirms, " 'Knolege is power, knolege is safety . . . knolege is happiness.' "[30]

Jefferson's educational theory grew out of Enlightenment philosophy, underscoring the importance of useful science for human liberty and social progress. He drew upon many classical and modern sources, and among the moderns Locke, Tracy, and Priestley figured prominently. What Jefferson borrowed he refashioned within the crucible of his own experience as student, as *philosophe* and *idéologue*, and as statesman, to articulate and apply a singular and influential program of education for a democratic society. At its base were to be ward schools, supported by local taxes and governed by locally elected supervisors. The ward schools were designed to provide primary education in the essentials of reading, writing, and common arithmetic free to all boys and girls for a period of three years according to the 1779 bill, and afterward at their parents' expense, except in those cases where, because of exceptional talent handicapped by personal poverty, public support was warranted. From the ward schools of primary education boys could proceed upward to district schools, which offered secondary education, and beyond, ultimately to the university. Jefferson's entire plan mixed democracy with elitism. The justification of primary, general education for all at public expense was that it both promoted their personal happiness and enhanced their usefulness in a republican society. To exercise the suffrage it was essential that men know and understand the issues at stake. Pertinently, Jefferson did not condone compulsory education, which he considered to be an infringement upon parental rights, but he insisted upon literacy as a requirement for the franchise, believing that it would induce parents to send their children to school. While all boys and girls were entitled to primary education at public expense, every boy able to pay for his own education could proceed up the ladder to higher education as far as his talents, inclinations, and family's encouragement would take him. By contrast, the opportunities of the poor boys were realistically curtailed. Jefferson recognized, without lament, the basic division of society into a vast class of workers and farmers, on the one hand, and a small class of learned persons, including members of the professions, on the other. He also recognized that nature had strewn exceptional talents among mankind without regard to economic status. The highest levels of education, attainable by the well-to-do on their own, should, he urged, be accessible to the exceptionally talented poor. Thus from each ward school the brightest poor boy could proceed at public expense to the district school, where he would again enter into keen competition with other poor boys in order to remain until he completed his secondary education in the first place and, secondly, to continue up the ladder to the university. By competitive means, Jefferson explained, "the best geniuses will be raked from the rubbish" (NV 146). The aim throughout was not only the personal development of the individual but also the benefits that society would gain. The curricula and professorships Jefferson proposed at the university level fit his scheme of socially useful education. Suffice it to observe that he excluded theology, that he favored ancient and modern languages, that he was wary of who would be appointed to the professorship in law, even attempting to prescribe the texts in this politically volatile field, and that he emphasized useful subjects, such as "technical philosophy" (architecture and engineering) and agriculture. The Head was to serve the Heart, which in turn was to be influenced by the Head.

Jefferson's conception of wards as basic units of organization, applied to politics as well as to education, is a cardinal element in his republicanism. Small communities realize direct, participatory democracy from which the best men are selected to serve as representatives in higher, more comprehensive, and more complex governmental organizations, just as the brightest boys are culled from the primary schools to begin their way competitively up the educational ladder. In both types of institutions, educational and political, the objective is the same: to educe the best men to the top for the benefit of all. At the heart of this program is a belief in a natural aristocracy which Jefferson shared with his Federalist friend John Adams, as he explained in one of his letters.

> I agree with you that there is a natural aristocracy among men. The grounds of this are virtue and talents. . . . There is also an artificial aristocracy, founded on wealth and birth, without either virtue or talents. . . . The natural aristocracy I consider as the most precious gift of nature, for the instruction, the trusts, and government of society. . . . The artificial aristocracy is a mischievous ingredient in government, and provision should be made to prevent its ascendancy.[31]

Jefferson's espousal of a natural aristocracy at first appears to contradict his axiom of the equality of men affirmed in the Declaration of Independence. For if men are naturally unequal, some being superior in talents and virtues to others, how can it be said that they are equal? At this point it is germane to respond that the political inequalities institutionalized in the European aristocracies and monarchies are unnatural. To assert that men are equal is political dynamite intended to explode foreign hierarchies based on invidious distinctions. While the paradox of affirming both equality and natural aristocracy is softened, however, it is not dissipated.

VI

This paradox is resurrected in more disturbing form when the actual station of Jefferson is considered—a slaveholder proclaiming human equality and liberty. It was an irony which his contemporaries, opposed to the American Revolution, did not fail to exploit: Thomas Hutchinson, the exiled Tory governor of Massachusetts, alleged hypocrisy. Recently it has stimulated investigations of historians. Thus Edmund S. Morgan has penetratingly analyzed the paradox within the context of the society from which it arose, contending that in Virginia a belief in republican equality rested on slavery. As Morgan says, "Aristocrats could more safely preach equality in a slave society than in a free one. Slaves did not become leveling mobs, because their owners would see to it that they had no chance to. The apostrophes to equality were not addressed to them."[37] And examining Jefferson's role in regard to slavery, David Brion Davis has found that it is worse than ambiguous, glittering in words but poor in deeds.[38] For his time and station Jefferson attacked slavery in strikingly vehement terms. Among his most famous efforts against slavery were the clause his rough draft of the Declaration of Independence contained condemning George III for the slave trade and his legislative and constitutional attempts in Virginia in 1779 and 1783 respectively to manumit the descendants of slaves born after 1800. Although defeated, he nevertheless affected a vigorous anti-slavery rhetoric, to which he resorted long after he abandoned further activities in behalf of abolition and emancipation.

Few thinkers have matched Jefferson's sensitivity to the corrupting influence of slavery upon those associated with the institution. With rare insight he wrote in the *Notes on Virginia* in response to the query concerning manners: "The whole commerce between master and slave is a perpetual exercise of the most boisterous passions, the most unremitting despotism on the one part, and degrading submissions on the other. Our children see this, and learn to imitate it; for man is an imitative animal" (NV 162). Furthermore, he had the foresight to apprehend that slavery must end, although his vision was framed in fear. As Jefferson confided, "I tremble for my country when I reflect that God is just" (NV 163). Despite his awareness of the injustice of slavery, Jefferson became more solicitous of the rights of states as he grew older, and above all, he feared the aggrandizement of the national government upon the southern states. His "fire-bell in the night," to use his own phrase, was the Missouri Compromise.[34] At the same time his attitude toward the status of the black in American society was disturbingly ambivalent. While he desired emancipation, he descried the possibility of an integrated American society in which former masters and slaves would live and work together. As he said in his *Autobiography*, written in his seventy-sixth year:

> Nothing is more certainly written in the book of fate, than that these people are to be free; nor is it less certain that the two races, equally free, cannot live in the same government. Nature, habit, opinion have drawn indelible lines of distinction between them. It is still in our power to direct the process of emancipation and deportation, peaceably, and in such slow degree, as that the evil will wear off insensibly, and their place be, *pari passu*, filled up by free white laborers. If, on the contrary, it is left to force itself on, human nature must shudder at the prospect held up.[35]

An additional restraint on Jefferson's activities in behalf of the abolition of slavery, apart from his concern for his political station and private reputation in a slaveholding society, was the crudely scientific (or pseudo-scientific) belief in the natural inferiority of blacks. The author of the *Notes on Virginia*, who desired recognition in the learned circles of enlightened Europe, and who had, in a characteristically un-American way, defended the equal humanity of Indians, filled his pages with derogatory, racist statements concerning blacks. Ruling out the incorporation of emancipated blacks into American society, Jefferson said, "Deep rooted prejudices entertained by the whites; ten thousand recollections, by the blacks, of the injuries they have sustained; and many other circumstances, will divide us into parties, and produce convulsions which will probably never end but in the extermination of the one or the other race" (NV 138). And to these considerations, which he considered political, he added others, which he called physical and moral. Among the signs of physical inferiority, he dilated on the ugliness of being black, remarking, for example, that the superior beauty of whites is confirmed in "their [the blacks'] own judgment in favour of the whites, declared by the preference of them, as uniformly as is the preference of the Oran-ootan for the black women over those of his own species" (NV 138). Remarks such as these, many of which persist almost unaltered in the thought and language of American racism, poured from his pen.

Does Jefferson's racism contradict the general philosophy of government he professed in the Declaration of Independence? *Prima facie* it seems inconsistent with the proposition that men are created equal. But so on first reading does his doctrine of natural aristocracy seem incompatible with the assertion of human equality. The way out of the impasse is to acknowledge that Jefferson probably meant something by the proposition of human equality quite different from what we have come to think he meant. In the original rough draft, after stating that all men are created equal, he added the now deleted phrase "and from that equal creation." Consequently, a proper interpretation of Jefferson's intent is that all men are created equally and independently; that, regardless of differences in the individuals and in their ethnic natures, they are equal in respect to their having been created by God Who, at the moment of creation, gave them rights to life, liberty, and the pursuit of happiness. Jefferson repeatedly condemned slavery as an encroachment not upon the equality of blacks but upon their liberty. Jefferson supported his belief that blacks constitute a distinct race inferior to whites by judgments that are correctly discerned to be unfounded and prejudicial. He thought, however, that these judgments were warranted by experience—in other words, that they were scientific. Of course they may be branded as racist; but their real defect is that they are false.

Nevertheless, Jefferson had the candor to face the troublesome challenge ethnicity poses for egalitarianism. We may be no more successful in handling this challenge than Jefferson's nineteenth-century successors were in coping with slavery. For Jefferson in 1776 and for several decades thereafter other challenges were more imminent. In the perspective of history we are able to observe that he was bound to his own class of Virginia slaveholders, that his Heart could not terminate those social relationships which distorted his perceptions of blacks, even though in amazing other ways his Head and Heart had grasped principles which transcended his time and place. It should be no wonder that, in the dialogue between the Head and the Heart, it is the Heart which says, "We have no rose without it's thorn; no pleasure without alloy. It is the law of our existence; and we must acquiesce."[36]

Is this merely a lame apology for a major architect of American democracy who, all his achievements and pretensions notwithstanding, remained a racist? Does Jefferson need our apology? Listen to what he wrote John Adams in 1820: "We have, willingly, done injury to no man; and have done for our country the good which has fallen in our way, so far as commensurate with the faculties given us. That we have not done more than we could, cannot be imputed to us as a crime before any tribunal."[37]

NOTES

1. *Jefferson and the Rights of Man* (Boston: Little, Brown, 1951), p. 72.

2. TJ to W. S. Smith, Paris, October 22, 1786, *The Papers of Thomas Jefferson*, edd. Julian P. Boyd et al., 20 vols. (Princeton: Princeton University Press, 1950–1982), x 476.

3. TJ to Maria Cosway, Paris, October 12, 1786, ibid., 444. Subsequent references to this letter are given in parentheses in the text.

4. *The Commonplace Book of Thomas Jefferson: A Repertory of His Ideas on Government*, ed. Gilbert Chinard (Baltimore: The Johns Hopkins University Press, 1926); *The Literary Bible of Thomas Jefferson: His Commonplace Book of Philosophers and Poets*, ed. Gilbert Chinard (Baltimore: The Johns Hopkins University Press, 1928); and Adrienne Koch, *The Philosophy of Thomas Jefferson* (New York: Columbia University Press, 1943).

5. Quoted in Edwin T. Martin, *Thomas Jefferson: Scientist* (New York: Schuman, 1952), p. 219.

6. Thomas Jefferson, *Notes on the State of Virginia*, ed. William Peden (New York: Norton, Inc., 1972), pp. v, xi. Hereafter NV. Later references to this work are given in parentheses in the text.

7. John Adams to TJ, Quincy, December 16, 1816, as quoted in Gilbert Chinard, *Jefferson et les idéologues* (Baltimore: The Johns Hopkins University Press, 1925), p. 257.

8. TJ to John Adams, Monticello, January 11, 1817, as quoted in ibid., p. 259.

9. TJ to John Adams, Monticello, March 14, 1820, as quoted in ibid., pp. 275–76.

10. TJ to Clark Sheldon, Monticello, December 5, 1825, as quoted in ibid., p. 282.

11. See Andrew J. Reck, "The Declaration of Independence as an 'Expression of the American Mind,'" *Revue Internationale de Philosophie*, 121–122 (1977), 401–37, and "The Philosophical Background of the Amer-

ican Revolution," *The Southwestern Journal of Philosophy*, 5 (1974), 179–202.

12. Carl Becker, *The Declaration of Independence* (New York: Vintage, 1970), p. 130.

13. Jefferson's "Original Rough Draft" of the Declaration of Independence, *Papers*, ed. Boyd et al., I 423.

14. See also Morton White, *Science and Sentiment in America* (New York: Oxford University Press, 1972), pp. 55–70. White now considers that his account in that work "exaggerated the extent to which some of Jefferson's references to the moral sense signified an abandonment of moral rationalism." See Morton White, *The Philosophy of the American Revolution* (New York: Oxford University Press, 1978), p. 101n5. In his later book White insists that the Declaration uses the word "self-evident" in the Lockean sense, but finds the clue to the interpretation of Jefferson's intentions in the philosophy of Jean Jacques Burlamaqui. On the other hand, Gary Wills, *Inventing America: Jefferson's Declaration of Independence* (New York: Doubleday, 1978), finds that "self-evident" in the sense of Locke or Reid will not suffice to establish the sorts of moral and political presuppositions proclaimed by Jefferson (pp. 181–92), and locates the major influence on Jefferson in the moral sense doctrine of Francis Hutcheson. Both White's book and Wills's book aim to displace Locke as the philosopher of the Declaration of Independence, White substituting Burlamaqui and Wills proposing Hutcheson. See my reviews of these books in the *Review of Metaphysics*, 32 (1979), 572–74.

15. TJ to Peter Carr, Paris, August 10, 1787, *Papers*, ed. Boyd et al., XII 14–15.

16. See Andrew J. Reck, "Natural Law in American Revolutionary Thought," *Review of Metaphysics*, 30 (1977), 686–714, and "The American Revolution: A Philosophical Interpretation," *The Southwestern Journal of Philosophy*, 8 (1977), 95–104.

17. *The Age of the Democratic Revolution*, 2 vols. (Princeton: Princeton University Press, 1959), I 214–15.

18. TJ to James Madison, Paris, September 6, 1789, *Papers*, ed. Boyd et al., XV 392.

19. *Autobiography of Thomas Jefferson*, ed. Dumas Malone (New York: Capricorn, n.d.), p. 89.

20. "Notes on Locke and Shaftesbury," *Papers*, ed. Boyd et al., I 548.

21. "A Bill for Establishing Religious Freedom," ibid., II 545. All quotations are from this edition. The clauses in italics are not contained in the 1786 Statute or in Jefferson's own publication.

22. See Leonard W. Levy, *Jefferson and Civil Liberties* (Cambridge: Harvard University Press, 1963), pp. 3ff. Levy, whose penetrating book unveils "the darker side" of Jefferson as civil libertarian, nevertheless judges that, in regard to religious freedom, he "displayed a principled consistency." The "darker side" of Jefferson has been successfully exploited in the novel *Burr* (New York: Random House, 1973) by Gore Vidal, who apparently seeks to

redeem our sullied present by fictionally reconstructing a more sullied past.

23. TJ to John Adams, Monticello, April 11, 1823, *The Writings of Thomas Jefferson*, edd., Andrew A. Lepscomb and Albert E. Berg, 20 vols. (Washington, D.C.: The Thomas Jefferson Memorial Association, 1904), xv 427.

24. TJ to Thomas Cooper, Monticello, August 14, 1820, ibid., 266.

25. TJ to John Adams, Monticello, August 15, 1820, ibid., 274–75. In this letter and in the letter to Thomas Cooper just cited, Jefferson footnoted his suggestion that the "heresy" of spiritualism or immaterialism stemmed from Athanasius and the Council of Nicaea in 324. Ultimately, of course, he attributed it to Plato, whom he intensely disliked not only for his foggy mysticism but also for the distortion of the teaching of Socrates.

26. TJ to Benjamin Rush, Washington, April 21, 1803, ibid., x 380.

27. Ibid., 383–85.

28. It was first lithoprinted by vote of Congress in 1904. An accessible and accurate edition is Thomas Jefferson, *The Life and Morals of Jesus of Nazareth*, ed. Henry Wilder Foote (Boston: Beacon, 1951).

29. Roy J. Honeywell, *The Educational Work of Thomas Jefferson* (Cambridge: Harvard University Press, 1931), p. 67.

30. TJ to George Ticknor, November 15, 1817, quoted in ibid., p. 146.

31. TJ to John Adams, Monticello, October 28, 1813, in *Writings*, edd. Lepscomb & Berg, XIII 396.

32. *American Slavery, American Freedom* (New York: Norton, 1975), p. 380.

33. *The Problem of Slavery in the Age of Revolution, 1770–1823* (Ithaca: Cornell University Press, 1975), pp. 164–84.

34. TJ to John Homes, Monticello, April 22, 1820, *Writings*, edd. Lepscomb & Berg, xv 249.

35. Ed. Malone, p. 62.

36. TJ to Maria Cosway, Paris, October 12, 1786, in *Papers*, ed. Boyd, x 451.

37. TJ to John Adams, Monticello, March 14, 1820, *Writings*, edd. Lepscomb & Berg, xv 241.

3

Emerson and America's Future

ROBERT C. POLLOCK

Late of

Fordham University

EMERSON'S ESSAY "The American Scholar" is rightly regarded as a second declaration of independence. Indeed, Emerson's thinking in its entirety may be seen as an attempt to explicate what Americans are committed to if they are to follow through to the last consequence what is implicitly contained in the Declaration of Independence. One scholar, commenting on an observation by F. O. Matthiessen, writes that for him "not only Emerson, but also Hawthorne, Thoreau, Whitman, and Melville, 'felt that it was incumbent upon their generation to give [artistic] fulfillment to the potentialities freed by the Revolution, to provide a culture commensurate with America's political opportunity.'"[1]

The scholar who has singled out these words of Matthiessen's himself goes on to say, "Particularly among transcendental poets, an effort was made not only to free America's art and America's judgment of art from the disciplines of the dominant European standards of taste, but also to free the individual American, whether artist or critic, from all rigidly instituted standards of esthetic judgment."[2]

Emerson understood full well the liberating role of aesthetic consciousness in the expanding life of man. But his mission lay elsewhere, in seeking a path of human existence that called for nothing less than a revolutionary approach to life itself in its entirety. So far from being simply an intellectual, he was concerned to show that this revolutionary approach is no mere doctrine, but a source of power, since it would liberate in profusion the energy requisite to carrying on a continuous war against whatever curtails a human being's right to live on the widest possible range.

People were longing to operate beyond the scope of custom and habit. Institutionalized thinking was beginning to show its heavy hand. Many were yearning for a new kind of revolution, one that would liberate human experience itself. Philip Rahv in *Image and Idea* makes some brilliant observations on this matter. Selecting Henry James as an outstanding example of the American preoccupation with experience, he writes:

> the lesson he taught in *The Ambassadors,* as in many of his other works, must be understood as no less than a revolutionary appeal. It is a veritable declaration of the rights of man—not, to be sure, of the rights of the public, of the social man, but the rights of the private man, of the rights of personality, whose openness to experience provides the sole effective guaranty of its development.[3]

Emerson himself was fully aware of the new imperative that had surfaced within the New World and for him it required a ceaseless resistance against whatever would impose restrictions upon the individual's freedom to function intellectually, aesthetically, and imaginatively from the center of his own personal being. As one who was forever consulting experience, he knew that the expansion of personal life called for a unity of functioning that embraced all the dimensions of human existence. New England transcendentalism was much concerned with wholeness of life. For those who espoused it, life meant wholeness of life, or it meant nothing. Emerson's own version can be identified as a passion to achieve a vision of reality comprehensive enough to accommodate things ordinarily viewed in isolation—a vision which would bring the power of the individual into full operation. People everywhere were rushing into life, and there were among them those who longed to rid themselves of a domesticated intelligence. On the other hand, there was a mounting obsession with material success, a mechanistic conception within the sciences which was suffocating the spirit and, within religion itself, a stifling of its own vital forces. In seeking to overcome this fragmented condition of human existence, no one was more qualified than Emerson to take on so formidable a task. The motivation was powerful within a world in which the issues were being sharply defined. Emerson was also well equipped culturally and intellectually for the task. As we must remember, he was an extraordinarily cultivated and sophisticated man who was, moreover, in touch with the primitive and elemental forces in American life that had been kept alive by the moving frontier. He was comfortable in a number of literatures and in a way that was far from academic. We can gauge what this vital concern for human experience, as imbedded in these literatures, signified in view of what he himself wrote concerning his Puritan ancestry. In the daily life of the Puritans " 'the whole Jewish history became flesh and blood.' " [4] What is interesting here is that it was precisely the experiential response of the Puritans that so conspicuously stood out in his mind. It would appear that as a child of the Puritans he was well able to relate to it. But Emerson must have realized that his own capacity to translate ideas and beliefs into experience had achieved mammoth proportions with regard to his vast readings. Undoubtedly he would have been astonished to find that the Puritans were, like himself, quite able to deal with multiple worlds. Thus their fervor for things religious was matched by a fervor for things scientific. This is vividly seen in Jonathan Edwards, who absorbed Newtonian science into his very bloodstream and into the whole fabric of his experience. Where others had dealt with Newton in a purely intellectual and formalistic way, Edwards penetrated into something far deeper: namely, a profound experience touching on a mystical dimension in the Newtonian world view which was lost sight of by later Newtonians. Like Edwards, Emerson was a veritable alchemist in his power to transmute intellectual material into something extraordinarily personal and intimate. We can gain some idea of his experiential involvement in his readings when we see him actually undertaking what, in his circumstances, would have appeared a rather daring feat—a translation of Dante's *Vita Nuova*.[5] Ralph L. Rusk writes, "Naturally in such a *tour de force* his lock steps were sometimes missteps, but he manages to keep much of the fragile beauty of the book."[6] As for a figure like Goethe, however far Emerson may have gone in his readings of this great poet and cosmological thinker, he surely gained vital contact with him through Margaret Fuller. She had a passion for communication, which in her knowledgeable enthusiasm for Goethe stood him in good stead. His openness to experience, as we can see, carried him everywhere, as though he instinctively knew that as an intellectual builder he would depend, for the architectural solidity of his thinking, on his capacity to meet human experience on a broad front. Accordingly, it came quite natural to him to seek intimate contact with a Plato or a Plotinus, a Coleridge or a Wordsworth. But that did not suffice, for he also delved into the wisdom of the East, which he found mentally and spiritually unbinding in leading him into the immensities for which he so greatly yearned.

Emerson longed to communicate to his countrymen the message of human liberation. Nothing less than a full-scale message would suffice, one that called for an immense widening of human perspectives. The generality of Americans were becoming habituated to a New World experience that had captured their imaginations. Within the New World the sense of material things had been considerably strengthened and with it a feeling of a wide-open future and what went with it—new mental habits as regards process and change. Emerson had no intention of diminishing a pattern of awareness that represented a real maturation of human consciousness. His own solutions remained very much within a larger and more meaningful scheme of things. He aimed, in fact, to launch Americans toward realities seen in their widest cosmic frame. Hence, so far from negating the American experience, he was seeking to open it up still farther and in every possible direction. He had too much Yankee good sense not to know that far from proclaiming his truths in a vacuum, his message had distant echoes in their souls. Nothing could be more alien to his spirit than to sap the life energy of a pioneering people. In essence he was, within the conceptual sphere, a pioneering man and what we might call an energy person. Thus he was concerned at all times to put into his compatriots' hands "new weapons in a magazine of power." And, as he saw it, nothing less than a cosmic breadth of view, one that illumined the commonly shared experience, would bring that about. The soul, he proclaimed, "invites every man to expand to the full circle of the universe."[7] To a people in tune with his central message he could say: "Nothing is secure but life, transition, the energizing spirit. . . . People wish to be settled; only as far as they are unsettled is there any hope for them."[8] Again, addressing himself to the American sense of new beginnings, he spoke thus: "No man ever came to an experience which was satiating, but his good is tidings of a better. Onward and onward! In liberated moments we know that a new picture of life and duty is already possible." [9]

Emerson found himself in the position of having to articulate powerful insights which hovered over many an American mind and from which it was averting its gaze. Whitehead has made an observation on the founders of Christianity which can be suggestive in appraising Emerson. Of these founders he writes, "that with passionate earnestness they gave free reign to their absolute ethical intuitions respecting ideal possibilities without a thought of the preservation of society. The crash of society was certain and imminent." [10] Emerson in a large sense was in a somewhat similar situation, inasmuch as he was confronting a nation that appeared to be squandering its vast potential for human development in an unrestrained stampede for material gain. Indeed, it would appear as though its very lifeblood as a great nation was in danger of ebbing away.

America stood at the crossroads of a new epoch, characterized by man's reaching out to a new view of himself as an intellectual–spiritual being. Emerson had a profound awareness of the new aspirations, but he also saw that a thin line separated the dream from the nightmare in American life. Things were enslaving the spirit, and man had shrunk to dwarf-like proportions. He felt the overpowering need to proclaim truths that could guide America toward her true destiny.

Whitehead speaks of truths which haunt humanity and "which mankind has grown to the stature of being able to feel though perhaps as yet unable to frame in fortunate expression." [11] It was precisely to such higher truths that Emerson dedicated himself. People might call him a romantic visionary or an optimist since he appeared to be engaged in an impractical, and even quixotic, enterprise. What they fail to see is that, given his wide historical perspective, these so-called impractical truths reveal themselves as the life force of man's drive to higher levels of perception and experience. To Emerson it was clear that such truths must be considered the absolute prerequisite of an intellectually and spiritually re-energized humanity. Perhaps in the light of the foregoing remarks, we can grasp the integral necessities that made Emerson, first and last, a cosmic man unable to find his bearings on any matter save by relating it to cosmic realities. "To be" meant for him to be within a universe. "Universe" was, for him, no mere idea but rather a living experience in which a powerful sense of interrelation and interdependence reverberated throughout his entire being. Even in regard to the beautiful, he could write that in order to be beautiful a thing must have "a certain cosmical quality, or a power to suggest relation to the whole world, and so lift the object out of a pitiful individuality."[12]

Emerson's universe is a great harmonic order in which nothing escapes a divine principle. Yet for him such a universe, so far from exhibiting a static character, reveals itself as a vast and dynamic profusion of forms marked by perpetually surprising similitudes and relationships. It was a universe in which flux and novelty reigned supreme. "There are no fixtures in Nature." The divine power, as one commentator writes,

> refuses the tried path, the old form. An infinite variety which age cannot wither nor custom stale is its prerogative. At this point the doctrine of self-reliance . . . assumes at a stroke a new interest and dignity. If difference be the mark and measure of the presence of the divinity, self-reliance, which is the expression of that difference, is the removal of the barrier to the influx of God into the heart.[13]

Thus Emersonian self-reliance is no mere expression of titanic egoism, for, seen in its widest possible context, it gives new force to the idea of the divine presence, not only within man in a superlatively special way, but within an infinite variety of living things. Above all, it is a world in which deep speaks to deep and each thing has its divine space and therefore its own unique interiority. As Emerson says, "The remotest spaces of nature are visited, and the farthest sundered things are brought together, by a subtle spiritual connection."[14] Again he writes, "The greatest delight which the fields and woods minister is the suggestion of an occult relation between man and the vegetable. I am not alone and unacknowledged. They nod to me, and I to them."[15]

As we can see, Emerson cannot be dealt with save as a cosmic-minded man. Taking his measure as such, we can estimate the inadequacy of interpreting any aspect of his thought within a too narrow compass, as, for example, when we view his doctrine of self-reliance in strictly social terms. How often too has his doctrine of the Oversoul been belittled by those who have ignored his cosmological framework! Yet much that is misconstrued or passed over as of little consequence blazes forth with new significance once we enter into his universe.

Whitehead makes an observation on the poet Shelley which is illuminating while broadening our view of Emerson.

> What the hills were to the youth of Wordsworth, a chemical laboratory was to Shelley. It is unfortunate that Shelley's literary critics have, in this respect, so little of Shelley in their own mentality. They tend to treat as a casual oddity of Shelley's nature what was, in fact, part of the main structure of his mind, permeating his poetry through and through. If Shelley had been born a hundred years later, the twentieth century would have seen a Newton among chemists.[16]

Intrigued by these words of Whitehead's, Professor Carl Grabo of the University of Chicago, following upon his own investigations, wrote a book entitled *A Newton Among Poets*. He tells us in his Preface how he was affected by Whitehead's challenge to the critics and decided to look into the matter for himself. He makes known his conclusion to the effect that Whitehead was entirely right and "justified in his strictures."[17] He writes further: "Criticism has ignored Shelley's interest in science or belittled it. . . . There has been much talk of Shelley's exquisite lyricism and very little of Shelley's hard intellectual meaning. . . . The study of Shelley's science has proved a revelation to me, and my findings, however inadequate and incomplete, will, I think, prove a revelation to others."[18] We learn from Grabo that Shelley's interest in science was far from that of a specialist. In Grabo's own words, "the problem which he sought to solve is, in its terms, the problem which we have set ourselves: to reconcile materialistic with mystical thought or, as we inadequately phrase it, 'science with religion.'" Critics overlook much in their interpretations of Shelley's poetry precisely because they fail to take account of his scientific concepts. Certainly the generality of critics, in missing his scientific interests, could not take full cognizance of the metaphysical strands in his thought which formed his mental universe. Controversy has arisen out of Grabo's thesis. However we may view the matter, this has proved profitable insofar as interpreters have had to take into account, in one way or another, the scientific and cosmological dimensions in Shelley's thinking.[19]

Gerald Holten, a physicist, writes of "these great syntheses which once comprised our intellectual and moral home—the cosmic view of the Book of Genesis, Homer, Dante, Milton, Goethe"[20]—which intellectuals have left far behind. Emerson himself was concerned with precisely the kind of synthesis we associate with a Dante or a Goethe, a synthesis that takes in the larger life of man. It would appear that he understood full well that such a synthesis, one of cosmological proportions, was a universal achievement within human history. Most likely he would have been in accord with the view of Joseph Needham, author of the magnificent volumes entitled *Science and Civilization in China,*[21] that the understanding of nature is one single enterprise on the part of mankind. Contact on the broad front of Eastern and Western cosmologies and the modes of knowledge and experience which they entail have broadened considerably what a full-scale cosmological picture would comprise. When we speak of a cosmological orientation, with Emerson in mind, we are taking cosmology in its broadest meaning, as a world picture which motivates an entire culture and involves the whole being of man.

Whitehead writes: "In each age of the world distinguished by high activity there will be found at its culmination, and among the agencies leading to that culmination, some profound cosmological outlook, implicitly accepted, impressing its own type upon the current springs of action."[22] This kind of all-encompassing integration of which Whitehead speaks ceased to function as a human goal due to the divided consciousness. Mechanistic science made inevitable the divided consciousness in narrowing down the meaning of cosmological to the point where it no longer answered to the conception that Whitehead seems to have in mind. A full-scale cosmology has, as a result, lain in abeyance since the seventeenth century. Nevertheless, the way to a larger view of things was already being opened up by such great figures as Goethe and Coleridge, and we surely can add here the name of Emerson.

Today scientists and historians of science are leading the way in the revising of scientific history in the direction of a more integral study of the diverse currents of thought, belief, and experience which have contributed to the development of the sciences. Thus, even mystical currents are now taken seriously as agents in the scientific development. We are not surprised to find scientists who feel free to deal seriously with Newton, not simply as scientist, but

as a total human being, in recognizing that his mystical and al-
chemical outlook may well have been an important factor in his
scientific thinking.

We are now in a position to appreciate Emerson's sustained
attempt to undermine the belief in a divided consciousness, in
which the whole complex life of the psyche, homeless and without
a universe, is relegated to no man's land. Today things have gone so
far in the right direction that we can applaud Thoreau's great
affirmation, "The fact is I am a mystic, a transcendentalist, and a
natural philosopher to boot." [23]

After having our fill of the lamentably acosmic approach to
Emerson on the part of commentators, it is indeed refreshing to
come upon a man like Buckminster Fuller, engineer, architect,
mathematician, who has occupied the Eliot Norton Chair of
Poetry at Harvard, and who is, besides, well on the inside of modern physics, and whose intellectual genealogy according to a biographer, Hugh Kenner, goes straight back to Emerson. Here we
have a thoroughly scientific and cosmological man who in some
important aspects is in intellectual rapport with Emerson. It seems
clear that it is precisely because he is in a superlative degree cosmic-
oriented and in tune with the new physics that he can, with
enviable ease, reinstate metaphysical thinking and a transcendent
viewpoint into the life of the mind. Kenner has brought to our
attention things in Fuller that enable us to couple his name with
that of Emerson. For instance, he says that when Fuller "slips from
number and structure into a mysticism that annoys scientists, or
from man's affairs into geometric talk that bewilders literary folk,
he makes a transition not only natural to him but faithful to a
kinship between the traditions of Emerson and Pythagoras." [24]
Emerson would have savored the idea of a scientist's being so intimately one with the whole scheme of things that he could be
called, in Ezra Pound's words addressed to Fuller, " 'friend of the
universe.' " [25]

Now it would appear that we are reaching a point where we shall
have to deal with Emerson as Whitehead and Grabo and now
others have done with Shelley. There are interesting analogies between Emerson's cosmology and Buckminster Fuller's. Needless
to say, there are also significant differences between them. But the
similarities are nonetheless of a character that throw new light on

Emerson who, like Fuller, was opening new doors into cosmological thinking.

Before dealing with Fuller, let me return, if only briefly, to what I have already touched on in Emerson's cosmology. The most obvious thing about it is its total concern for the absolute connections among all things. In our own time, relations have come to the forefront in speculative thought, and Emerson would have been delighted. He was captivated by this idea and, considering his extraordinary capacity for experience, we can measure the extent to which relationship permeated his whole life. We find numerous observations of relationship. This fact alone should warn anyone who has made a mere individualist out of Emerson to tread warily. "A man is a bundle of relations, a knot of roots, whose flower and fruitage is the world."[26] "[Man's] power consists in the multitude of his affinities, in the fact that his life is intertwined with the whole chain of organic and inorganic being."[27] Again, nothing can escape "the magic circle of relations."[28] Still again he can say: "contrary and remote things cohere and flower out from one stem."[29] What always caught his eye was the polarizing effect of relationship. He found such relationships within the nooks and crannies of cosmic and human existence. He found them in centrifugal and centripetal forces, in electricity, galvanism, and chemical affinities. It also came easy to him to handle the opposites of the human condition. No one could be more socially alert and no one more keenly observant of other people and more eager to penetrate their minds. Yet, for him, all this would have remained void of substance apart from his own capacity to guard his privacy and solitude. Solitude and society were inextricably interwoven. The need for community was fused with the need to lose oneself within the wilderness. Such a paradox of polar opposites was not to be abolished but had rather to be carefully contained within the fullness of human existence. He could see, too, that a high state of contemplation, to remain faithful, was tied in with a powerful urge to apply oneself to the particular work at hand. They formed together a single pattern of experience. Again, within the depths of concrete existence it became plain that living within time, really within time, was vitally bound up with living beyond time. "God delights to isolate us every day, and hide from us the past and the future."[30] With respect to the past, he tells us, "Man

is explicable by nothing less than all his history."[31] Yet elsewhere
he can say, "The one thing we seek with insatiable desire is to forget ourselves, to be surprised out of our propriety, to lose our sem-
piternal memory and to do something without knowing how or
why; in short to draw a new circle."[32] And again, "I simply experiment, an endless seeker, with no Past at my back."[33]

Emerson is forever insisting on experimentation. Hence his
warning, "Let me remind the reader that I am only an experi-
menter."[34] How else is one to deal with a world within which
things are in a perpetual state of co-energizing relationships that
can generate the most unexpected possibilities? A state of constant
alertness regarding such possibilities becomes the *sine qua non* of
such a world. "No man," he says, "can antedate his experience, or
guess what faculty or feeling a new object shall unlock, any more
than he can draw today the face of a person whom he shall see
tomorrow for the first time."[35] Since for him new doors were always opening into the world, it was impossible for him to settle
down into doctrinaire thinking. Rusk, his biographer, writes, "It
was one of Emerson's triumphs to escape the ignorance of the
educated, or at least their biased judgment, and revel in the display
of vigor on no matter what intellectual plane."[36]

It is interesting that Emerson, who was so essentially an explorer
in the world of experience, could also convey to us the near impossibility of reaching far into it. How easily we tend to isolate
ourselves from life, and so we find Emerson agonizing over the
fact that two years after the death of his beloved son Waldo he
had not really absorbed the experience. In the same vein he writes:
"The Indian who was laid under a curse that the wind should not
blow on him, nor water flow to him, nor fire burn him, is a type of
us all."[37] Invulnerability to experience seems to be the major afflic-
tion of the human race. No one understood better than Emerson
how marvelously equipped man is for experience, and on diverse
levels. And yet he knew the bitterness of frustration in seeking to
break through the crust of external facts into meaningful vision.
People have spoken of his lack of a tragic view of life. Perhaps the
difficulty lies in our failure to perceive the many ways in which
tragedy throws a deep shadow over us. In dealing with Emerson,
the trouble may well be that in seeking a tragic dimension, we are
looking in the wrong place. No one knew better than he the gap

between the vast human potential for vision and the actual state of affairs. Nonetheless, he had no alternative but to communicate to others that potential for vision that he had glimpsed in himself.

The struggle to remain within the actual movement of life was no light matter for him, for life embraced the uncharted regions of his own being and the universe itself. Emerson could not survey the strange and marvelous powers within himself without being lifted up into what we might call the "seventh heaven" of cosmic perception. In our own contemporary terminology, his inner spaces became inextricably one with the outer spaces. He could experience his thought, not as something locked up within himself and private, but as

> a great public power on which he can draw, by unlocking, at all risks, his human doors, and suffering the ethereal tides to roll and circulate through him; then he is caught up into the life of the Universe, his speech is thunder, his thought is law, and his words are universally intelligible as the plants and animals. The poet knows that he speaks adequately then only when he speaks somewhat wildly, or "with the flower of the mind"; not with the intellect used as an organ, but with the intellect released from all service and suffered to take its direction from its celestial life.[38]

Emerson was familiar with pre-Darwinian evolutionary doctrine, which he found acceptable, but he went on to fuse it with a vertical dimension. For him, life remained inexplicable as a closed-in affair, separated from the immensities. The thinking of Plato and Plotinus had evidently made it impossible for him to regard reality one-dimensionally. "Our being is descended into us from we know not whence. . . . I am constrained every moment to acknowledge a higher origin for events than the will I call mine."[39] These philosophers had deepened his conception of mind as a metaphysical, and not merely a psychological, entity, with inmost connections to transcendent realities. Only a multi-level reality could provide the context that would enable a person to rise beyond the temptation to lock the spirit within one form or another of institutional life. In a deep sense he was a true pragmatist of the Jamesian variety for he sought to situate himself within reality, not as something distilled only through his intellect, but as something glimpsed within the complex processes of life. He placed a very high value on his intellect, but at the same time he saw intellect as situated within the whole psyche of man with its subconscious, conscious, and supra-conscious levels. He was certainly a pragmatist in his wonderful penetration into the primacy of perception itself as inherent in the mind's power to enlarge its vision of the world or, as he would say, to draw a wider circle. Perception itself is visionary, but only when it keeps faith with expanding consciousness of man. The intellectual vision of reality must cohere with the perceptual vision. I would suppose this is what Emerson has in mind when he sees himself as a "transparent eyeball." Certainly what he also means is that perception is rooted within the whole inner being of man. As he says, "To speak truly, few adult persons can see nature. Most persons do not see the sun. At least they have a very superficial seeing. The sun illuminates only the eye of the man, but shines into the eye and heart of the child."[40] Emerson was guided in his thinking by poetic perception. Thus, as he sees it, the function of the poet is to transform the world around him into living images capable of resonating the soul and giving it the power and freedom to soar.

Let us now go on to Buckminster Fuller, who, according to the aforementioned biographer, Hugh Kenner, was influenced not only by mystical Pythagoreanism but also by the transcendentalism of his great-aunt Margaret Fuller's friend, Ralph Waldo Emerson. This is set forth in a volume entitled *Bucky: A Guided Tour of Buckminster Fuller*, a selective and chronological detailing of his life. In relating Fuller's thought to transcendentalism, Kenner goes so far as to say, "It is hard to find a sentence in Emerson that Bucky Fuller would reject."[41] In Fuller, it may be that we are undergoing a new turn in the evolution of our culture, nothing less than a metamorphosis of the engineer into the transcendentalist. Such a strange happening may be just a bit too much to contemplate. Yet, if we move over into the terrain of contemporary physics, we are actually witnessing the transformation of the old-time physicist into something startlingly different. In his world the mind has been given its freedom to take off into the outermost and submiscroscopic spaces; and within these wider perspectives, it finds itself confronted by a wholly new picture of the universe which in going directly counter to common sense invites a thorough reconstruction of thinking itself. The fact that scientists can

accept the term "quark" to designate a weird particle, a term borrowed from James Joyce, or that physicists can describe what nature seems to be like by comparing it to a Jackson Pollock painting,
suggests how far the physicist has journeyed into a totally new kind
of reality and one that moves quite easily into a world of paraphys-
ics, which itself finally makes contact with parapsychology. Given
Kenner's own cosmic sense, we can understand why he pounces on
instances of Emerson's cosmic awareness. Thus he tells us how
natural it came to Emerson to observe that "'when the force of
gravity brings down a carpenter's axhead, the planet itself splits
his stick.'"[42] Then, too, he notes that when Emerson says that
"'man's wisdom is to hitch his wagon to a star,'" he was not just
being poetic. As Kenner says, "It would astonish ten thousand
commencement speakers to learn what prompted that famous
sentence: the spectacle of harnessed tidal power, which 'engages
the assistance of the moon, like a hired hand, to grind, and wind,
and pump, and saw, and split stone, and roll iron.'(And since coal
is solar energy, for that matter, railway wagons are hitched to a
star.)"[43] This fusion of images is itself an instance of Emerson's
power through language to widen perception, in drawing diverse
things together with startling effects. Here we have the image of a
lowly wagon, most likely a covered wagon, pitting its fragile and
even rickety-looking being against the mighty forces of nature, yet
urged on, as it were, by a still vaster force symbolized by the starry
heavens.

Standing before an audience of two thousand members of the
American Association of Neurosurgeons, Fuller expounded with
all the resources of analogy the radical distinction between mind
and brain.[44] Surely in meeting head-on this great mass of neurosurgeons, he had wandered into a lion's den. Kenner tells us that
Fuller is by no means setting out to discount body knowledge. His
point "is to undercut the real robot-mongers, the Skinners for
whom we are nothing but machines, for whom all passion is a
surge from the endocrines, all behavior habits shaped by stimuli,
all thought a traffic-pattern through synapses. Mind is not Brain,
he keeps telling them. He is right."[45] With his usual passion,
Fuller set out to show that we cannot function in the universe that
we now envision unless we differentiate the mind from the brain,

that is, unless we see with crystal clarity that we think with our minds, not with our brains. Fuller is attempting to show the neurosurgeons that a scientific demonstration of the mind/brain relationship will reveal the truth of his contention that the mind is not brain, or in any way a mere epiphenomenon of the brain.

What we must grasp is that we are living in a synergetic universe, and synergies are disclosed, for instance, by the attraction for one another of two or more objects. We are thus dealing with a vast system of objects which themselves are "energy–event aggregates—mutually intercoordinating phenomena." But the all-important point here is that wherever we study any kind of whole system at all—it could be the earth or our bodies—we are dealing with interconnecting behavior of the parts which cannot be predicted. Unpredictedness is at the heart of reality.[46] The behaviors to be sought are always unknown until through experiment they are revealed. Computers cannot be instructed to watch out for them. That is entirely impossible. We would be instructing them to look out for the unknown. Computers can keep track of a complex of behavior but the "metaphysically operative mind" alone can discern heretofore unknown unique interrelations.[47]

Today man confronts a universe that is mostly invisible. This constitutes a real new moment in man's evolution. Add to this the fact that he is now moving into the unknown, and so far from being discouraged or downcast by this event, he knows exhilaration and is now face to face with the strange truth that mind is at its best when it faces into the unknown.

Fuller cannot go along with the idea that the mind simply evolved. He doubts that view as a viable solution to the overriding mystery of mind. Mind, he conjectures, came from elsewhere, from the domain of the Great Mind. At the forefront of Fuller's thought is his belief in "the a priori comprehensive and permeative mystery of the universe." This omnipresent *a priori* mystery is the real beginning of education, he contends—the experimental realization of absolute mystery. Fuller makes a very important point in connection with synergetic interrelationships. He asserts, however,

[It] is deliberately side-stepped,
Or is just overlooked
By most educators,

And is politically acknowledged
Only as orthodox religions.[48]

We can see still farther into Fuller's oft-repeated insistence on the great need for a lucid understanding of mind/brain differentiation in his belief that in being cosmically oriented, the mind is centered on an *a priori* mystery, or, as he says, "the mystery of mysteries, the wisdom of wisdoms."

Humans grope for *absolute* understanding,
Unmindful of the a priori mystery
Which inherently precludes
Absolute understanding.[49]

It is in experimental evidence
That the origins of science
Are inherently immersed
In an a priori mystery.
This explains why
The history of science
Is a history of
Unpredicted discoveries
And will continue
So to be.[50]

And again,

Out of the a priori mystery
From time to time
Mind flashes a new
Generalized principle,
Which though absolutely unique
Always accommodates and integrates
With all the previously discovered
Generalized principles.[51]

We cannot help thinking here of Emerson's concept of "the intellect released from all service, and suffered to take its direction from its celestial life." We must emphasize that Emerson, like Fuller, has a metaphysical view of the mind far removed from the contemporary outlook which would imprison the mind in an exclusively psychological or sociological or even biological universe. Emerson is clearly in that tradition that stretches back to Plato. A metaphysical outlook and the conception of a metaphysical mind are, quite naturally, tied in with a cosmology. Without a cosmology, as generally speaking is the case today, there seems to be no place for a metaphysical mind.

Fuller's concept, universe, would seem to be in accord with Emerson's. As Fuller says:

Thus, the human mind
Has collected, combined and refined
All experiences of all humanity,
In all-remembered time,
Into one single concept,
Universe,
Which is, *ipso facto*,
The ultimate generalization.[52]

Fuller provides us with a beautiful statement of his creed.

. . . I realized o'erwhelmingly
That if humanity is going to survive
It will be only because it commits itself
Unselfishly, courageously and exclusively
To its most longingfully creative inclinations,
Visionary conceptions
And intuitively formulated objectifications;
For the mind's intellections—
In contradistinction to the brain's automatics—
Apparently constitute humanity's
Last and highest order of survival recourse.[53]

Fuller's geodesic dome is regarded by Kenner as a metaphor of where we are today. The geodesic dome stands as a reminder of what can be done by man when he dares to free all his powers in drawing upon invisible forces in the ongoing reconstruction of the world. Without going into the matter here, Fuller has demonstrated the well-nigh unbelievable results obtainable when we bring tetrahedonal geometry into relationship with the network of interlocking invisible forces. What he has produced in the dome is an affront to common sense, an impossibility made real. We are told how in the development of his thought Fuller began by examining the nature of the universe as a manifestation of God and came to the conclusion that its essence was not matter but design.[54]

One would gather that in Fuller's cosmology God is viewed as an artist, a designer who works according to a preferred pattern in which the most powerful and astonishing results are obtained by utilizing materials that make the most efficient use of invisible forces. The design represents the right use of the right materials that bring into operation invisible forces through which we can produce an object regarded as impossible by the experts. The geodesic dome does not depend on heavy objects such as flying buttresses. It has been described with Fuller in mind as "self-sufficient as a butterfly's wing and as strong as an eggshell . . . [and as] really a kind of benchmark of the universe, what the seventeenth century Mystic Jacob Boehme might have called 'a signature of God.' "[55] The geodesic dome has been called a heavenly wigwam. It brings to light that the universe, seen through the eyes of Buckminster Fuller, enables us, and to a fabulous degree, to do more and more with less and less in bringing the invisible forces of the universe to bear in working with matter. This is the process he calls ephemeralization. Emphemeralization represents the ever-increasing intersection of the visible with the invisible. Kenner describes Fuller's spectacular dome, "a giant 250-foot steel and plexiglass 'skybreak bubble.' It is as free as a soap bubble of internal supports . . . and had it been a half-mile in diameter it would have been capable of drifting away."[56]

Comparisons between Emerson and Fuller come thick and fast. Emerson's vertical view of the universe with its mysterious source as an absolutely energizing principle of our world seen as manifestation, a source that man experiences in the workings of his own mind, surely is in line with that of Fuller. Emerson's doctrine of nature as a vast system of interrelations that issue forth in novelty would be recognizable at once as central to Fuller's thought. If Emerson escaped the ignorance of the educated, he was also repelled by the "impudent knowingness" of the learned. In an Emersonian universe, in which the unexpected is always happening, knowledge as a finished product is unthinkable. Fuller himself is full of the theme of the computer-type mind that can, by itself, become a destructive force in the world, obsessed as it is by its own partial knowledge that is at the opposite pole of the Leonardo-type man, or, as Fuller also describes him, the Comprehensive Man. Emerson's concept of Man Thinking fits nicely into this whole picture. We can also make sense out of Emerson's statement that "a foolish consistency is the hobgoblin of little minds."[57] Fuller, himself accused of inconsistency, responds simply that he is forever in the process of learning. Within our universe, there is no end to that process. Margaret Fuller found herself intoxicated with Emerson's mind and spoke of his glorious inconsistency.

Emerson saw the work of the poet as that of bringing all human achievements, even that of the engineer, into poetry, thus revealing their epiphanic character, that is, as a manifestation of the divine. Emerson actually pictured the time when mankind

> will raise to a divine use, the railroad, the insurance office, the joint-stock company, our law, our primary assemblies, our commerce, the galvanic battery, the electric jar, the prism, and the chemist's retort, in which we seek now only an economical use. . . . When science is learned in love, and its powers are wielded by love, they will appear the supplements and continuations of the material creation.[58]

The horizontal movement of evolution, bound up as it was in Emerson's thinking with a vertical movement, is thus a process toward the triumph of the epiphanic. Fuller's whole idea of ephemeralization, in which invisible forces are brought into visible operation and seen as an historical process, is certainly in harmony with the Emersonian outlook.

To go on to our final statement about Emerson: as we know, he pleaded with Americans for an original relation with the universe. Here we have a fine example of the basic similarity of viewpoint in the thinking of Emerson and Fuller. We have seen that cosmic orientation is the core of their way of looking at things, an orientation which, in making contact with what is most vital and promising in their own times, enters deeply into the process of human history. As Emerson well knew, an original relation was at the heart of the matter in the realization of the American potential for human liberation. The New World in its very essence made intellectual and affective reorientation to the universe a prime imperative. America, we must remember, was as much a state of mind as a social entity. In this respect Whitehead offers a poetic image that is illuminating. "The creativity of the world is the throbbing emotion of the past hurling itself into a new transcendent fact."[59] America itself, we might say, is a new transcendent fact, one which makes nothing less than a far-reaching re-evaluation of the human condition an inescapable reality of American life. "Man," says Emerson, "is great in his transitions." But the transition that is America is of a prodigious sort! Consider the contradictory aspects of the New World experience. America regenerated a mythic sense that carried the imagination back to primeval times. Newcomers from the Old World found themselves in "this vast, empty Eden of ours"—Emerson's phrase—and were transported in a sort of "twilight zone" experience into a timeless world. On the other hand, America was a triumphant call to a new adventure within time. Thus we have a strange new blend of experiences in which temporal consciousness co-exists with a sense of what transcends time. No one was immune from this psychic pattern. Thoreau was saturated with it. Melville, very much aware of the American adventure within "the wilderness of untried things," epitomizes in his thinking these two aspects of the American mentality to the point of seeing them as almost opposed. Thus he could speak of renouncing "innovating willfulness," in favor of "reverence for the archetype."[60] The Boston historian Francis Parker, a man of delicate sensibilities, was yet haunted by the wilderness images. And it was Emerson himself who, according to Norman Foerster, said that "'Europe stretches to the Alleghenies; America lies beyond.'"[61] Emerson was perpetually aware of the primal power of the West. In his lecture tours West, he was forever delighted by the awesome luxuriant wildness of Western scenery, from which the symmetry and elegance of a walled-in garden were absent.

America was clearly a new world of experience. Emerson was a conceptual pioneer. He was, in fact, a frontiersman of experience. Emerson looked out on the American scene and, as Harry Levin notes, he caught the "tensions that threaten to turn the dream into nightmare,"[62] peering into the abyss of lawlessness, competitive imperialist expansion, racial aggression. Americans were being hurled mindlessly into the future. A wholly new conception of man was required, one which would enable the individual to situate his consciousness within a far greater context than America itself, and would allow the individual to grasp what it means to feel the flow of a creative force within him that is at one with the creative force of the wilderness and the universe itself. America of the dream called for a new kind of individual, who refuses to be domesticated, who can enter into "the danger of difference" and is able to look into the future as the passage from one quality of experience to a still higher quality. A countervailing force to the materialist splurge of Americans could come only from individuals who, in the Emersonian spirit, were willing to carry on an endless struggle in forcing their ideal into act. To move across frontiers to a higher quality of life, one must be powered by the willingness to "accept . . . a transcendent destiny; and not minors and invalids in a protected corner, not cowards fleeing before a revolution, but guides, redeemers and benefactors, obeying the Almighty effort and advancing on Chaos and the Dark."[63] "Whoso would be a man, must be a nonconformist."[64] "Wherever a man comes, there comes revolution."[65]

I have described the direction of Buckminster Fuller's thinking in order to throw into relief that fusion "of spirituality and a cosmic sense which Emerson knew to be coeval with the human spirit."[66] Bringing to mind some Americans who have felt the direct influence of Emerson may serve to bring out still farther that larger vision of things within which he operated.

Recalling what literary critics have done to Shelley in overlooking his scientific and cosmological outlook, let me first quote from an article by Irving Howe:

> Emerson is everywhere. From Whitman to Mailer, from Melville to William Carlos Williams, from Thoreau to Wallace Stevens, it is Emerson who dominates, our angel with broken wings. Over and over again one hears in American writing echoes of his call for the self-reliant man, follower of instinct and conscience, with the two happily blurred in the gassy regions of the Oversoul. Over and over again one hears echoes of Emerson's ethicized romanticism asserting man's share in the godhead, providing a semi-religious sanction for democratic largesse, indeed, for individualist overreaching. . . . Emersonian "transcendentalism" comes to seem toothless, a genteel evasion.[67]

Let me juxtapose with this statement of Howe's the rather striking fact that none other than Nietzsche himself, in his formative years, included Emerson among his favorite authors. While Nietzsche, as we might expect, would throw in a rebuke or two along with his praise, nonetheless he seems to have sized up Emerson as a powerful human specimen. He obviously felt at home with Emerson, a fact that would suggest a feeling of kinship with him.

Whitman, we remember, in Leaves of Grass, put himself on record as a person and a human being. And that he did so, we must attribute in some degree to Emerson. It would seem that in his work Whitman was celebrating an openness to the universe which Emerson regarded as the necessary condition to the discovery of what it means to function as a person. If Emerson brought Whitman to a boil, he brought a great many others with him. Certainly at the very least, we must credit Emerson with creating an intellectual atmosphere which would allow the individual the freedom to unlock, at all risks, his human doors, and self-reliantly we may add, into the universal life.

Emerson's influence on American literary figures is a well-established fact. Yet there were other powerful individuals outside the literary world who have acknowledged this influence. Many have distinguished themselves in many fields. Here we shall consider a few of them, individuals who responded in a highly creative way to the Emersonian vision that in them, as in others, helped to bring out something characteristic of the American genius when it gives free reign to the frontier spirit. They had discovered for themselves that Emersonian self-reliance meant more than "individualist overreaching," in that it called for a vision of things that makes plain what it signifies for a person *to be*. Emerson would have called such people "soul-guided" and as such they can be viewed as individuals who are filled with what is often regarded derisively as a facile Emersonian optimism. As soul-guided, it would appear that they trusted a deeply rooted belief that the inmost structure of things was on their side.

Let me begin with Louis Sullivan. Sullivan philosophized, according to a biographer, "on the model of Whitman and Emerson."[68] This great architect set himself the titanic task of creating an architecture that would transform the mind of the people. He aimed at turning bronze, terra cotta, steel into a poem that would transform the materials of the earth into a work of art that would function as an awakener of perception and spirit. He understood only too well the Emersonian injunction "Insist on yourself." He was constantly at war with those who would make architecture a subsidiary of commercial interests. To the end he remained unyielding. Sullivan belonged in the company of those "mighty men who built heroically," his own phrase. His skyscraper was a proud and soaring thing, exulting in its sheer height. Frank Lloyd Wright says he made the skyscraper "sing, a new thing under the sun."

The man who designed the Brooklyn Bridge also came under the influence of Emerson. Emerson, John Roebling[69] discovered, was a man after his own heart. He read "Nature" with delight and was metamorphosed by it from an engineer into an artist. He had at last found the vision through which he could project a bridge into the vast scheme of nature as something that rightfully belongs there. He was electrified by the thought, always uppermost in his mind, that "the bridge will be beautiful." He was engaged in building something that the best engineering minds had already decided was impossible. Interestingly, he was among the first to recognize the resilience of steel wire, a resilience that has its roots in the electromagnetic world of the unseen. He wove this wire into massive cables of great strength and flexibility. Today, after more than a century of tremendous wear and tear, the Brooklyn Bridge stands as a proud testimonial to a visionary mind.

Frederick Law Olmstead, the designer of great parks which humanized America—Central Park among them—surely belongs in the Emerson company. One of his intellectual heroes was Emerson. As he said, Emerson and " 'other real prophets . . . gave me the needed respect for my own constitutional tastes and an inclination to poetic refinement in the cultivation of them that afterwards determined my profession.' " [70] Emerson's doctrine of self-reliance had become the very chemistry of his being. What he sought as a landscape designer was to create in the very heart of the city an alternative experience which would add a new quality to urban life. He was the principal environmental planner of his time. Olmstead, a biographer writes, "emerges from the shadow of neglect as a man extraordinarily effective in a range of socially creative undertakings and as one dedicated passionately and intelligently—even, sometimes, successfully—to conserving the beautiful and healthy, and to remedying the ugly and harmful in the American scene a full hundred years before the environment . . . became a matter of popular concern." [71] This biographer makes it abundantly clear that Olmstead merits an honorable place in the company of American heroes. We find him expressing a central theme of his life in the Emersonian advice given to his son. " 'You will find it is what you have *been*, and not what you have done, that you care for.' " [72] Yet as a man of vision, he remained throughout his life a true doer.

Frank Lloyd Wright also belongs with Emerson. His biographer tells us how firmly transcendentalism took root in his mind. He writes, "It was primarily Emerson who spoke through all the subsequent philosophizing of Frank Lloyd Wright." [73] In true Emersonian fashion, he was concerned with an organic architecture. The Emersonian sense of energy-liberating interrelationship marks all his works. Thus, we find his structures exhibiting an interplay of indoor and outdoor space, and of light and space. Regarded as the most abundantly creative genius of American architects, who inaugurated a new era in architecture, he was nonetheless shunned by the architectural establishment. In Europe, he was acclaimed. In America, he was, for almost a generation, regarded by many as something of an outlaw. There were architects who viewed his structures, before they were set up, as impossible.

Still another in the far-reaching Emersonian circle was Charles Ives, whose musical innovations anticipated later developments in music. Like a true Emersonian, he was able to see how, as far as he was concerned, his business experience and his experience as a composer belonged together. Needless to say, his unorthodoxy was a thorn in the side of the conventional musician. His *Concord Sonata* reflects the influence of the Concord transcendentalism. Its wide-ranging artistic independence is its central feature. His *Second Piano Sonata* echoes the spirit of New England transcendentalists, in its four sections: Emerson, Hawthorne, The Alcotts, Thoreau. A real synergistic enthusiast, who should delight the heart of Buckminster Fuller, he brought a great variety of experiences into one network of inter-energizing relationships. He delighted in polytonality, atonality, and conflicting rhythms. His music is one great celebration of sound. All sound is potential music. Ives was the liberator of sound. He was the Whitman of music. Let me finish by quoting from his work *Essays Before a Sonata*:

> There is an "oracle" at the beginning of the *Fifth Symphony*; in those four notes lies one of Beethoven's greatest messages. We would place its translation above the relentlessness of fate knocking at the door, above the greater human message of destiny, and strive to bring it towards the spiritual message of Emerson's revelations, even to the "common heart" of Concord—the soul of humanity knocking at the door of the divine mysteries, radiant in the faith that it *will* be opened—and the human become divine![74]

NOTES

1. Charles R. Metzger, *Emerson and Greenough: Transcendental Pioneers of an American Esthetic* (Berkeley and Los Angeles: University of California Press, 1954), p. 26.

2. Ibid.

3. *Image and Idea: Twenty Essays on Literary Themes* (New York: New Directions, 1957), p. 9.

4. Quoted in Charles Feidelson, Jr., *Symbolism and American Literature* (Chicago: The University of Chicago Press, 1953), p. 90.

5. Dante Alighieri, *Vita Nuova*, trans. Ralph Waldo Emerson, ed. J. Chesley Mathews (Chapel Hill: University of North Carolina Press, 1960).

6. *The Life of Ralph Waldo Emerson* (New York: Scribner's, 1949), p. 300.

7. "Address," *The Complete Works of Ralph Waldo Emerson*, ed. Edward Waldo Emerson, 12 vols. (Boston and New York: Houghton, Mifflin, 1903–1934), I 130. All subsequent citations by volume and page number refer to this edition.

8. "Circles," II 319–20.

9. "Experience," III 75.

10. *Adventures of Ideas* (New York: Macmillan, 1933), p. 19.

11. Ibid., p. 11.

12. "Beauty," VI 303.

13. O. W. Firkins, *Ralph Waldo Emerson* (New York: Russell & Russell, 1965), p. 340.

14. "Nature," I 52.

15. Ibid., 10.

16. *Science and the Modern World* (New York: Macmillan, 1925), p. 123.

17. *A Newton Among Poets: Shelley's Use of Science in* PROMETHEUS UNBOUND, repr. ed. (New York: Gordian Press, 1968), p. vii.

18. Ibid., pp. vii–viii.

19. See *Shelley's* PROMETHEUS UNBOUND: *A Variorum Edition*, ed. Lawrence John Zillman (Seattle: University of Washington Press, 1959), p. 197.

20. "The False Images of Science," in *The Mystery of Matter*, ed. Louise B. Young (New York: Oxford University Press, 1965), p. 647.

21. 6 vols. (London: Cambridge University Press, 1954).

22. *Adventures of Ideas*, pp. 13–14.

23. *The Journal of Henry D. Thoreau*. V. *March 5, 1853–November 31, 1853*, edd. Bradford Torrey and Francis H. Allen (Boston: Houghton Mifflin, 1906), p. 4.

24. *Bucky: A Tour of Buckminster Fuller* (New York: Morrow, 1973), p. 150.

25. R. Buckminster Fuller, *Intuition* (Garden City, N.Y.: Doubleday, 1972), inscription.

26. "History," II 36.

27. Ibid.

28. "Education," X 128.

29. "The American Scholar," I 85.

30. "Experience," III 67.

31. "History," II 3.

32. "Circles," II 321.
33. Ibid., 318.
34. Ibid.
35. "History," II 38.
36. *Life of Emerson*, p. 318.
37. "Experience," III 49.
38. "The Poet," III 26–27.
39. "Over-soul," II 268.
40. "Nature," I 8.
41. P. 149.
42. Quoted in *Bucky*, p. 148.
43. Ibid., pp. 148–49.
44. *Intuition*, p. 49.
45. *Bucky*, p. 268.
46. Fuller, *Intuition*, p. 29.
47. Ibid.
48. Ibid., p. 50.
49. Ibid., p. 40.
50. Ibid., p. 39.
51. Ibid., p. 43.
52. Ibid., p. 147.
53. Ibid., p. 80.
54. "The Dymaxion American," *Time*, January 10, 1964, p. 47.
55. Ibid., p. 50.
56. *Bucky*, p. 133.
57. "Self-Reliance," II 57.
58. "Art," pp. 368–69.
59. *Adventures of Ideas*, p. 227.
60. Harry Levin, *The Power of Blackness* (New York: Knopf, 1967), p. 10.
61. "Factors in American Literary History," in *The Reinterpretation of American Literature*, ed. Norman Foerster (New York: Russell & Russell, 1959), p. 29.
62. *Power of Blackness*, p. 34.
63. "Self-Reliance," II 47.
64. Ibid., 50.
65. "Address," I 144.
66. Robert C. Pollock, "Ralph Waldo Emerson: The Single Vision," in *American Classics Revisited*, ed. Harold C. Gardiner (New York: Scribner's, 1958), p. 26.
67. "The American Voice—It Begins on a Note of Wonder," *The New York Times Book Review*, July 4, 1976, p. 2.
68. Willard Connely, *Louis Sullivan As He Lived: The Shaping of American Architecture* (New York: Horizon, 1960), p. 218.
69. David Barnard Steinman, *The Builders of the Bridge: The Story of John Roebling and His Son* (New York: Harcourt, Brace, 1950).

70. Quote in Laura Wood Roper, *FLO: A Biography of Frederick Law Olmstead* (Baltimore and London: The Johns Hopkins University Press, 1973), p. 40.

71. Ibid., p. xv.

72. Quote in ibid., p. 476.

73. Finis Farr, *Frank Lloyd Wright* (New York: Scribner's, 1961), p. 15.

74. *Essays Before a Sonata and Other Writings*, ed. Howard Boatwright (New York: Norton, 1961), p. 36.

4

Chauncey Wright and the Pragmatists

EDWARD H. MADDEN
The State University of New York
at Buffalo,
Emeritus

IN HIS AUTOBIOGRAPHICAL SKETCH for the Harvard *Class Book of 1858* Chauncey Wright wrote, "From the earliest period of my conscious life I have shrunk from everything of a startling or dramatic character. I was indisposed to active exercise, to any kind of excitement or change." That this attitude persisted is evident from the uneventful character of his later life.[1] After graduation from Harvard he worked on the mathematics staff of the *Nautical Almanac* until 1870. In 1860 he was elected a fellow of the American Academy of Arts and Sciences, of which he was secretary for a while. He lectured at Harvard in philosophy and psychology in 1870, and in mathematical physics in 1874. A high spot in his life was his visit to Darwin in 1872. Between 1864 and 1875, when he died, he wrote numerous articles and reviews for the *Nation* and *The North American Review*. Charles Eliot Norton, Wright's closest friend in later years, published Wright's essays posthumously in 1877 as *Philosophical Discussions*; and James Bradley Thayer, his lifelong friend, published his *Letters* posthumously in 1878.

Wright occasionally gave private courses in his rooms. Henry W. Holland remembered Chauncey from such a course as "an extraordinary teacher for anyone who really wanted to study,— always ready with explanations and illustrations of difficult points, always patient and interested."[2] Wright's tutorials flowered into pleasant philosophical discussions so that other interested individuals sought out conversations. And Wright did not disappoint them. He was at his best in his own study with his gray dressing gown on and his perpetually filled pipe billowing smoke. It was through this easy interchange of ideas that men like Charles S. Peirce, William James, and Oliver Wendell Holmes, Jr., came to feel the influence of his sharp wit. Peirce and James especially learned a great deal from him about the nature of philosophical analysis—how to clarify, criticize, and compare—in addition to getting a *feel* for the dialectical drift of the philosophical argument. They were also influenced, both positively and negatively, by Wright's own specific philosophical commitments. I shall be concerned here with three important and instructive ways in which Wright and the two pragmatists were at odds.

I

One issue that sharply separates empiricists and pragmatists is the self-containedness, or not, of "the given."[3] For the classical British empiricists and their lineal descendants, the expression "x is hard" means that x exhibits a certain property the meaning of which is provided denotatively by instances of certain direct sensory experiences. This view is traditionally described by saying the empiricist insists on the self-containedness of a sensory given. The meaning of a sensory term does not transcend the immediate awareness of experience. Yet for Peirce and other pragmatists (though not for James), the expression "x is hard" is an hypothesis that predicts that if I rub glass across it, the glass will not cut it, etc. The meaning of the sentence for Peirce is the whole set of such possible consequences.[4] Peirce, in short, claimed that all empirical propositions, not simply the theoretical ones of science, have the nature of hypotheses. Peirce's notion that the meanings of simple empirical terms and propositions transcend the givenness of immediate experience is what is meant by the pragmatist's denial of the self-containedness of a given.

Wright never interpreted sentences like "This diamond is hard" as an hypothesis. For him only sentences that contain theoretical terms—such as "This object is in uniform motion"—count as hypotheses. Nor did he ever suggest that the meaning of a sentence consists in its whole set of experienceable consequences; he only insisted that theoretical terms, to be admissible scientific notions, must have some sensory credentials, either by yielding sensory consequences themselves or by yielding such consequences in conjunction with other theoretical terms.[5] Moreover, Wright insisted that the meaning of basic sensory terms is wholly given by denotative instances of what the terms refer to, and he rejected any effort to give them discursive "if–then" definitions. In short, he wholly agreed with the British empiricists that "the given" is self-contained. Hence, Wright cannot be said to anticipate Peirce's (or any other pragmatist's) interpretation of the meaning of propositions about sense experience. For Wright, scientific principles must be interpreted as working hypotheses, but basic empirical propositions cannot be so interpreted. He must be understood as providing the logic of scientific inference that Peirce and others projected into pragmatic epistemologies.

In a series of letters to F. E. Abbot, Wright developed a concept that later commentators have described as a "functional apriori." At first glance, this concept might appear to conflict with Wright's insistence on the self-containedness of the sensory given,[6] but analysis reveals no conflict at all. My detailed response has two parts: (a) What was the notion of a "functional apriori"? and (b) Why does it not conflict with my interpretation of a fundamental difference between Wright's epistemology and Peirce's (and, no doubt, Dewey's as well)?

In his letters to Abbot, Wright insisted that the perception of relations was just as basic and irreducible as the perception of qualities. The perception of both "x is hard" and "x is between y," however, involves more than a single item of "hardness" or a single item of "betweenness."[7] Neither properties nor relations are perceived in a vacuum; they all result by comparison and contrast from previous perceptual experience.[8] Hence, no instance of the given is by itself sufficient to provide denotative meaning of a sensory term. For Wright, then, the given is not self-contained and always reaches beyond itself to provide full meaning. So perhaps Wright was not, after all, far from the pragmatic fold on this crucial point.

That this argument and conclusion are faulty can be seen from the following considerations. There is no doubt that the operation of Wright's functional apriori "goes beyond" the immediately sensory given in some sense, but the whole issue hinges on what this sense is. The crucial point is that such "apriori" knowledge goes beyond any specific instance of "red" or of "between," but does not go beyond the class of such instantiations. No instance can be an instance of a kind unless there is an apriori classifying of it along with other instances. Without such classification there would be no recognition of x as an instance of a kind. All these points Wright clearly insists upon. But such "going beyond" the given in any specific case is quite different from going beyond it in the sense of treating "hard" as if it were a dispositional concept and giving a set of if–then statements as the analysis of the meaning of "This diamond is hard." That x will scratch glass if it is pushed across its surface, etc. plays no meaning role whatsoever in Wright's analysis of "hard" as predicated of a certain particular. The meaning of "hard" is given by any denotative instance of what the word refers to, though one cannot *know* or recognize anything as such an instance without the functioning of the mnemonic apriori.

It is important to distinguish carefully between the meaning of propositions, on the one hand, and coming to know that they are true, on the other. Wright's concept of a functional apriori concerns the latter but not the former. To recognize that x is hard, one needs to see it in relation to other hard objects, soft things, and so on (where "see" does not entail being conscious of comparing), but the meaning of the proposition itself—x is hard—is not thereby given a discursive definition in terms of concepts like scratching, which would be the case if the pragmatic interpretation of it as an hypothesis were correct. It is the latter case where the self-containedness of the given, and the concept of the given itself, are being denied; and it is precisely this sort of thing that Wright was not doing. It is true that for Wright *knowledge* of the given goes beyond any specific instance of it. Nevertheless, the knowledge that one has as a result of this apriori "going beyond" is *of the given*.

It is true that one might stipulate that "going beyond" any specific instance of the given breaks its self-containedness, and in this case Wright would automatically be denying the self-containedness of a sensory given. But this sense of "going beyond the given" is not one that other commentators and I have in mind when we speak of "denying the self-containedness of the given." We mean by the latter phrase that other concepts play a definitional role in connection with sensory concepts, that a discursive definition-in-use of such terms is possible, that denotative definition is in fact never sufficient to give meaning to a term. Wright clearly rejected all these claims, while Peirce insisted upon at least some of them.

II

The relations between Wright and James, both intellectual and personal, were more intimate than those between Wright and Peirce, and I have dealt with them in detail elsewhere.[9] Two issues on which the contrast between the two is particularly interesting are those on the will to believe and the question of women's rights. On the will-to-believe issue, James held a weaker and a stronger position, the weaker showing Wright's influence while the stronger one, formulated under the influence of Renouvier, conflicted with it. On the question of women's rights it is interesting to see James cast in an uncharacteristically conservative position: Wright defended J. S. Mill's position in the *Subjection of Women* while James worried over it.

A. The problem of the will to believe arises when the objective evidence, after it has been honestly consulted, is *insufficient* to decide an issue one way or another. What, then, given the fact that the evidence is insufficient, does a person have a right to believe? That is the basic question James considered in the first four essays in *The Will to Believe and Other Essays*. After reviewing James's mature position, we will return to Wright's influence on his views.

James answered the question in a complex way. Suspending judgment when the evidence is insufficient makes perfectly good sense in science; we can *afford* to wait for a decision between wave and particle models because our cosmic hopes and aspirations are not wrapped up in the outcome. But the case is quite different in religion. Assume, after honest inquiry, that the evidence for and against the existence of God is inconclusive to a person; assume, too, that this person cares much to believe in God since it would give morality an ultimate sanction and would confer great benefit on the person in his everyday life, making it possible for him to cope with difficulties that would otherwise be insurmountable. If all of this is the case, then, James said, having done all that is ethically required—viz., honestly consulting the evidence—this person has a perfect right to believe what his affective and volitional needs require. And we must be quite clear that James granted the agnostic the same right to make the opposite decision. What annoyed James about Clifford and Huxley was their insistence that a man has a *duty* to be a religious agnostic since the evidence is inconclusive, a position James felt to be an intolerant one. Under the guise of duty they were improperly importing scientific values into the area of religious concerns. Moreover, James felt that they were willing to suspend judgment because, as scientific materialists, the religious hypothesis was not really a live option for them.

James was not content with this weak form of his right-to-believe doctrine; he added a stronger claim in which affective and volitional elements play a more vital role. Not only are there situations in which a person has a right to believe without adequate evidence, but there are also situations in which a willingness to believe without adequate evidence is a condition for obtaining that very evidence. If I meet a person whom I like and wait for signs of his friendship before believing that he is my friend, these signs may never come. But if I am willing to believe that he is my friend and act accordingly, the signs of his friendship may well be forthcoming. But what analogy does such an ordinary experience—examples of which James multiplied endlessly—have to religious experience? James replied that if religion is a live hypothesis for a person, then he believes that God must be a personal being if he does exist, a "thou" in place of an "it." Consequently, relations of a kind existing between human beings might possibly exist between God and man, and so analogies between the similar relations might well exist. Now, if a show-me agnostic should insist upon proof before believing in God, then he may never be given the necessary proof by God. "We feel . . . as if the appeal of religion to us were made to our active good-will, as if evidence might be forever withheld from us unless we meet the hypothesis half-way."[10]

For the weaker version of his right-to-believe doctrine James was indebted to his old Cambridge friend Chauncey Wright, regular visitor at the James home on Quincy Street; and for the stronger version and overall voluntarism, to Charles Renouvier, a friend and correspondent throughout James's mature years, one whose writings James read to great advantage both for his personal and for his philosophical development.[11]

In 1875 James had reviewed P. G. Tait's *Unseen Universe* for the *Nation* and in this short piece he had already formulated several themes which were later to appear in his four will-to-believe articles. He wrote that Tait, in spite of gyrations to avoid it, exhibited the same simple teleological trust that the search for truth will succeed as everyone else exhibits, no matter how "rational" and apparently nonvolitional their approaches seem to be.

> "We for our part not only hold that such an act of trust is licit, but we think, furthermore, that any one *to whom it makes a practical difference* (whether of motive to action or of mental peace) is in duty bound to make it. If 'scientific' scruples withhold him from making it, this proves his intellect to have been sicklied o'er and paralyzed by scientific pursuits."[12]

Wright was not impressed by voluntaristic views, but he was more disturbed by what he felt to be James's misuse of the phrase "duty to believe" and looked for an early opportunity to cross philosophic swords with his young friend. In his customary spot on the sofa in the living room of the Quincy Street home, Wright replied to a question from Henry James, Sr., by saying that he "had found no *typographical* errors" in William's review of Tait, and William, as Wright had intended, asked for an explanation of this emphasis.[13] Wright's reply was that William had misused the concept of duty in its epistemic context. The only *duty* we have in this context is to consult honestly all the available evidence; when the evidence is genuinely unpersuasive, a person has a *right* to believe anything his natural bent prefers until further evidence is forthcoming. If this natural bent is toward a belief in God, Wright continued, then he has a right to such a belief, just as another person who is not affectively involved in the question of God's existence has an equal right to suspend judgment. James was finally convinced that he had misused the concept of duty and agreed with Wright at the end of the discussion that the only duty is to consult the evidence impartially. That he agreed with Wright is further and more importantly borne out by the fact that he used Wright's argument against his own earlier view to refute the agnosticism of Clifford and Huxley. These bulldogs of science erred in the direction opposite to that of his own early view. They insisted that it was a person's *duty* to suspend judgment, to be an agnostic, when the evidence is inconclusive. James's thrust was that Clifford and Huxley, to be sure, had the right to be agnostics, but that he equally had the *right* to believe without adequate evidence.

James wanted more, however, than this weak sense of a right to believe; he also felt the pull of the Pauline doctrine that one must be willing to believe without adequate evidence before the evidence is recognized or even forthcoming. James's voluntarism and fideism, his claim that the will is "prior" to the intellect, which binds together most of his writings on the will to believe, he owed largely to his early reading of the works of Charles Renouvier. Chauncey tried hard to stamp out these influences toward voluntarism and fideism, but he fought a losing battle.

B. Wright argued against the "subjection" of women, defending their right to vote and their right to legal equality, but his motivation was, not a sentimental attachment to the rights of women, but a utilitarian attachment to liberty in principle (*Letters* 159–60). Utility, he wrote, is the basis alike of law and of liberty. The need for laws restricting certain kinds of acts is an obvious consequence of the greatest happiness principle. But laws that infringe individual tastes and preferences without being necessary for security are impertinent and defeat the utilitarian goal.

> Believing as I do, that human beings generally, even children, have hitherto been much more in subjection to authority than they ought to be (both directly and indirectly, or through the sanctions of punishments and rewards) . . . and seeing that, so far as women are treated differently from men, it is mainly in consequence of some traditional and prevailing sentiments, which are not justified by any more obvious utility than an unreasoning conservatism,—I am in general ready to protest against this present state of things and in favor of larger liberty [*Letters* 160].

But, Wright concludes, it is only because women's condition is less improved on the whole than men's that their rights need to be signalized in a special manner.

It is under the rights of individuals, then, that I would place the rights of women; and it seems to me that those who agitate specially for the latter are not usually actuated by the true principle of liberty, since what they demand is not equal exemption of all persons from oppression . . . but they ask an increase of the range of authority by conferring it equally on all. So far as this is really regarded as an indirect means to the end of true liberty, it may be justified; but the usual motives are, in fact, the love of power and a wish to share it, and a false notion that inequality is in itself unjust [Letters 163].

Grace Norton asked Chauncey to consider, finally, to what degree women can be said to be in "subjection." After all, she wrote, the force of character and wide experience, rather than the fact of sex, determines the ruler and the ruled in all immediate personal relations (Letters 161). Chauncey agreed with this point in part but noted:

men have so arranged the affairs of life that, for the most part, they or their sex have the best opportunities for acquiring these qualifications for ruling. . . . No doubt, a prince is better able to rule than a peasant, and therefore has a better right; still, society is just as responsible for the peasant's subjection, since it has made the inequality by the difference in their education [Letters 161].

Grace Norton suggested that only women in the lower classes were subjected; that women in the higher classes had educational and other opportunities through which their influence could be exerted. Quite so, Wright replied, but are not the women in the lower classes those

who stand most in need of protection from just laws and just public sentiments,—for whom, indeed, and not for the others, a reformation of the laws is needed? I do not think that Mr. Mill has overlooked the existence of a class,—large even in England, I suppose, but much larger with us,—who are in advance of the laws and the general sentiments of society, and are practically independent of them. Such a class justifies, indeed, his hopes, but could not have justified his silence. It was not of them or for them, but rather to them, that he spoke [Letters 161].

Moreover, whether or not women in America are in any important respect in subjection, Wright continued, it remains a fact that most men not only think they are but think they should be. "That their subjection, however, is not of the nature of servitude, but rather of religious obligation, is a part of the arrogant opinion, which springs from a sentimental estimate of 'the fact of sex,' and blinds men to the truth that personality is a still greater fact . . ." (*Letters* 162).

James not only did not have anything positive to say about or contribute to the women's rights' movement but actually demonstrated upon occasion a somewhat patriarchal streak. This attitude appears in his *North American Review* critique[14] of Horace Bushnell's *Women's Suffrage: The Reform Against Nature* and J. S. Mill's *The Subjection of Women*, where he criticized both, but for quite different reasons. Bushnell had claimed that although women's rights were in some ways wrongfully abridged, the abridgment of their participation in government was not one of them. Women are "naturally subject," "subordinate," and so on. James observed:

> So far so good. If Dr. Bushnell is contented to urge this as an ideal, a matter of inexplicable sentiment, he remains in a strong position. The universal sense of mankind hitherto, and its almost universal sense now, will uphold him. But he is naturally tempted to illustrate the doctrine and enforce it by arguments derived from different orders of considerations, which to our mind are far from making it more imposing, but rather, being unsound themselves, tend to infect it with its own decay, and so undo the authority it possesses in its brute dogmatic form [NAR 557].

In his review of Mill's book, James accused the author of being emotional when writing his treatise, and he asserted that Mill, had he been more rational, would not have been so liberal in his remarks. James was troubled by Mill's claim that men are generally ignorant of the true intellectual capacities of women and uneasy about his view that the disadvantages that women suffer are not organic but artificial and can actually be eliminated through proper education. He rejected Mill's egalitarian view of love because it confused, he believed, the feelings of love and friendship. "Independence," he wrote, "is Mr. Mill's personal ideal, and his notion of love confounds itself with what is generally distinguished as friendship;—each party being able to subsist alone, and seeking a mate, not to supply an essential need, but to be enjoyed as a mere ally, or great moral luxury" (NAR 562). James also worried that Mill's view of love would encourage a high divorce rate and wondered why Mill did not address this problem in *The Subjection of Women*. Moreover, he could not help but feel that women were much better off in America than in England.

Much of what he attacks exists here but in feeble form. The legal abuses are in large measure obsolete; the element of brutality which he makes so prominent in the masculine feeling of superiority is foreign; American husbands are as a rule less sensitive about their wives occupying a position of independent publicity than those of whom Mr. Mill writes; and Mrs. Grundy is not the tyrannical reality to Americans which she is to English matrons [NAR 561].

It is only fair, however, to point out that James exhibited in this early review the same sense of fairness that is so justifiably associated with his name. He wrote that if his attitude were wrong, then Mill's position was revolutionary and ahead of his time (NAR 565).

Did James later in his life identify with the struggle for women's rights? I have discovered no writing where he subsequently agreed with Mill. To be sure, he came close to this view. He was deferential to women's judgments and believed that they had the right to determine what was in their own best interests. He was not offended by active suffragettes and held Jane Addams in high esteem. He even applauded women hiking in knickerbockers. Taking all this into account, I cannot see that it bears witness to an ultimate acceptance of Mill's position. His position remained markedly different from that of Chauncey Wright, who, as we have seen, supported Mill at the time he wrote *The Subjection of Women*. Chauncey, like William James, had a feeling for the underdog, but on the issue of women's rights his realization of the plight of the underdog was sharper than that of his friend.[15]

NOTES

1. For a detailed biographical study of Wright, see my *Chauncey Wright and the Foundations of Pragmatism* (Seattle: University of Washington Press, 1963), pp. 3–30 (hereafter cited as *Foundations*), and *Chauncey Wright* (New York: Washington Square Press, 1964), pp. 1–19.
2. *Letters of Chauncey Wright*, ed. J. B. Thayer (Cambridge: Wilson, 1878), p. 214 (hereafter cited as *Letters*).
3. *Foundations*, pp. 79–81.
4. Ibid.
5. Chauncey Wright, *Philosophical Discussions*, ed. C. E. Norton (New York: Holt, 1877), p. 47.

6. J. J. Chambliss, "Chauncey Wright's Enduring Naturalism," *American Quarterly*, 16 (1964), 628–35.

7. Ibid., 630–31.

8. Ibid., 631.

9. *Foundations*, pp. 43–45.

10. William James, *The Will to Believe and Other Essays in Popular Philosophy*, repr. ed. (New York: Dover, 1956), p. 28.

11. For Renouvier's influence, see Wilbur H. Long, "The Philosophy of Charles Renouvier and Its Influence on William James," Unpubl. Ph.D. dissertation, Harvard University, 1925. What appears to be the only extant copy of this useful piece of scholarship is in the Hoose Library of Philosophy, University of Southern California.

12. Quoted in Ralph Barton Perry, *The Thought and Character of William James*, 2 vols. (Boston: Little, Brown, 1936), I 529.

13. *Foundations*, p. 45.

14. *The North American Review*, 109 (1869), 557–65; hereafter cited as NAR.

15. For a valuable discussion of James's social views in general, see Gerald Myers, *William James* (New Haven: Yale University Press, 1986), pp. 425–45.

5

Charles S. Peirce:
Action Through Thought—
The Ethics of Experience

VINCENT G. POTTER
Fordham University

ON APRIL 19, 1914, Charles Sanders Peirce, scientist, logician, philosopher, died of cancer after several years of great suffering. Aged 75, he left this life a frustrated and isolated man, still working on his manuscripts, without a publisher, without students, and nearly penniless. This man, for the most part unappreciated in his lifetime, virtually ignored by the academic world of his day, is now recognized as perhaps America's most original philosopher and surely her greatest logician.

Peirce, of course, is credited with being the father of the American Pragmatic Movement, to date America's only indigenous philosophy. Yet I suspect that his thought might be judged "un-American" in many ways since it certainly does not live up to the stereotype of American thinkers still widespread here and abroad. According to that image, Americans are supposed to be the great technicians; they have the know-how; they are successful in the practical affairs of business, commerce, and industry. But as speculative thinkers, as men of cosmic vision, as men whose ideas shape civilization, Americans are a sorry lot. Not a Kant, not a Hegel, not a Heidegger, among them! I hope this consideration of Peirce will do something to dispel such an oversimplification and substantiate the pragmatic movement's philosophical sophistication. The "American Mind," to use Emerson's phrase, is speculatively complex and rich.

Permit me just to mention some of Peirce's philosophical positions that might be considered quite "un-American" according to the familiar stereotype. Peirce held a version of Scholastic Realism over against Nominalism, including Positivism, in all its forms. He was convinced that metaphysics is a genuine theoretical science and that physical science receives its principles of investigation from philosophy. He held that theory and practice should have nothing immediately to do with one another; that education is not primarily for teaching but for research (learning); that action is not the be-all and end-all of thought; that pleasure, success, better living, are not properly and specifically human goals at all. In short, Peirce the pragmatist, in the name of that very method, foreswore the practical, the immediate, the useful, as of any real consequence for either science or philosophy. I dare say this will come as a surprise to many philosophers from abroad and is already an embarrassment to some American thinkers who pride themselves on being in the mainstream of America's philosophical tradition.

The title of this volume contains the terms "experience" and "doctrine." Peirce has an enormous amount to say about the former and precious little about the latter. In fact, he rarely, if ever, uses that term. More usually he talks about beliefs and how they are acquired and fixed. Beliefs, he holds, are to be brought to the test of experience, and insofar as they shape conduct, they influence what our future experience is likely to be. It is more to my purpose, then, to discuss the relation of doctrine and experience according to Peirce in terms of the relation between beliefs (theoretical and practical) and practice. Doctrine, it should be clear, is a special case of belief, that is, a belief or beliefs of a certain kind. I hope in particular to show that, in the case of Peirce, the charge frequently leveled against Pragmatism—namely, that it emphasizes practice to the detriment of theory—is unwarranted and indeed false, even if Peirce sees an important connection between them.

I would like, therefore, to begin with the major facts of Peirce's life, and then to take up the following issues:

(a) Peirce's separation of theory from practice;

(b) the meaning of the pragmatic maxim in terms of "practical consequences"; and

(c) Peirce's understanding of the relation of Instinct and Reason as grounding the ultimate continuity between theory and practice expressed in the maxim.

PEIRCE'S CAREER

Who, then, was Charles Sanders Santiago Peirce?[1] He was born on September 10, 1839, in Cambridge, Massachusetts, the second son of Benjamin and Sarah Hunt Peirce. His father, a professor at Harvard and one of the greatest American mathematicians of the day, played a decisive role in Charles's upbringing and formal education. He early introduced Charles to mathematics, the physical sciences, and logic. At the age of 8 Charles took up the study of chemistry on his own, and at 12 set up his own small laboratory. About the same time he composed a short history of that science. At 13 he had read and mastered his elder brother's logic textbook. As 15 he entered Harvard College, and, four years later, in 1859, graduated, one of the youngest in his class. For all his genius, however, Charles's scholastic record was undistinguished. He described himself as "a very insouciant student."

Peirce's interest in philosophy began during those undergraduate days. He read and expounded as best he could Schiller's *Aesthetische Briefe* to his friend and classmate Horatio Paine. He studied Kant's *Critique of Pure Reason* so thoroughly that he knew it almost by heart. Still, due in large measure to his father's influence, he chose to become a scientist. In 1863 he received from Harvard his Bachelor of Science in Chemistry *summa cum laude*, the first ever to do so. Meanwhile, in 1861, Peirce had joined the United States Coast and Geodetic Survey with which he remained for thirty years, holding many important posts and doing much original work in photometry and gravitation. The only book he ever published was entitled *Photometric Researches* (1878), and he won international recognition for it. In connection with this research, he received one of the very few official votes of confidence in his career when in 1877 he was elected a fellow of the National Academy of Arts and Sciences and a member of the National Academy of Science.

His interest in philosophy never diminished. Rather it strengthened as his scientific work confirmed, as he saw it, his philosophic views. His early efforts were concentrated in the fields of logic and the philosophy of science. In these areas he anticipated much of present-day work. The technical papers that he published between 1867 and 1885 established him as one of the greatest formal logicians of his day. He lectured at Harvard as an official member of the staff three times between 1864 and 1871, and it was about this time that the "metaphysical club," as Peirce later called it, was formed, an informal discussion group which met fortnightly to discuss philosophical problems. Among its members were some of the finest minds of the day: Oliver Wendell Holmes, Jr., William James, Chauncey Wright, Francis Abbot, and Nicholas St. John Green, to mention a few. It was in this imposing intellectual milieu that Pragmatism first saw the light of day. At about this time, too, Peirce's interest in logic led him to read the great Scholastics—Aquinas, Scotus, Ockham, Bacon—and to declare unequivocally for Scholastic Realism as against Nominalism in every form. This exposure to the famous controversy over universals decisively influenced his brand of Pragmatism.

Although it is certain that Peirce first discussed and formulated the pragmatic maxim in these informal meetings, the first definite statement of it did not appear until 1878 in a paper, published in *Popular Science Monthly,* under the title "How to Make Our Ideas Clear." The maxim reads as follows: "Consider what effects, which might conceivably have practical bearings, we conceive the object to have. Then, our conception of these effects is the whole of our conception of the object" (5.402).[2] This version is admittedly crude, and indeed it led to misunderstanding and to misinterpretation by other philosophers who called themselves pragmatists. Peirce would take great pains to rectify that and to clarify his real meaning.

Despite his eagerness to teach, despite his ability and originality, Peirce never had the opportunity to do so for more than eight years of his whole life. Apart from his early Harvard lectures, his only academic post was at The Johns Hopkins University, and this he held for only five years (1879–1884). After that he mounted a university podium only to deliver an occasional series of lectures by invitation. Despite the direct and personal intervention of William James with Harvard's president, Eliot, Peirce was refused an appointment to a chair.

Yet Peirce was an inspiring lecturer. Too advanced, perhaps, for the ordinary student, he challenged the more gifted, and was respected and highly esteemed by all. He organized at Johns Hopkins a second metaphysical club for his students. Among those who attended was John Dewey, then a graduate student. Peirce's rejection by university administrations has been the topic of speculation. It was perhaps due in part to his difficult personality, in part to his domestic problems. With regard to the first, Paul Weiss sums up his personality in this way, "he was always somewhat proud of his ancestry and connections, overbearing towards those who stood in his way, indifferent to the consequences of his acts, quick to take affront, highly emotional, easily duped, and with, as he puts it, 'a reputation for not finding things.' "[3] With regard to the second, his marriage in 1862 to Harriet Melusina Fay (granddaughter of the prominent Episcopalian bishop, John Henry Hopkins) ended in divorce in 1883 while Peirce was teaching in Baltimore. His career there ended the next year. Subsequently he married Juliette Froissey of Nancy, France, to whom he remained devoted all his life, and who survived him. In 1887, having inherited a small legacy, Peirce, aged 48, retired to a small farm near Milford, Pennsylvania, where he lived out his life studying and writing. He was continually in financial straits. Once he applied to the Carnegie Foundation for help in publishing a series of books on philosophy, but, to the subsequent chagrin of the Foundation, he was turned down. Peirce was in quasi-exile. Near the end it was only the touching fidelity of William James that fed and sheltered him. Upon his death, his widow sold his papers to Harvard where they remain.

Such was the brilliant and tragic career of Charles Peirce. Though he never published a book on philosophy, his articles and drafts fill volumes. It has only been since the publication of the *Collected Papers* in the '30s that the philosophic community has been able to appreciate the depth and scope of his speculation. Peirce is beginning to find his place in American thought—a place of the first rank.

THREE ISSUES

Let us now consider the three substantive issues mentioned above, namely:

(a) the separation of theory and practice,
(b) the meaning of the pragmatic maxim,
(c) the relation and role of Instinct and Reason.

Theory and Practice

Peirce consistently and repeatedly maintained not only that theory had nothing whatsoever to do with practice, but also that it ought not to have anything to do with it. Peirce makes his most sustained case for this view in a series of lectures delivered at Harvard in 1898.

During the spring and summer of 1897 Peirce worked on eight lectures to be given in a series at Cambridge.[4] His invitation to give the series was the result of William James's efforts to bring him to the Harvard campus in some capacity or other. Two years earlier James unsuccessfully intervened in Peirce's behalf with President Eliot for a permanent position to teach "Philosophy of Nature." Eliot flatly refused even to have Peirce considered, so James had to settle for inviting him to give a lecture series. In December 1897, Peirce sent James an outline of eight lectures, all of them on logic. James wrote back lamenting the choice of topic since " 'there are only three men who could possibly follow your graphs and relatives.' " In a most friendly way, and out of the sole motive of having Peirce's lectures be a success, James advised him to " 'be a good boy and think a more popular plan out' "—a plan which would hold the audience's interest. James remarks, " 'Separate topics of a vitally important character would do perfectly well.' "

Peirce's reaction was predictable. The logician–mathematician–scientist was hurt and deeply disappointed. He wrote back accepting the conditions without enthusiasm and without holding out any hope that he could thus give his hearers any real idea of his philosophy since all his ideas repose " 'entirely upon the theory of logic.' " He remarks that no doubt James has correctly gauged the capacities of his students, and he cannot resist adding, " 'It agrees with all I hear and the little I have seen of Cambridge.' " He goes on to compare the Cambridge students with those whom he has been tutoring in New York City. For the latter the method of graphs proved quite easy because their minds were stimulated by New York life. " 'Your Harvard students of philosophy find it too arduous a matter to reason exactly. Soon your engineers will find it better to leave great works unbuilt rather than go through the necessary calculations.' "

Peirce then set to work redoing the entire series. This revised version he entitled "Detached Ideas on Topics of Vital Importance." In Cambridge, however, they were advertised under the inoffensive title "Reasoning and the Logic of Things." Despite James's suggestions, a great deal of logic found its way into those lectures. Royce wrote to James that they put him on a completely new direction.[5] But they were also the occasion for some of Peirce's most ironic and satirical remarks on "the practical" in education.

Consider the title Peirce suggested for the series. Nothing could be more foreign to his view of philosophy than a set of "detached ideas," and nothing could be less promising a subject for philosophical discourse than "vitally important topics." If one thing is clear, it is that for Peirce philosophy must be done systematically and that it had little or no immediate relevance for "life" and its vital concerns. According to Peirce,

> Philosophy is that branch of positive science (i.e., an investigating theoretical science which inquires what is the fact, in contradistinction to mathematics which merely seeks to know what follows from certain hypotheses) which makes no (special) observations but which contents itself with so much of experience as pours in upon every man during every hour of his waking life [5.13n].[6]

Philosophy has three branches, Phenomenology, Normative Science, and Metaphysics, which are related to each other as First, Second, and Third. Phenomenology is a First in that it makes no judgment or evaluation of what is experienced, accepting it merely for what it is; Normative Science is a Second in that it sets up a standard against which things are to be judged as true or as good or as beautiful; Metaphysics is a Third in that it mediates between phenomena and norms—that is, it is the realm of the Real. Hence, since Metaphysics involves the other two, it is the science of the Real *par excellence*.[7] Yet Peirce is fond of saying that metaphysics is gibberish, and meaningless, not intrinsically, but because of its backward state. That backward state is due fundamentally to the neglect of Kant's advice to build metaphysics architectonically, i.e., in the manner in which a house is constructed—on a broad and solid base, and out of materials tested for the purpose (see, e.g., 1.176–79, 5.5, 6.7–34). This architectonic structure must be put together with exact logical care. "What is needed above all, for metaphysics, is thorough and mature thinking; and the particular requisite for success in the critic of arguments is exact and diagrammatic thinking" (3.406).

In a word, there can be no sound metaphysics unless it be systematic and based on logic. Finally, metaphysical philosophy can advance if and only if it is conducted by "laboratory men" whose sole motivation is the pursuit of truth wherever it may be found (see, e.g., 5.412, 1.618–20). Furthermore, the purpose of any theory is "to furnish a rational account of its object" (2.1), and so it aims directly at nothing but knowledge.

Peirce is combating two rather common views of theoretical investigation. The first we might call the "doctrinaire view"; the second, the "utilitarian view." According to the first, science and philosophy are looked upon as a body of acquired truth which is to be taught and to be learned for the instruction and betterment of mankind. It is expected, of course, that the possession of this truth will have immediate beneficial effects upon individuals and society. According to the second (frequently held in conjunction with the first), the sole legitimate motive for scientific or philosophical inquiry is the application of the results for the immediate personal or social benefit of mankind. Technology becomes science's ultimate motive and justification; ideology becomes philosophy's.

According to Peirce, the doctrinaire view simply misses science as a "living historic entity." "As such it [science] does not consist so much in *knowing*, nor even in 'organized' knowledge, as it does in diligent inquiry into truth for truth's sake, without any axe to grind, nor for the sake of the delight of contemplating it, but from an impulse to penetrate into the reason of things" (1.44).

The second view, he contends, corrupts the scientific enterprise from the beginning because it prejudices the outcome and restricts the extent and scope of research. Such a view might be called "logical hedonism" inasmuch as it falls victim to the same mistake as moral hedonism does: it confuses the usual upshot of research with its effective motive force. Just as moral hedonism mistakes some form of "pleasure" for the moral good, so logical hedonism mistakes some form of "utility" for the truth. Such an error, in Peirce's view, generally results in achieving neither genuine satisfaction nor authentic utility (1.619).

Peirce once said that the pragmatic maxim was nothing but Jesus' recommendation "By their fruits you shall know them" (Mt 7:20). He might also have justly pointed out that the ethical principle of investigation proposed here is also in the New Testament in the parable of the lilies of the field (Mt 6:28–33; Lk 12:27–31), which he might have paraphrased as "Seek first the Truth, and all these things will be added to you."

Let us consider Peirce's understanding of "topics of vital importance" in some detail. In the first lecture of the Cambridge series, "Philosophy and the Conduct of Life," Peirce begins with the remark that the Greeks:

> expected philosophy to affect life—not by any slow process of percolation of forms, as we may expect that researches into differential equations, stellar photometry, the taxonomy of echinoderms and the like will ultimately affect the conduct of life—but forthwith in the person and soul of the philosopher himself, rendering him different from ordinary men in his views of right conduct [1.618].

This I would call the "Immediate Relevance" thesis.[8] Peirce exempts Aristotle from this mentality because he was not altogether Greek. He writes: "Now, Gentlemen, it behooves me, at the outset of this course, to confess to you that in this respect I stand before you an Aristotelian and a scientific man, condemning with the whole strength of conviction the Hellenic tendency to mingle philosophy with practice" (1.619).

Practice, the conduct of life, utility, what would forthwith make one a better or more successful man—none of this has or should have anything to do with science or philosophy since, as we have seen, they would undermine those disciplines and endanger the moral integrity of the philosopher and the scientist. What Peirce considered the backward state of philosophy in his day is directly attributable to the fact that it was largely in the hands of those he called "seminary men" who "have been inflamed with a desire to amend the lives of themselves and others, a spirit no doubt more important than the love of science, for men in average situations, but radically unfitting them for the task of scientific investigation" (1.620).

Peirce thought that all men might be put into three classes[9] according to what they considered to be the highest good in life.

If we endeavor to form our conceptions upon history and life, we remark three classes of men. The first consists of those for whom the chief thing is the quality of feelings. These men create art. The second consists of the practical men, who carry on the business of the world. They respect nothing but power, and respect power only so far as it is exercised. The third class consists of men to whom nothing seems great but reason. If force interests them, it is not in its exertion, but in that it has a reason and a law. For men of the first class, nature is a picture; for men of the second class, it is an opportunity; for men of the third class, it is a cosmos, so admirable, that to penetrate to its ways seems to them the only thing that makes life worth living. These are the men whom we see possessed by the passion to learn, just as other men have a passion to teach and to disseminate their influence. If they do not give themselves over completely to their passion to learn, it is because they exercise self-control. Those are the natural scientific men; and they are the only men that have any real success in scientific research [1.43].

"Vital importance" has two senses, and Peirce's irony depends upon the play between them. In the literal sense, vitally important topics refer to questions of physical life and well-being in the common, ordinary course of things. In the extended sense, they refer to those questions of ultimate significance which make life worth living at all. If one is convinced that the literal is the only sense, then neither philosophy nor science need play any role in that life. Attending to one's natural sentiments and instincts in these matters will afford one a much better chance of success. On the other hand, if one is convinced that coming to know the truth about oneself and about the universe is what makes human life specifically human and, therefore, affords man his only genuine fulfillment, then the pursuit of philosophy and science becomes a way of life, and questions of everyday business take a secondary and relatively modest place of importance.

The practice which Peirce would divorce from theory is the "conduct of life," that which takes place in the arena of practical affairs, whether the decisions concern ordinary business or great crises.

In the great decisions, I do not believe it is safe to trust to individual reason. In everyday business, reasoning is tolerably successful; but I am inclined to think that it is done as well without the aid of theory as with it. A *logica utens*, like analytical mechanics resident in the billiard player's nerves, best fulfills familiar uses [1.623].

But in practical affairs, in matters of vital importance, it is very easy to exaggerate the importance of ratiocination. Man is so vain of his power of reason! . . . It is the instincts, the sentiments, that make the substance of the soul. Cognition is only its surface, its locus of contact with what is external to it [1.626 and 628].

Peirce claimed that he could strictly prove all this, "but only by assuming a logical principle . . ." (1.629). Peirce, then, is convinced that this attitude toward theory and practice is itself recommended by reason!

Were I willing to make a single exception to the proposition I thus enunciate that theory and practice be kept separate and to admit that there was one study which was at once vitally important and scientific, I should make that exception in favor of logic; for the reason that if we fall into the error of believing that vitally important questions are to be decided by reasoning, the only hope of salvation lies in formal logic, which demonstrates in the clearest manner that reasoning itself testifies to its own ultimate subordination to sentiment [1.672].

At the same time, Peirce observes that if you accept this "conservative sentimentalism" and modestly rate your own reasoning powers in matters of vital importance, then you will find that the very first command laid upon you by instinct itself would be to recognize a higher business than your business. "Thus while reason and the science of reasoning strenuously proclaim the subordination of reasoning to sentiment, the very supreme command of sentiment is that man should generalize . . ." (1.673). I will return to this point in the final part of this essay.

Pragmatic Maxim

In 1896 James's *The Will to Believe* appeared, dedicated to Peirce. In these Cambridge lectures Peirce substitutes, in matters of theoretical investigation, the "Will to Learn." "I hold that what is properly and usually called belief . . . has no place in science at all. We *believe* the proposition we are ready to act upon. . . . But pure science has nothing at all to do with action . . ." (1.635).

This brings us to the second issue: the meaning of "practical consequences" in the pragmatic maxim. There is something paradoxical about the remark just cited above since the pragmatic maxim of 1878 was formulated in the context of the fixation of belief. In those early papers, Peirce argued that the whole point of inquiry is to fix belief, and that the best way to do that is by the scientific method. How, then, can he now claim that belief has no place at all in science? As a first step toward making some sense out of this, I think we should recall the distinction between science as a lived enterprise and science as an established body of truths, i.e., of theoretical beliefs. Genuine doubt, not mere "paper doubt," is the stimulus of scientific inquiry. When the irritation of such doubt is removed, inquiry ceases. Fixation of belief in that sense may be the upshot or outcome of inquiry, but it cannot be its immediate motive. Only the Will to Learn, to pursue genuine doubt wherever it may lead, not the Will to Believe, to fix belief and so to cut off investigation, can play a role in science as a lived enterprise of inquiry.

Furthermore, Peirce considered the notion of "theoretical belief" to be odd. At best, it could mean only that certain scientific laws and theories are provisionally accepted by the scientific communities. Only in this sense is there a body of "scientific truth" and so of "theoretical beliefs."

A practical belief is a habit of deliberate behavior, that upon which we are prepared to act. A theoretical "belief" is an expectation concerning future experience either actual or merely possible. While it is true that "every proposition that is not pure metaphysical jargon and chatter must have some possible bearing upon practice" (5.539), as the pragmatic maxim says, still it must have some "possible bearing," that is, it must consider what conceivable practical consequences the proposition may have, and this is so even in purely theoretical propositions. Conceivable practical consequences or possible bearing in practice is quite distinct from practical consequences in the sense of practice—action here and now. In Peirce's words, while every theoretical belief is at least indirectly a practical belief, this is not the *whole* meaning of a theoretical belief. A theoretical belief is an expectation or anticipation of future experiences, actual or merely possible, not in the sense that it anticipates some muscular sensation (as in a practical belief), but in the sense that it is "the stamp of approval, the act of recognition as one's own, being placed by a deed of the soul upon an imaginary anticipation of experience, so that, if it be fulfilled, . . . the person will claim the event as his due, his triumphant 'I told you so' implying a right to expect as much from a justly regulated world" (5.540).

Since all beliefs essentially involve expectation (5.542) and so look to the future, the "theoretical beliefs" of science must too. What is expected from them *directly*, however, is not some bodily reaction. *Indirectly* and *ultimately*, through the mediation of thought, such "muscular sensation" may be anticipated. What is *directly* anticipated by theoretical belief can only be another *thought*. Consider some of Peirce's examples.

To say that quadratic equation which has no real root has two different imaginary roots does not sound as if it could have any relation to experience. Yet it is strictly expectative. It states what would be expectable if we had to deal with quantities expressing the relations between objects, related to one another like the points of the plane of imaginary quantity. So a belief about the incommensurability of the diagonal relates to what is expectable for a person dealing with fractions; although it means nothing at all in regard to what could be expected in physical measurement. . . . Riemann declared that infinity has nothing to do with the absence of limit but relates solely to measure. This means that if a bounded surface be measured in a suitable way it will be found infinite, and that if an unbounded surface be measured in a suitable way, it will be found finite. It relates to what is expectable for a person dealing with different systems of measurement [5.541].

Consequently, even if every proposition must have a reference to some conceivable application to practice in order for it to have any definite meaning at all, still, when the pragmatic maxim is applied to "theoretical beliefs," the "practical consequences" are purely a matter of thought. Even in practical beliefs, insofar as they have been articulated and critically scrutinized, they too have been transformed through thought into rules for deliberate (rational) conduct.

It would be too long to repeat here what I have said elsewhere concerning Peirce's efforts to disassociate himself from other "pragmatists" who he thought pushed the maxim too far so as to make action the be-all and end-all of thought.[10] It is enough to note that he argued to the contrary.

If it be admitted . . . that action wants an end, and that that end must be something of a general description, then the spirit of the maxim itself, which is that we must look to the upshot of our concepts in order rightly to apprehend them, would direct us towards something different from practical facts, namely, to general ideas, as the true interpreters of our thought [5.3].[11]

Peirce's pragmatism recognizes a fundamental connection between thought and action, between theory and practice, without confusing the two and without inverting the order of the relation. Thought *ultimately* applies to action, and theory ultimately applies to practice, at least in the sense of reference to conceivable action and to conceivable practice. But this is quite a different thing either from making thought consist in action and theory consist in practice, or from making thought's ultimate purpose action and theory's ultimate purpose practice. Action through thought is only the upshot of investigation; it is neither its purpose nor its legitimate motive.

Instinct and Reason

I would like now touch briefly on our third and final theme: the relation between Instinct and Reason as the ground of the pragmatic maxim and as the explanation of the continuity between theory and practice. In Peirce's opinion, all scientific inquiry supposes a Realism, in the sense that the Real is coextensive with the Knowable. There is no Kantian noumenon. If this is so, the Real constitutes a network of relations such that everything is connected with everything else or, to put it another way, that the Real is everywhere continuous. *Natura non facit saltus.* This continuous Real is systematically explored through abduction, deduction, and induction. But, since neither deduction nor induction yields any new knowledge about the Real, abduction is at the heart of all discovery. But, according to Peirce, abduction is nothing but instinctive reason. It is the power which nature provided, in the course of evolution, for man to survive in an evolving cosmos by enabling him to meet radically new situations and, at the same time, to help bring about radically new situations. While Peirce holds that there is probably no instinct for logicality, in the sense of an immediate feeling of logical connection that guarantees the correctness of any inference, still he does admit instinctive reason, which may be wrong more often than right, but which is right often enough to allow us to make discoveries of some of nature's laws.

Galileo appeals to *il lume naturale* at the most critical stages of his reasoning. Kepler, Gilbert and Harvey—not to speak of Copernicus—substantially rely upon an inward power, not sufficient to reach the truth by itself, but yet supplying an essential factor to the influences carrying their minds. It is certain that the only hope of retroductive reasoning ever reaching the truth is that there may be some natural tendency toward an agreement between the ideas which suggest themselves to the human mind and those which are concerned in the laws of nature [1.80–81].

Perhaps under the influence of Chauncey Wright, Peirce accepted a thoroughgoing evolutionism. He held, then, that human reason must be an evolutionary development of animal instinct. "Side by side, then, with the well-established proposition that all knowledge is based on experience . . . we have to place this other equally important truth, that all human knowledge, up to the highest flights of science, is but the development of our inborn animal instincts" (2.754). Peirce bases this opinion precisely on *il lume naturale*, the faculty for guessing right without which scientific knowledge would have been impossible.

That Reason is in continuity with the animal instincts of feeding and breeding (although not identical with them), that Reason itself is instinctive, man's specific instinctive power as it were, led Peirce to adopt a position which he called Critical Commonsensism. As the name suggests, it is sympathetic to the Scottish School, and yet critical of it in some details. Peirce, in fact, identified his pragmaticism with such Critical Common Sense. There are some beliefs that are indubitable because they are instinctive. Such beliefs are acritical and essentially vague. Nonetheless, they are at the very heart of the power to reason itself, and function as a necessary counterbalance to scientific fallibilism. That there is order in the universe is one such belief. That God is real is another (see 5.508; 8.262).[12]

Instinctive Reason, with its vague instinctive beliefs, inserts man into an evolving world, not merely as a product of the creative process, but also as an active, cooperative agent. Since Reason gives him the power of reflection and a high degree of self-control, man holds the unique and privileged position of co-creator:

it is by the indefinite replication of self-control upon self-control that the *vir* is begotten, and by action, through thought, he grows an esthetic idea . . . as the share which God permits him to have in the work of creation [5.403n3].

I do not see how one can have a more satisfying ideal of the admirable than the development of Reason so understood. The one thing whose admirableness is not due to an ulterior reason is Reason itself comprehended in all its fullness, so far as we can comprehend it. Under this conception, the ideal of conduct will be to execute our little function in the operation of creation by giving a hand toward rendering the world more reasonable, whenever, as the slang is, it is "up-to-us to do so" [1.615].

NOTES

1. For a fine biographical sketch of Peirce, see Paul Weiss, "Charles Sanders Peirce," *Dictionary of American Biography*, 14 (1934), 398–403. For further biographical details, see the following pieces by Max H. Fisch: "Peirce as Scientist, Mathematician, Historian, Logician, and Philosopher," in *Proceedings of the C. S. Peirce Bicentennial International Congress*, edd. Kenneth L. Ketner, Joseph M. Ransdell, Carolyn Eisele, Max H. Fisch, and Charles S. Hardwick, Texas Tech University Graduate Studies 23 (Lubbock: Texas Tech Press, 1981), pp. 13–34; "The Range of Peirce's Relevance," in *The Relevance of Charles Peirce*, ed. Eugene Freeman, Monist Library of Philosophy (La Salle, Ill.: Open Court, 1983), pp. 11–37; "Introduction," in *Writings of Charles S. Peirce: A Chronological Edition*, ed. Christian Kloesel, 3 vols. (Bloomington: Indiana University Press, 1982–1986), I xv–xxxv, II xxi–xxxvi; and "Supplement: A Chronicle of Pragmaticism, 1865–1879," *The Monist*, 48 (1964), 441–66.

2. References to Peirce's works are taken from *Collected Papers of Charles Sanders Peirce*, edd. Charles Hartshorne, Paul Weiss, and Arthur Burks, 8 vols. (Cambridge: The Belknap Press of Harvard University Press, 1931–1958). References are by volume and paragraph.

3. "Charles Sanders Peirce," p. 402.

4. For an account of this episode in Peirce's life, and for the correspondence between Peirce and James, see R. B. Perry, *The Thought and Character of William James*. II. *Philosophy and Psychology* (Boston: Little, Brown, 1935), pp. 417–21.

5. Royce's letter to James in 1901 is cited in ibid., p. 421.

6. "By a positive science I mean an inquiry which seeks for positive knowledge; that is, for such knowledge as may conveniently be expressed in a categorial proposition" (5.39).

7. For a discussion of the relation of philosophy's branches to the categories, see V. G. Potter, *C. S. Peirce on Norms and Ideals* (Amherst: The University of Massachusetts Press, 1967), pp. 18–24.

8. For a more extensive treatment of "Immediate Relevance" in philosophy, see V. G. Potter, "The Irrelevance of Philosophy," *Thought*, 49 (1974), 145–55.

9. In his *Spiritual Exercises* Ignatius Loyola speaks of three classes of men, only the third of which are sufficiently detached from their own immediate satisfaction to take the measures necessary to achieve the end in view. The passage is found under the Second Week's "Three Classes of Men."

10. See my *Norms and Ideals*, pp. 3–7; "Normative Science and the Pragmatic Maxim," *Journal of the History of Philosophy*, 5 (1967), 41–53; and "Peirce's Pragmatic Maxim," *Tijdschrift voor Filosofie*, 35 (1973), 505–17.

11. Peirce revised the maxim several times to make his meaning clear; see, e.g., 5.18.

12. For an extended development of Peirce's views on God, see my " 'Vaguely Like a Man': The Theism of Charles S. Peirce," in *God Knowable and Unknowable*, ed. Robert J. Roth, s.j. (New York: Fordham University Press, 1973), pp. 241–54; and "C. S. Peirce's Argument for God's Reality: A Pragmatist's View," in *Wisdom and Knowledge: Essays in Honor of Joseph Papin II* (Villanova: Villanova University Press, 1976), pp. 224–44; as well as Donna M. Orange's *Peirce's Conception of God: A Developmental Study*, Peirce Studies 2 (Lubbock: Institute for Studies in Pragmaticism, 1984).

6

"Life Is in the Transitions":
Radical Empiricism and
Contemporary Concerns

JOHN J. MCDERMOTT
Texas A & M University

> You see also that it stands or falls with the notion I have
> taken such pains to defend, of the through-and-through
> union of adjacent minima of experience, of the confluence
> of every passing moment of concretely felt experience with
> its immediately next neighbors.
> WILLIAM JAMES[1]

I

THE DECIDED INCREASE in publications, both editions and com-
mentaries, has pointed to a definite renascence of interest in American classical philosophy as represented by Peirce, James, Royce,
Dewey, Santayana, and Mead. Two major tasks await such a revival of interest: first, presenting and clarifying the textual tradition; second, utilizing the insights of that tradition in an effort to
confront the significant problems of our time. In this essay, I focus
on the second task, relating James's radical empirical empiricism
to some of our more recent problems, in the hope that different
formulation may assist remediation. Although James was basically
a late-nineteenth-century thinker, his thought is highly relevant to

An earlier version of this chapter appears in John J. McDermott, *The Culture of Experience: Philosophical Essays in the American Grain* (New York:
New York University Press, 1976), pp. 99–117.

contemporary culture; indeed, the philosophy of William James acts as a vestibule to much of twentieth-century life.

Before I proceed to the substance of these issues, two methodological concerns are in order. First, in formulating relationships between contemporary concerns and the thought of William James, care must be exercised that his language and ideas not be wrenched out of their setting so as to create anachronistic and misleading patterns of influence. It cannot be contended, for example, that James anticipated the specifics of new developments in depth psychology, theories of interpersonal relations or proxemics, the new subtleties of cultural anthropology, and the vast import of developments in transportation and electronic media. James was a man of the Industrial Revolution, of steamships, the telegraph, and the train. His experienced sense of time, while "speeded up," was fundamentally antique, that is, measurable by the traversing of space.

Despite these cautions, James's thought nonetheless functions in an extraordinarily anticipatory way. For one thing, if James was not the first, he was the most outspoken proponent of a distinctively contemporary view of cosmology, unabashedly post-Copernican and highly sensitized to the role of novelty and the constitutive role of human life. He was also committed to an overthrow of the centuries-old "substance"-oriented description of reality, and attempted to replace it with a relational and process-oriented metaphysics, far more flexible and in keeping with the subsequent developments in the disciplines of our own time. James's critique of previous positions paved the way for a more free-wheeling approach to the problems of inquiry and description, and though not worked out in detail, his own theories and approaches, however inadvertently, foreshadowed major shifts in priorities and concerns in psychology, the arts, and even social psychology.

The significance of James's thought for social psychology leads to the second methodological question. How, it may be asked, can such significance be ascribed to a thinker so notoriously concerned with the individual and so singularly free of apparent insight into matters social or into the sociological context for inquiry, later explicated so brilliantly by John Dewey? A first response to this question has to do with James's language. Granted: he does not invoke a sociological vocabulary. Nonetheless he assumes a fundamental social matrix in his epistemology; for the pragmatic method has to do with consequences, testing and experimentation as subject to verification in a world of experience other than one we simply think about. Put another way: James was adamantly opposed to evaluating ideas relative only to other ideas, professing that ideas carry their weight as applied to actual situations, many of them inevitably social.

Secondly, unless a sociology is explicitly reductionistic, it must honor some assumptions about the nature of human activity from a philosophical and psychological perspective. James's thought on human behavior, while nurtured on his abiding sensibility to individual experience, is yet characterized by perceptions significantly germane to social psychology. And as both G. H. Mead and John Dewey have attested, their own developments in social theory would be inconceivable without James's breakthroughs in psychology and his metaphysics of relations.

These methodological cautions concluded, let me set up the approach to the present considerations. After a brief reminding exposition of James's doctrine of relations, I shall examine in some detail two contemporary problems in what, I trust, is the Jamesian manner, and attempt to recast the diagnosis of our present situation, characterized as it is by the language of alienation and anomie, in the direction of less emphasis on the quest for human certitude and more emphasis on affectivity and the texture of our actual experiences. For James, after all, "Experience itself, taken at large, can grow by its edges."[2] The manifestations of living occur in time, with both events and meanings internal to that process, never yielding to a transcendent point of view.[3]

II

As is well known, James stated the basic contentions of his philosophy, that is, radical empiricism, on a number of occasions. Despite some surface ambiguity, a careful reading of James will show it to be clear, both textually and thematically, that for him pragmatism is a methodological application of his radical empiricism. In that sense, to call James simply a pragmatist is misleading, and, indeed, without radical empiricism as a metaphysical base, pragmatism is subject to the savage philosophical critique it has received.

In 1897, as part of the Preface to *The Will to Believe*, James wrote:

> Were I obliged to give a short name to the attitude in question, I should call it that of *radical empiricism*. . . . I say "empiricism" because it is contented to regard its most assured conclusions concerning matters of fact as hypotheses liable to modification in the course of future experience, and I say "radical" because it treats the doctrine of monism itself as an hypothesis. . . .
>
> He who takes for his hypothesis the notion that it [pluralism] is the permanent form of the world is what I call a radical empiricist. For him the crudity of experience remains an eternal element thereof. There is no possible point of view from which the world can appear an absolutely single fact.[4]

In 1904, James wrote to François Pillon that " 'My philosophy is what I call a radical empiricism, a pluralism, a "tychism," which represents order as being gradually won and always in the making.' "[5] And finally, in 1909, James offered his clearest version of radical empiricism when he wrote a Preface to *The Meaning of Truth*, a book intended to answer the critics of his *Pragmatism*:

> Radical empiricism consists first of a postulate, next of a statement of fact, and finally of a generalized conclusion.
>
> The postulate is that the only things that shall be debatable among philosophers shall be things definable in terms drawn from experience. [Things of an unexperienceable nature may exist ad libitum, but they form no part of the material for philosophical debate.]
>
> The statement of fact is that the relations between things, conjunctive as well as disjunctive, are just as much matters of direct particular experience, neither more so nor less so, than the things themselves.
>
> The generalized conclusion is that therefore the parts of experience hold together from next to next by relations that are themselves parts of experience. The directly apprehended universe needs, in short, no extraneous trans-empirical connective support, but possesses in its own right a concatenated or continuous structure.[6]

For the present purposes, two major themes emerge: first, that in our experience at large we are given continuity but not Unity; and, secondly, that this continuity is due to our affective or feeling grasp of the relationships that set up in all our activities, conceptual as well as perceptual. This second claim is what James calls a "statement of fact" and what Arthur Bentley[7] calls the "Jamesian datum," capable of experimental verification. If it is not so that relations are equally and affectively experienced as the poles of the relationship are, then James's thought is but a string of brilliant asides, declining considerably in positive and philosophical merit. Further, given that his negative statement about the impossibility of seeing the world whole or as a single fact is seemingly true, as twentieth-century thought attests over and over, his doctrine of relations provides the only meaningful source of intelligibility. The accuracy of James's "statement of fact" is, therefore, no idle matter, for with the rejection of an overarching, transcendent principle of explanation, man is forced back into an unreflective "taking things as they come" or the intellectual encapsulations of a solipsism. Let me sketch an approach, accepting James's radical empiricism and consistent with its claims, to the discussion of two contemporary concerns, alienation and repression.

III

One of the cardinal concerns of our century has been the increased presence of the experience of alienation. The language of articulation for this situation has been either Marxist, following the renewed awareness of the *Economic and Philosophic Manuscripts* (1844), or existentialist, following the writings of Camus, Sartre, Marcel, Jaspers, and Heidegger. In both traditions, however profound their differences, there exists the common theme of deep distrust of the classical European institutions, the Church, class structure, and philosophy, especially the claims fostered by centuries of confidence in the ultimate intelligibility of nature as open to reason. The collapse of these claims in a series of intellectual revolutions, from Copernicanism, through Luther, Hume, Kant, the Romantic poets, Marx and Nietzsche, abetted by the irrational terrors of the Holocaust, has generated a rootlessness and despair in much of Western contemporary thought. The writings of Cioran and Ellul are a witness to the loss of hope, and the vigorous interest in Eastern thought as well as the writings of Joyce and N. O. Brown yield a return to the doctrine of the cycle and the rejection of historical novelty.

By contrast, an analysis of alienation from the perspective of James's experience and thought will prove illuminating. Although James[8] has said that one is not educated unless one has "dallied" with suicide, as he did, and although the focus of most interpreters on James's multiple neuroses—such as his psychosomatic neurasthenia, insomnia, and transcontinental restlessness—has led Gay Wilson Allen[9] to imply that James was on the edge of a nervous breakdown all his life, James's anthropology, nonetheless, was not characterized by alienation. The reasons for this are extremely instructive, not only relative to an interpretation of James's life but as a harbinger of a creative response to our own problems. Taking fundamental issue with the interpretation of James as a neurotic and insecure person, I submit that the key to his philosophy can be phrased as, first, his rejection of a derivative ethics and of a derivative sense of self, and, second, his affirmation of local intelligibility as present in the experience-continua of human activity. This rejection and affirmation feed off each other. James is willing to chance the dangers of radical novelty, even in the deepest recesses of personal life precisely because he believes that all our experiences are affectively related and carry with them distinctive meanings. Paradoxically, James holds that the real threat to human life is security, for it prematurely blocks us from sources of intelligibility that often yield themselves only on behalf of personal risk.

For James, alienation is the inability to make relations. To accept a derivative ethics or an a priori meaning of the self, as in the classical doctrine of the soul, is to abort the making of relations. On the other hand, to be without such an inheritance is not to be cut adrift completely, for while "My belief, to be sure, can't be optimistic . . . I will posit life (the real, the good) in the self-governing resistance of the ego to the world. Life shall [be built in] doing and suffering and creating."[10] In effect, James sees the human task as constituting meaning, not ab ovo from the power of the mind as in philosophical idealism, but in selective and rejective response to the press of events upon us.

Alienation can be described as the experience of disconnections in those areas of life in which we are vulnerable. No event, situation, or circumstance is by nature alienating. Human beings have withstood, nay flourished under, the most objectively dehumanizing and terrifying of experiences. Just as the liver is the relational manifold of our bodies, so we have a psychological relational manifold, which has as its task to anticipate needs, set balances, and warn us against misleading directions. James writes in the *Pragmatism*: "Woe to him whose beliefs play fast and loose with the order which realities follow in his experience; they will lead him nowhere or else make false connexions."[11] James is not pointing to ultimate alienation, that is, the inability to make sense of the world, for that is a result of an illegitimate expectation in the first place. Rather, he is pointing to the instances of alienation that occur when we do not guard against the twin dangers of prometheanism and the laissez-faire acceptance of the world as conceived by others. When James states that " 'The inmost nature of the reality is congenial to *powers* which you possess,' "[12] he affirms a metaphysical possibility but he offers no guarantee. Although James is fond of talking about powers, energies, and leads, he also assumes a highly developed sense of self-awareness and self-protection. After all, the abandonment of an inherited self, while liberating, is nonetheless challenging and even dangerous. If the world is not given as meaningful and the self is but our capacity to be meaningfully present, then the making of relations becomes equivalent to who we are.

There are a number of ways in which we are alienated, that is, prevented from making relations. The traditional meaning of alienation, to be "cut off," we describe as relation-starvation, and given James's understanding of human activity, it is but one source of alienation. Other sources can be described as relation-saturation and relation-seduction. Before I detail these terms, a brief statement of James's fundamental world-view will be helpful. Reality is a network of concatenatedly related objects or things, rendered as such by human conceptual decision, in keeping with the possibilities and limitations structured by nature on its terms and historically rendered by previous human activity. Human experience is an "aware flow" within the activities of reality at large, which in turn is also in process, unfinished, and broken into by novelties relative to the patterns already set up. For the most part we live our lives focally, that is, within a familiar range of experiences rendered clear to us by our conceptual systems or simply accepted by habituation. Ideally this focus opens outward, reaching toward a fringe of experiences, often vague and inarticulate but subtly continuous and profoundly meaningful. Religious experience, unusual psychic experiences, aesthetic experiences, drug experiences, psychophysical breakthroughs as in yoga, and the range of allegedly neurotic and psychotic experiences are potentially rich possibilities at the fringe.

Speaking diagnostically, then, about human well-being, James's philosophy offers the following cautions and suggestions. First, if our focus is concave, either we tend to duplicate our experiences or, at a minimum, no matter their actual differences, the experiences are slotted in an already articulated and accepted conceptual scheme. James refers to this as " 'vicious intellectualism,' " which is the "treating of a name as excluding from the fact named what the name's definition fails to include. . . ."[13] This attitude becomes increasingly defensive, even shrill, in overestimating the importance and reach of our focus and in time develops a hostility to experiences not already included within our range. In effect, we tend to identify and evaluate experiences only in terms already familiar to us and sanctioned by us.

Self-encapsulating, this approach results in relation-starvation and in an increasing narrowness of person. What is to be lamented is, not the decrease in the quantity of relations formulated, although that is often, if not necessarily, a factor, but the absence of novelty, differentia, and, in short, the developing inability to be open to experience. In this pillbox mentality, novelty is ever a threat so we burn out the relational ground around us. Little that is not duplicative or replicative comes to our consciousness. It is as if we lived our lives in imitation of the way we were taught to diagram sentences as children. We were told to focus on subject (noun/pronoun), verb (active/passive), and object (direct/indirect). Yet most of the action is found in our use of gerunds, participles, adjectival clauses, and propositional phrases—to say nothing of expletives, argot, and grunts. In a work, relation-starvation is cancerous. More specifically, it is a cancer of the psychological "liver," for not only does it represent the stark absence of most novelty but, what is more serious, it generates an increasing incapacity to make anything of the little novelty that does break through. To live within an increasingly concave focus is to give the impression of security and confidence. Yet this masks a deep experience of alienation, for with a decrease in the capacity to make relations, the experiences we have already undergone become threadbare and lifeless.

By contrast, if our focus is convex, we have the advantage of reaching out and thereby reconstituting our frame of reference, flooding us with enormous possibilities, for, as James tells us, anything that makes a difference anywhere makes a difference elsewhere.[14] These differences may be slight or they may be dramatic, thus forcing us to reconstitute the importance of experiences undergone long ago. James contends that every experience we have is fringed with relational possibilities. To live in the world is to be in the presence of inference. James's view of the fringe is not that of a world separate or totally unknown. It resides within the possibilities of the perceptual field, linked by relationships open to human awareness, even if not to clear and defined statement. We make our way to and throughout the fringe hand over hand as it were, with all senses on the *qui vive*, alert to pitfalls and dead-ends, ever within hailing distance of our point of origin. Just as we have no inherited self, so too we have no permanent foothold. We do, however, "selve" ourselves in the vast, teeming flow of experience, and in so doing, we constitute a foothold, ever-changing but ever-present.

I caution here that the liberating possibilities that emerge in opening ourselves to new experiences and to the novel relational implications of heretofore ordinary experiences are not brought off without attendant dangers. The first of these dangers is relation-saturation. For many of us, the obviousness of our daily lives heightens the temptation of sheer novelty, such that a change of interpersonal relations, scene, or lifestyle often carries with it the promise of an enriched life. Yet the piling up of novelties does not guarantee a significant breakthrough in the quality of our experiencing. The crucial task is always the same; whatever our experiences, we must be able to break them open so that we savor their fullest implications, relative to our needs and hopes. It is essential that we proceed from extensive self-diagnosis, enabling us to make decisions on the kind of novelty that is genuinely nutritious for us. Some of us need multiple novelty of a linear kind, stretched out through changes of place, thing, and person. Others find novelty in the ramifications of the same event, worked through in deeper and deeper patterns of articulation. I am reminded here of the long aesthetic journey of the two "Pablos," Casals and Picasso. The first, Casals, built into his cello, explodes it from inside so that the same piece, the same note, is never quite the same. He creates multiple relations out of an intense and creative version of the same locus. The second, Picasso, picks up scraps, pieces, textures, and themes from the world at large and assembles them to make new worlds. Just as the world speaks to itself, as salamanders to mud, so Picasso has everything speak to everything else, in an endless variety of ways. Quantity, then, is not the key to the experience of novelty. Relation-saturation occurs when we move through our lives, touching while untouched. We become voyeurs rather than participants, piling up a string of "experiences" in name only, hashmarks vicariously undergone and fundamentally unrelated. In time, we lose the capacity to make relations and we undergo a subtle form of alienation. Seemingly "with it," we are carried from novelty to novelty, more like flotsam than of our own doing.

One further danger lurks behind our quest for novelty, that of relation-seduction. I agree with James that the extreme fringe of our conscious life is revelatory of possibilities otherwise hidden from view. In pursuing these possibilities we must be careful not to "space" our relations too far apart. Extreme discontinuities in the kind of experiences we have can cause us to be "spaced out" beyond the fundamental patterns of familiarity necessary to self-sustenance. To leap over the working relationships in our experiencing is to be seduced by the promise of radical novelty, often to the extent of blocking a return to the necessities of ordinary experience. Extreme hallucinogenic experiences or the mind-bathing of religious cults are instances in point, for despite their acknowledged intensity and possible illumination, they often sever us from the remaining range of our life-enhancing relationships. In spite of the promise of liberation, many of these highly novel experiences are a trap. Unless we come to them overland, anticipated relation by relation, their very intensity can sear off our past, rendering us "strung out." We should seek to experience a wide fabric of relations rather than a single event that renders the rest of our lives trivial and tawdry. In the concrete, relation-seduction is most explicitly present in that event that presents to us either the most profound liberation or the most singular alienation, namely, our suicide. Our experience of suicide must be continuous with the needs, patterns, and anticipations of our life; otherwise it is the supreme insulating cut, the ultimate discontinuity, marked by the presence of no return.

Given the philosophical approach of William James, alienation is not an ultimate term, proceeding from the language of being and non-being, of meaning and nihilism. Rather, James's language is one that calls for nutrition and warns of starvation, points to liberation and warns of entrapment, that is, the language of affairs and processes rather than that of traditional metaphysics. And despite his strident emphasis on individuality, James's approach is relevant more to Marx's analysis of social alienation than to the social philosophy of the British empiricists or of the utilitarians. James is a philosopher of descriptions and diagnoses, who offers us a "phenomenology" of the Lebenswelt. And, in the long run, the import of James's philosophy is that an analysis of human activity turns out to be an "ultimate" metaphysics, for there is no reality to be discussed apart from our participation and formulation. In The Varieties of Religious Experience, he writes, "so long as we deal with the cosmic and the general, we deal only with the symbols of reality, but as soon as we deal with private and personal phenomena as such, we deal with realities in the completest sense of the term."[15]

IV

Turning now to a second contemporary concern, the problem of repression, I again find James's thought to be helpful. The term "repression" can bring to mind a variety of definitions and analyses. It is commonplace to associate repression with the activities of human sexuality as interpreted by Freud. In the area of pedagogy, both Maria Montessori and John Dewey have elucidated the repressive implications of traditional educational institutions and practices. And from Rousseau through Marx to more recent critics such as Sartre, Marcuse, and N. O. Brown, the repressive penalties of political institutions are well detailed. The analysis and comparison of these and other versions of the meaning of repression are a major undertaking all its own. I have in mind here something more modest: namely, a demythologizing of the term "repression" such that it could have some positive connotations. Using James's functional approach to our conscious life, the term "repression" takes on a very different meaning. This is not to say that other interpretations of repression as damaging to personal life are misguided, only that they are too exclusive.

It is to be noted that James, despite his affection for the mysteries of the fringe of consciousness, did not hold to the presence of a secret self, whether it be traceable to the classical claim of a "soul" or to the Freudian claim of an unconscious. James would regard the layers of consciousness, *id, ego,* and *superego,* as abstractions, devoid of subtlety. So, too, he would regard as reductionistic the flock of post-Freudian nostrums, each of them giving a different single principle of accountability. Perhaps we can say that for James, there is no ultimate explanation of either our personal or our historical situation. What we do have is a series of grapplings, context by context, more or less resolving, more or less enriching.

In the stream of consciousness, clarity is attained by negation, that is, by cutting off the myriad of relations that proceed from any given experience and suturing these cuts so that one can name the remainder. Such clarity is often necessary to prevent us from being overwhelmed by the implicitness and inferentiality of our experiences. What we call knowledge is a pragmatically inspired compromise to enable us to hold our own somewhere between our need for identity and our need to grow, that is, to be open to leads and ramifications. *In the Jamesian context, repression means the shelving of an event such that it is temporarily banished from the realm of its own implications.* Such an approach need not be dangerous to the person, for within the functional exigencies of human activity some leads should not be followed, depending upon the overall assessment of the weakness and capacity of the person involved.

It has to be granted that Freud's contention that repression leads to a festering and sublimated articulation, often violent, has considerable empirical support. A major reason for this situation, however, is that within the fabric of Western culture human beings are burdened by the pressure to come clean, to have our experiences hang together in a causal and rational sequence. Psychoanalysis and its more recent offshoots, such as encounter groups, transactional analysis, and varieties of psychodrama, have as their predecessor the resolute possibilities of the long-standing tradition of Christian confession. Despite the claim of an aggressive unconscious at work in human life, ironically, contemporary therapy from Freud forward is addressed to a rational resolution of these hidden difficulties. James would reject both ends of this description. He uses terms such as "fringe" and "subliminal" to accentuate the reaches of conscious life, holding that we have access to all aspects of our experience while denying that we can account for any experience undergone in any final or complete sense. A radical empiricist holds that experiences "speak" to one another and their relations are as much a part of our experience as the poles of the relationship.

> Life is in the transitions as much as in the terms connected; often, indeed, it seems to be there more emphatically, as if our spurts and sallies forward were the real firing-line of the battle, were like the thin line of flame advancing across the dry autumnal field which the farmer proceeds to burn. In this line we live prospectively as well as retrospectively. It is "of" the past, inasmuch as it comes expressly as the past's continuation; it is "of" the future in so far as the future, when it comes, will have continued it.[16]

If every experience has to be undergone such that we are affectively aware of its relations, fore and aft, then it might well be necessary under certain circumstances to mute the implications until a more propitious time. We cannot deny having had a specific experience but we may be able to hold off the relational bathing that every experience brings. Granted that the strategy of functional repression is always a distinctively personal decision, I can, nevertheless, point to some generalized situations in which such a strategy is feasible. First, I point to those experiences which we look forward to, with intensive anticipation, yet which prove to be abortive. I have in mind here not only the classic rites of passage, such as our first party, first sexual contact, and first public performance, but also a host of subsequent events in which our imaginative projection of realization turns out, in fact, to be sullied. Unless we are very mature, we run the risk in such situations of tying failure to intensity of effort, an extremely crippling relationship. Better, then, that we should shelve or "repress" our failure until we can set up subsequent patterns of realization following upon intention and anticipation. In that way, human life comes very much to resemble our use of a "junk-drawer," into which we put our memorabilia, rarely to be taken out and then only when the pain has lessened or ceased.

A second occasion of functional repression has to do with those positive experiences whose implications are so extensive that a vast rearranging of our priorities and sensibilities would be required if we were to absorb them into our immediate frame of reference. Not every good is good for us. Love generates loyalty and loyalty generates exclusivity. Time spent is time taken from somewhere, someone, else. Everything we experience extracts a price, and often we must say no if we are to say yes, although both responses are to potentially enriching occasions. In time some of these conflicts are resolvable, whereas my third example of functional repression holds out no such hope. I refer to those experiences which now stand outside the possibilities of remediation or resolution because of the passing of time, as, for example, guilt attendant upon the death of others or frustration due to forever missed opportunities. For these events, there is no healing, only a lifelong process of slowly ameliorative absorption into a wider range of understanding. On such events, James is quite clear, seeing them rooted in the actuality of our experience, while interpretively, they float loose, unrealizable, warnings to the fact that "whatever separateness is actually experienced is not overcome, it stays and counts as separateness to the end."[17]

As with the earlier discussion of alienation, so too with this consideration of repression, it is necessary to realize the importance of James's functional approach and his steadfast suspicion about apodictic judgments. No experience is unrelated as undergone, for at the minimum the "haver" of the experience proceeds from a perceptual point of view and thereby constitutes a context for and to some extent the quality of the experience. How the experience is had is inseparable from our knowledge of the experience. In his essay on "The Thing and Its Relations," James writes:

In a concatenated world a partial conflux often is experienced. Our concepts and our sensations are confluent; successive states of the same ego, and feelings of the same body are confluent. Where the experience is not of conflux, it may be of conterminousness (things with but one thing between); or of contiguousness (nothing between); or of likeness; or of nearness; or of simultaneousness; or of in-ness; or of on-ness; or of for-ness; or of simple with-ness; or even of mere and-ness; which last relation would make of however disjointed a world otherwise, at any rate for that occasion, a university "of discourse."[18]

The upshot of this is that for James repression need not have its point of origin in an unintelligible motivation or irrational source. Similar to all our experiences, repression occupies a role in the sliding stream of events, which, for reasons of deep personal self-awareness, functions on behalf of quiescence, hiddenness, and a time-biding until the organism can relate the repressed event to a more ongoing, obvious dimension in the flow of our experience. Furthermore, in a world riven with tychastic events, experiences rendered out of sorts, repressed, or held at arm's length can be re-covered and rejuvenated because of favorable and surprising inter-ventions in our lives. In James's philosophy, no experience can be spoken for once for all. Opposing the absolutistic arrogance found in the conceptual systems of the philosophers, James writes in a "Notebook" in 1903 that

"All neat schematisms with permanent and absolute distinctions, clas-sifications with absolute pretensions, systems with pigeon-holes, etc., have this character. All 'classic,' clean, cut and dried, 'noble,' fixed, 'eternal,' *Weltanschauungen* seem to me to violate the character with which life concretely comes and the expression which it bears of being, or at least of involving a muddle and a struggle, with an 'ever not quite' to all our formulas, and novelty and possibility forever leaking in."[19]

V

The fundamental contribution of William James to any morpho-logical analyses of the human condition is that he thickens the dis-cussion. Radical empiricism involves an acceptance of a far wider range of continuous and experienced relationships than that usu-ally associated with the normal confines of the human self. It gives to novelty and chance a much greater role in our understanding of the fabric of the world. The philosophy of James calls for a never-ending series of descriptions and diagnoses, each from a specific vantage point but no one of them burdened with having to account for everything. For James, the world is much like "the pattern of our daily experience,"[20] loosely connected, processive, and plural-istic. The crucial factor in our understanding of the world we live in is the affective experiencing of relations. So multiply involved are we that the attainment of deep insight into our "inner life" leads us to participate in no less than the very rhythm of the world at large. If we live at the edge, what we find most in this rhythm are surprises, relational novelty, everywhere. Nothing is clear until the last of us has our say and the last relation is hooked. Rare among philosophers, William James believed this.

> In principle, then, as I said, intellectualism's edge is broken; it can only approximate to reality, and its logic is inapplicable to our inner life, which spurns its vetoes and mocks at its impossibilities. Every bit of us at every moment is part and parcel of a wider self, it quivers along various radii like the wind-rose on a compass, and the actual in it is continuously one with possibles not yet in our present sight.[21]

NOTES

1. "A Pluralistic Universe," in The Writings of William James: A Comprehensive Edition, ed. John J. McDermott (New York: Random House, 1967; repr. New York: Modern Library, 1968), p. 808. Unless otherwise cited, references to the work of William James will be taken from this volume, hereafter cited as Writings. For a more detailed statement of the meaning of radical empiricism, see John J. McDermott, "Introduction" to William James, "Essays in Radical Empiricism," The Works of William James, ed. Frederick Burkhardt (Cambridge: Harvard University Press, 1976), pp. xi–xlviii.

2. "A World of Pure Experience," Writings, p. 212.

3. Cf. "Knowledge of sensible realities thus comes to life inside the tissue of experience. It is made; and made by relations that unroll themselves in time" (ibid., p. 201).

4. Writings, pp. 134, 135.

5. The Letters of William James, ed. Henry James, 2 vols. (Boston: Atlantic Monthly Press, 1920), II 203, as quoted in Writings, p. xxxvi.

6. Writings, p. 136.

7. Cf. Arthur Bentley, "The James Datum," in Inquiry into Inquiries, ed. Sidney Ratner (Boston: Beacon, 1954), pp. 230–67.

8. Letters of William James, II 39, as cited in Writings, p. xiv.

9. Cf. William James: A Biography (New York: Viking, 1967), pp. vii, xii.

10. "Diary," Writings, p. 8.

11. "Pragmatism," Writings, p. 432.

12. "The Sentiment of Rationality," Writings, p. 331. This is also the sentiment of Walt Whitman: "The press of my foot to the earth springs a hundred affections. / They scorn the best I can do to relate them" (Leaves of Grass, #14).

13. "A Pluralistic Universe," *Writings*, p. 503; emphasis deleted. In his chapter of "The Stream of Thought," James holds that we tend to believe "where there is *no* name no entity can exist!" (*Writings*, p. 38). To the extent that this is true, we obviate most of the subtleties in our experiencing.

14. Cf. "Pragmatism," *Writings*, p. 379.

15. *Writings*, p. 768.

16. "A World of Pure Experience," *Writings*, pp. 212–13.

17. Ibid., p. 212.

18. "The Thing and Its Relations," *Writings*, p. 221.

19. Cited in Ralph Barton Perry, *The Thought and Character of William James*. II. *Philosophy and Psychology* (Boston: Little, Brown, 1935), p. 700.

20. "A Pluralistic Universe," *Writings*, p. 509.

21. Ibid., pp. 296–97.

7

John Dewey
and the Metaphysics
of American Democracy

R. W. SLEEPER
Queens College
The City University of New York

THE TITLE IS DESIGNED to signal a celebration, a commemoration of the bicentennial year of the Constitution and of that curious and continuing transaction we refer to as our American Democracy. It is also designed to celebrate the one philosopher who showed us how best to understand that Constitution, and the transaction that it set in motion, by means of his searching perspective. I refer to his metaphysical perspective, his transactional philosophy of nature and of experience.

The standard histories of political philosophy do not accord much credit to the contributions of Americans. As Henry Steele Commager pointed out some years ago: "It is customary, even fashionable, to disparage American political thought; after all, America has contributed little to formal political philosophy and boasts few political philosophers."[1]

> Yet it is no exaggeration to say that over a period of a century and three quarters American politics have been more mature and American political achievements more substantial than those of any other modern people. The contrast here between theory and practice is not really paradoxical, for in a very real sense the apparent bankruptcy of political theory is a product of the obvious prosperity of political practice.[2]

It is, I shall argue, the great merit of John Dewey's analysis of the principles and practices of democracy that he sought to place the "apparent bankruptcy" of American political theory in perspective. Less sanguine than Commager about the "prosperity of political practice," Dewey came to see the relationship between theory and practice in very different terms from the way in which it had ever been seen before. In the end he found warrant for ascribing America's successes in political practice to those early years in which theory and practice were closely joined. The failures could be ascribed to the widening gap between them: when theory no longer learns from practice and practice is no longer informed by theory. For the genius of American democracy is to be found in the experimental temper of the early years, the rejection of the *idée fixe* of ideology. Its aberrations are owed to the loss of that temper, to moments of unrestrained ideological fervor.

I

Traditionally the role of political theory has been almost exclusively axiological. Political norms, laws, and even ideals are drawn from, and based upon, metaphysical generalizations about the nature of man and society. Schematic structures are erected, which are taken to account for the place of man in nature and in history, structures that relate man to the highest authorities of morality, to "natural law," to God, or to the "Idea of the Good." The works of Plato and Aristotle come readily to mind, but also those of Epicurus and Epictetus, Cicero and Livy. In such thinkers theory dominates, and the problems of practice are scarcely acknowledged. With the transitional era, inaugurated by Augustine's *The City of God*, the balance begins to shift, and in Aquinas, Dante, and Machiavelli political practice is increasingly taken into account. Political practice is seen as "testing" theory in the work of Hobbes and Locke, Rousseau and Kant. But only at the close of the "modern" period is there the beginning of a sense of practice as a co-determinant of theory, along with metaphysically drawn axiological norms and ideals, in the "dialectical" politics of Hegel and Marx. But even then, as Dewey never tired of pointing out, the "dialectic" was dominated by a one-sided "idealistic" emphasis on the axiological element, and practice inevitably was measured against its standards. The "Age of Ideology" had begun.

It is central to Dewey's analysis that theory and practice are "reciprocally," not "dialectically," related. The "test" of theory by practice is designed to *modify* theory, not merely to exhibit it. The perspective here is that of the experimental temper of mind, not the dialectical. Theory and practice are thoroughly integral, functioning in the political process as they function everywhere in experience, in natural science as in art, in logical inquiry as in religion. In every field and dimension of human experience Dewey sees theory and practice as mutually effective, reciprocally functioning to resolve unsatisfactory and indeterminate situations into satisfying and determinate ones. In the background of Dewey's metaphysical and axiological perspective, theory and practice may, of course, be distinguished, one from the other. But inquiry considers them in isolation from each other only at the cost of profound and intractable irrelevance.

II

Political philosophy, like our American Constitution, is properly concerned with the nature of power and its distribution. In this, Dewey's contribution is no exception. But power is realized in and through action, in action and in withholding from action. It is displayed in going to war and in suing for peace, in passing laws and in revoking them, in revolution and in counter-revolutionary resistance. The key to power is action, and the key to the theory of power is the theory of action. Here political philosophy is of necessity carried into the realm of metaphysical inquiry. It must deal with metaphysical categories and assumptions, written or unwritten, whether carefully schematized or randomly presupposed. If we would understand a particular philosopher's political theory, we must examine the theory of action it embraces.

The claim is readily illustrated by reference to the familiar example of Aristotle's *Politics*. Unlike Plato, Aristotle gives us an explicitly articulated theory of action. Action does not leave us in doubt concerning the relations of ends and means, or the processes by means of which political power is obtained and distributed in practice. Moreover, the theory of action which Aristotle articulates is widely shared among the ancients—almost surely even by Plato himself—and it persists well into the modern world as well. For the central thesis of that theory is that every natural entity contains within itself the principles governing its own action.

It is worth noticing that this thesis is not one that Aristotle adopts simply for the purposes of his political thought. It is a thesis of his metaphysics that has application, as we have learned from his logic to say, as a "universal." That natural entities "change" in accordance with principles or "laws" that are intrinsic to the kind of entities they are is a claim that cuts across every field of inquiry. It is, as we have also learned to say—though not, in this case, from Aristotle himself—a feature of the very "essence" of natural entities as such, a feature of their "metaphysical" makeup which is intractably fixed and permanent.[3] Thus, Aristotle remarks in the *Physics*, all natural entities are distinguished from the products of art by this feature; the products of art, he says, "have no innate impulse to change."[4]

The political implications of this doctrine of natural action, or change, are readily apparent. For once we grant that man is by nature—or "essence"—a rational and political animal, the form and actuality of the "ideal state" is already embodied in the human soul, together with potentiality for achieving it through political means. Dewey himself, in remarking on the simple beauty of Aristotle's scheme, credited him with the view that "Everything ideal has a natural basis and everything natural has an ideal fulfilment."

III

The problem that Dewey finds with such a scheme, despite its admirable synthesis of naturalism and idealism, is that action and change are conceived of as eternally limited. The motion of an entity is constrained by the permanent "nature" or "essence" of the thing itself, its fixed natural endowment. The only possibilities for action and change are those that are already there in principle or "essence." Action as "self-action"—to use Dewey's term for it— can result only in the achievement of a fixed and limited range of possibilities. For the full range of possibilities is already given, κατὰ φύσιν, "in accordance with nature." The *telos* is fixed and determinate, and political action is constrained. It can take only a limited and, in principle, a predictable course.

Because there is always some "distance" between the ideal fulfillment of man's given nature and the actual conditions of existence, Aristotle allows for a variety of possible "good" polities. He lists them in the *Politics* together with their corrupt forms. Axiologically, the preferred forms are those most conducive to the realization of the innate capacities of their members. The corrupt states are those that fail in this *telos* through constitutional inadequacy. In the end, of course, there is only one "best" polity: it will have that form that best implements the innate principles of action inherent in man's nature. It will, in Plato's phrase, take the form of man "writ large."

Doubtless, from Dewey's perspective, the most striking feature of such a polity is the narrow conception of political liberty that it entails. Freedom must be conceived of merely as the absence of those external conditions that impede the development of the capacities with which man is said to be naturally endowed. Action, change, development—all these take place only within the limits that are antecedently set by nature and that, in every important respect, remain forever fixed and unalterable. While there is room in this scheme for a strong doctrine of "natural law," and hence of "natural rights," the scope of what we know as "civil liberties" is indeed severely constricted. There are no "individual" rights as such, for "individuality" as such can have only negative value. There is no room for genuine novelty or invention, no real cause for engaging in political experimentation, no reason for entertaining "new" ideas. From the metaphysical conception of the fixed and unalterable nature of man arises the paradigm of the "City of Man," the closed society that Augustine challenges in *The City of God*.

IV

The doctrine of man on which the Aristotelian theory of action is based reflects Plato's conception of the soul as containing the capacity of moving itself—i.e., of "self-action." Closely related to the cosmological theory of the "unmoved mover" and to the Stoic doctrine of the eternal *logos* of nature, this way of looking at action and change is very nearly a universal presupposition of the political philosophy of Graeco-Roman antiquity. Shared implicitly by Platonists and Aristotelians alike, it is basic to the Stoics from Cleanthes to Marcus Aurelius, Cicero, and Seneca. Even Epicurus, that "puritanical" hedonist, warned that we must learn to distinguish those pleasures that are both natural and necessary, and—in action—pursue only those that are strictly necessary in accordance with the nature with which we have been endowed. It was thus that, by general consensus, a conception of "natural law" was adopted by the jurists of the late Roman Empire.

The constraints on political liberty, implicit in Roman law, passed almost without modification into the Canonical law of the Church after Constantine. The Augustinian challenge to the dominant theory of man's "fixed" nature, and to the conception of "Christendom" that was implied in his account of the "City of God," remained almost dormant throughout the era that followed.

As late as Descartes, "self-action" was still a resonant theme. Each substance must act only within its own sphere, mind within the "mental" realm and body within the realm of matter. This denial of any substantive interaction, or change, in the context of the rise of modern science, had implications far beyond those of mind-body dualism. In an effort to heal the Cartesian schism in accordance with what he took to be the requirements of the new sciences, Spinoza risked the charge of "pantheism" and excommunication from the congregation of his fathers. Placing the eternal cause of "self-action" in a single substance, Spinoza postulated the conception of *Deus sive Natura*, acting as *natura naturans*. And he did so in order to preserve nature from having to include *interaction* between separate substances! It was a brilliant but unsuccessful maneuver. The conception of "self-acting" substance could not long endure the assaults of the new sciences.

The turn away from substantive "self-action" in the direction of philosophies that countenanced change in terms of "interaction" was truly a Copernican Revolution. For, commencing with Copernicus himself, and reaching a climax with Newton and Kant, new systems of metaphysics were devised to account for "action at a distance" as well as action between "substances." Eventually, of course, even the notion of "substance" itself came under attack.

But, at the outset, the new conception of "interaction'" was mainly conceived of as an extension of the old notion of self-action to include a kind of "collective" action in which entities "acting together" produce an aggregate effect. The entities themselves were conceived of as remaining relatively stable, and were still supposed to have intrinsically fixed natures.

v

The prime examples of the new conception of action and change were, of course, the fundamentals of the Newtonian science of mechanics. But not only did the laws of "action and reaction" challenge the hegemony of Aristotle's physics; they called into serious question his metaphysics as well. The consequences were far-reaching indeed. Not only was a new physical cosmology possible; it was necessary to rethink the entire basis on which the ages-old conception of "natural law" had been grounded. It would not be long before the challenge to the doctrine of fixed "natural law" in the sciences, already called into question during the events of the Protestant Reformation, and by the predicaments of Giordano Bruno and Galileo, would be followed by similar challenges to the prevailing foundations of political thought as well. Nor would it be long before Europe would undergo a series of major political changes that were "revolutionary" in scope and consequence, if not always in name. It is, indeed, in that context that our own "American Revolution" took place, and in that context that it is best understood.

Central to that context is the fact that Newton had set in motion a series of changes in our traditional world-view which centered in change itself, its nature and causes. No longer was time itself intrinsically cyclical, as Aristotle had supposed; *real* change over time—as Augustine had presciently suggested—was now considered possible. But for the explanation of *real* change, we must look beyond Newton's conception of interaction. For his laws of motion require, simply put, that the universe be composed of elemental and *unchanging* constituents. Not merely must all physical motion and change be determined by these unchanging components, but all chemical and biological change as well. The image of the world as a great "machine" powered by the mechanical interactions of these elemental and irreducible parts soon become a familiar one.

Dewey finds the political impact of this Newtonian world-view, with its new metaphysics of interactional motion, to be both profound and puzzling. While, on the one hand, some found in the Newtonian scheme a justification for universal determinism, others found in it the basis for a new and positive conception of human individuality and freedom. Of the latter—for Dewey brushed aside the determinists—many distinguished between man in a "state of nature" and man in a political environment. But there is none who more clearly illustrates the presupposition of an interactional "atomistic" basis of the political state than Rousseau. Thus: "Man was born free, and everywhere he is in chains."[5] The "social contract" which Rousseau conceives of as preserving original freedom, and as liberating man from his "chains," is precisely what is meant by a product of atomistic interaction operating mechanically. In Dewey's view, Rousseau's theory is clearly predicated on the collective—or mechanically aggregate—interaction of individual wills operating in a state of nature to produce the "general will" as the foundation of the state. Moreover, in a view that Dewey finds shared with Hobbes, Rousseau regards the individual will as "free" only when it meshes, in "gear-like" fashion, with the "general will" in the social contract. The clauses of that contract are such, as Rousseau himself puts it, that "all are reducible to one only, viz., the total alienation to the whole community of each associate with all his rights."[6]

For Dewey, Rousseau's conception of the social contract and the state to which it lends legitimacy is an almost perfect example of the sort of result that could not follow from the doctrine of "self-action" alone. It depends completely upon the interaction of individuals and the collective "mechanical" result—like a great and complex "parallelogram" of forces. The individuals themselves remain substantially unchanged under the terms of the contract. "Born free," each remains "free." Thus, as Rousseau reckons it, "each, while coalescing with all, may nevertheless obey only himself, and remain free as before."[7] The reckoning here is purely mechanical. Freedom is conceived as the proper "fit" between the individual will and the "general will" that is ensconced in the state. The part must conform to the total mechanism of the whole, a feature of Rousseau's scheme that has led more than one of his critics to see him as contributing less to the development of the idea of freedom than to the theory of the totalitarian state.

But that is surely a misreading of Rousseau. For it overlooks the interactional and atomistic metaphysics on which the holistic idea of the "general will" is predicated. To see what is involved in the process of fitting the individual will to the general will, of "coalescence" in Rousseau's sense, it is necessary to start with the naturally "fixed" essence of the individual who is born "free" in the first place. The will of such an individual can remain free if, and only if, it requires no *essential* modification of will in order for that individual to act in concert with the general will. This clearly requires that the general will conform to the fixed and determinate nature of the individual will, a condition notably absent from totalitarian theory. Whether it was intentional or not, the unchangeable nature of the individual will, presupposed as "free" by Rousseau, is thoroughly consistent with the Newtonian conception of the component elements of nature. Not unlike the "atoms" of Democritus, these are solid material bits of varied size and shape which readily lend themselves to combination into more complex entities through interaction among themselves. Whereas Aristotle tells us, in the *Physics*, that all natural things contain within themselves their own principles of motion and change, the elements of Newton's world contain no such principles. Rather, they are so designed as to have the properties that enable them to combine with each other mechanically *and* teleologically. Thus, in his famous work on *Opticks*, Newton tells us that "it seems probable to me that God in the beginning formed matter in solid, massy, hard, impenetrable, movable particles, of such size and figures, and with such other properties, in such proportion to space, as most conduced to the end for which he formed them. . . ."[8] From Newton's perspective, then, the construction of the world is not a matter of assembling complete "self-acting" entities, each having, as Aristotle held, "within itself a principle of motion." Nor is it a matter of shaping the parts to fit the whole, of "informing" matter in the fashion of Platonism. It is, instead, a process of working out the wholes for which the parts have been previously designed. It is like building a machine from pre-designed parts such as are already available rather than from parts that are capable of infinite mod-

ification. The available parts, being essentially incapable of modification, will determine the configuration of the whole. They will, in
a sense, "reveal" it.

It is this feature of the Newtonian world-view that is responsible for the widespread popularity of the "argument from design"
articulated by the new teleological theology of deism. Evident in
Newton's own theological writings, it forms part of the common
background of thinkers as widely different as Leibniz, Locke, and
Paley. Even the very different approaches of the Benthamite utilitarians and the Kantian transcendental idealists were not to escape
the powerful influence exerted by this Newtonian vision of the
world as the product of interacting "solid, massy, hard, impenetrable, movable particles." Though the teleology which Newton
himself saw as implicit in the interactions of these particles was
not uniformly interpreted or accepted, the conception of action as
"interaction" left a permanent mark on the thinking of an era that
was seeking out new forms of political organization, new moral
philosophies, and the structures of society congruent with them.
In Dewey's view, Rousseau's political philosophy of the "social
contract" represents just such an attempt.[9]

VI

I have gone on about Rousseau at such length only to lend emphasis to the importance in political theorizing that Dewey himself
places on the role of metaphysics, and in particular to bring out his
view of the central part played by action theory. But I hope that
these remarks will have a certain side-effect as well. For they are
meant to call into question the widely shared habit of thinking
of Rousseau's concept of the state as "organic" while failing to
observe that the very concept of "organism" was itself expressed
in terms that are inescapably "mechanistic." In the Newtonian
world, which Rousseau shared, it was considered appropriate that
metaphysics should deal with certain truths as a priori "necessities" of thought. These truths, it was considered by rationalists
and empiricists alike, were foundational to the natural sciences
and entirely independent of experience. One has only to think of
Locke's "necessary truths," or of Kant's valiant effort in defense

of the *a priori* categories of "pure reason," to grasp the point.

Yet these efforts to guarantee the certitude of science ended in failure. The Newtonian "mechanistic" world could not be saved in the end, for it rested on a mistake. Appropriately enough, it proved to be a mistake of *a priori* metaphysics that caused both rationalists and empiricists to assume that the "universal laws" of mechanics could suffice for the understanding of organisms. Into that flaw would be driven many wedges, hammered home by such diverse thinkers as Hegel and Darwin, Schopenhauer and Clerk Maxwell, Brentano and Nietzsche, Marx and Freud, until but vestiges remained of the once-imposing edifice of the "clockwork" universe. In the event more than one philosopher felt the need to start over, as it were, from scratch. The history of nineteenth-century thought is burdened with such efforts, the totalizing of novel insights that bypassed tradition, scorning the legacy of the past, and erected in complete discontinuity with it.

John Dewey's dissent from, and criticism of, this impulse is recorded in his popular lectures published in 1920 under the title *Reconstruction in Philosophy*. The preposition in the title is important; Dewey, at the time, envisaged reconstruction "in" philosophy and not, as so many of his predecessors had taken for granted, "of" philosophy. For continuity was something that Dewey felt strongly about.[10] Indeed, "continuity" became a prominent characteristic of his metaphysical perspective and a distinguishing feature of his reconstruction of the theory of action itself. It is this reconstruction, basic to his political and social thought, as well as to his theory of inquiry and philosophy of science, that drives his unique understanding of both the successes and the failures of our American Democracy.

VII

On Dewey's account, the trouble with the Newtonian "mechanistic" theory of interaction is that it starts out from the same presupposition of "fixed" interacting entities that was partly characteristic of the old "self-action" theories. Though these natural entities do not contain their own principles of action, they nevertheless remain immutably what they are throughout all the "changes" that occur in their interactions with other entities. There is a real, i.e., metaphysical, limitation imposed upon the range of possible changes that nature can allow.

But, as both Darwinian biology and Maxwellian physics had demonstrated, no such antecedently immutable elements had to be assumed in order to account for either the great regularity of natural occurrences or the immense variety of changes that actually take place in nature. When we get down to the most elementary particles of matter, and of the combined materials that we call "organisms," we find instead only *mutable* elements, each of which gets its specific character—or "nature"—from its active relationships with other constituent elements within the functional context in which it is found. Within each and every such context the actions of each constituent are as reflective of the actions of every *other* constituent as *their* actions are of *its* actions. Each constituent is what it is in continuous and reciprocal relation to, and with, every other constituent. This is a species of interactive relationships that is typical of what we understand today as "organic" as contrasted with the "mechanical." When viewed as *constitutive* of the individual entity, the web of such relations provides for that entity a uniqueness of character, or "individuality," that contrasts sharply with the "fixed essence" notion. It is this *"constitutive"* type of relationship that Dewey at first called "organic interaction" and, later, simply "transaction." [11]

Perhaps a brief quotation from Maxwell's 1876 book *Matter and Motion* will serve to shed some light on Dewey's insistence upon understanding all entities and their actions, motions, changes and powers in terms of "transactional" relations:

> If we confine our attention to one of the portions of matter, we see, as it were, only one side of the transaction—namely, that which affects the portion of matter under our consideration—and we call this aspect of the phenomenon, with respect to its effect, an External force acting on that portion of matter, and with respect to its cause we call it the Action of the other portion of matter. The opposite aspect of the stress is called Reaction on the other portion of matter. [12]

As physics developed after Maxwell, it soon became obvious that the type of interaction that had previously been thought of as restricted to the biological range of phenomena was equally characteristic of physico-chemical behavior as well. It was thus possible for Dewey to see how a theory of action, understood now as "transaction," could serve as the continuous connective tissue of a theory of nature *tout court*. Matter, living matter, human society—all could be conceived of as variously complex stages of continuously overlapping and interpenetrating transactions. Actions and powers, including political actions and political powers, could thus be understood in terms of transactional analysis. In fact, as Dewey would come to insist, they could be adequately understood *only* in that way.

The outstanding illustration of the range and scope of transactional analysis is Dewey's own brilliantly original treatise on metaphysics, *Experience and Nature*, published in 1925. Only the briefest sketch of the contents of that remarkable work can be given here, in the hope that it will be sufficient to illuminate the political theory for which it provides the critical background. At the outset it must be emphasized that Dewey reconceptualizes the role of metaphysics itself. Instead of regarding it as the "foundation" upon which the rest of philosophy is erected, Dewey conceives of metaphysics as the denotative "ground-map" of existence as such, or, as he preferred to say, of the "generic traits of existences of all kinds." Dewey conceived of *all* philosophy as inherently serving an axiological and critical function, so that when he says, in *Experience and Nature*, that "metaphysics is the ground-map of the province of criticism . . ." he indicates something of the axiological centrality that he ascribes to metaphysics.

As in Aristotle, it is "first philosophy" that draws upon the natural sciences, and investigates the relation—the *active* relation—between the real and the ideal. As in Kant, it is "critical" and examines the ways of knowing and of acting, of inquiry and morals. It is, in Dewey's own terms, later used by Strawson, a "descriptive" enterprise. Metaphysics, for Dewey, searches out the "generic traits" of existences encountered in our experience of nature; its "categories" are all *a posteriori*, framed as empirical generalizations of the broadest possible application.[13]

It is a consequence of the empirical and *a posteriori* character of metaphysics, as Dewey conducts it, that it should investigate those features of both nature and experience that make natural science possible as well as those features that support, or withhold support from, values and valuations. Such a metaphysics is, of course, eminently naturalistic; it makes no room for the transcendental arguments of Kantian idealism, or for the a prioristic arguments of Scholastic realism. In his rejection of dualisms of all sorts, Dewey moves beyond both realism and idealism by reconciling them, capturing both the objective strength of realism's grasp of the independently real and idealism's grasp of the subjective role of thought in the creation of meaning and value. It is a metaphysics that, in Dewey's words, "is bound to consider reflection itself as a natural event occurring *within* nature because of traits of the latter." [14]

By "reflection" Dewey meant "thought" and "reason," "inquiry" and "experiment," probing into the values no less than the facts of nature, investigating every transaction of intelligence, of the "live creature" wherever and whenever thinking takes place. Thinking is both a cause and an effect of nature, of changes taking place within the processes of nature. It is itself a natural process, subject to both the contingencies and the regularities that are among the generic traits of existences of all kinds. It is the fact that thinking is among these processes of nature which make its results in knowledge both precarious and contingent. Dewey hints at the political implications of this fact in a pungent passage: "Let us admit the case of the conservative; if we once start thinking no one can guarantee where we shall come out, except that many objects, ends and institutions are surely doomed. Every thinker puts some portion of the world at peril and no one can wholly predict what will emerge in its place." [15]

The plight of the thinking individual in nature is both as precarious and uncertain as knowledge. But, when viewed from Dewey's metaphysical perspective, both the predicament of the self and the uncertain character of knowledge are subject to ameliorating conditions that nature itself provides. A key passage from *Experience and Nature* examines those conditions:

> But the interests of empirical and denotative method and of naturalistic method wholly coincide. The world must actually be such as to generate ignorance and inquiry, doubt and hypothesis, trial and temporal conclusions; the latter being such that they develop out of existences which while wholly "real" are not as satisfactory, as good, or as significant as those into which they are eventually reorganized. The ultimate evidence of genuine hazard, contingency, irregularity and

indeterminateness in nature is thus found in the occurrence of think-ing. The traits of natural existence which generate the fears and adorations of superstitious barbarians generate the scientific pro-cedures of disciplined civilization. The superiority of the latter does not consist in the fact that they are based on "real" existence, while the former wholly upon a human nature different from nature in general. It consists in the fact that scientific inquiries reach *objects* which are better, because reached by a method which controls them and which adds greater control to life itself, method which mitigates accident, turns contingency to account, and releases thought and other forms of endeavor.[16]

In this perspective, then, individual thinking is "transactional" with both the conditions of nature and the thinking of other indi-viduals. While remaining ineluctably "individual," thinking re-quires the individual to expose his thinking to others, to enter into those associative transactions communication consists of, trans-actions without which the "scientific procedures of disciplined civilization" to which Dewey refers could not exist.

VIII

It is in this metaphysical perspective, then, that Dewey regards the human predicament, a situation of dynamic tension that provides him with a title for his most popular work of political thought, *Freedom and Culture*, published in 1939. In that work he develops the idea that democracy is an expression of the essential tension between the individual and those associated forms of life to which the self is inevitably drawn:

> All that we can safely say is that human nature, like other forms of life, tends to differentiation, and thus moves in the direction of the distinctively individual, and that it also tends toward combination, association.... The problem of freedom of cooperative individualities is then a problem to be viewed in the context of culture.... We have advanced far enough to say that democracy is a way of life. We have yet to realize that it is a way of personal life and one which provides a standard for personal conduct.[17]

That this tension is "dynamic" and "productive" has not always been obvious. That it is an inescapable condition of nature has been even less so. That it has been so frequently ignored may help to explain why freedom and individuality are so often sacrificed on the altar of stability and security.

In a different context entirely, Dewey approaches human experience with a very different objective while maintaining the same perspective, the same sense of the importance of the tension between the self and society. In metaphysical terms this is the universal tension between the precarious and the stable, here expressed in the area of aesthetic experience. The text is from *Art as Experience*, and in it Dewey lends emphasis to the creative potential present in all such situations of tension:

> There are two sorts of possible worlds in which esthetic experience would not occur. In a world of mere flux, change would not be cumulative; it would not move toward a close. Equally it is true, however, that a world that is finished, ended, would have no traits of suspense and crisis, would offer no opportunities for resolution. Where everything is complete there is no fulfillment. We envisage with pleasure Nirvana and a uniform heavenly bliss only because they are projected on the background of our present world of stress and conflict. Because the actual world, that in which we live, is a combination of movement and culmination, of breaks and reunions, the experience of a living creature is capable of esthetic quality. The live being recurrently loses and re-establishes equilibrium with his surroundings. The moment of passage from disturbance to harmony is that of the intensest life. In a finished world, sleep and waking could not be distinguished. In one wholly perturbed, conditions could not even be struggled with. In a world made after the pattern of ours, moments of fulfillment punctuate experience with rhythmically enjoyed intervals.[18]

It scarcely needs pointing out that what holds true of the aesthetic and the veridical qualities of experience, what makes them both possible and naturally occurring, also holds true of social and political experience. In a world of utter stability, of perfect individual security, political endeavor would have no meaning or purpose. In a world wholly chaotic it would be hopelessly impossible. In *our* world, however, political transactions are both possible and necessary. They are possible because of the human propensity to association, necessary, because of the precariousness of individual life.

The metaphysics—at this point, perhaps, we might say the "background theory"—of political experience is no different from that of the metaphysics of natural science, of art, or of morals. While the point should be obvious, it requires emphasis owing to the persistent habit of political philosophers of separating both the person and the *polis* from their natural environment. One need only consider those who, like Hobbes and Rousseau, conceive of "morality" as coming into being only in the context of the state, and of moral obligation as not pre-existing the "covenant" or the "social contract." Or consider John Rawls's complex conception of those who are in what he calls the "original position"—i.e., a position in which each person is hypothetically free of duties and obligations toward others, but engaged in a cooperative endeavor with others to choose, as he puts it, "in one joint act, the principles which are to assign the basic rights and duties and to determine the division of social benefits."[19] On Dewey's view, political theories erected on such bases as these must inevitably fail, for they wrest man from his natural environment and proceed to deal with him as an "artifact" to be artfully constructed by the "contractors" and social engineers. Moves like these, he argues, account for the wholly artificial character of many conceptions of political society. By contrast, Dewey insists that political society is wholly natural; that political transactions are but complex versions of the kinds of transactions that are continuously taking place everywhere in nature from the simplest physico-chemical interchanges of mass and energy to the most sublime achievements of culture in art, science, and philosophy.

Behavior in each of these dimensions or stages of nature—one hesitates to say "levels" owing to the danger of being taken as imputing to nature a fixed axiological hierarchy—exhibits a continuous basic pattern. Risking the charge of anthropomorphism, Dewey calls this pattern of transactional behavior "need–demand–satisfaction" activity. Thus:

By need is meant a condition of tensional distribution of energies such that a body is in a condition of uneasy or unstable equilibrium. By demand or effort is meant the fact that this state is manifested in movements which modify environing bodies in ways which react upon the body, so that its characteristic pattern of active equilibrium is restored. By satisfaction is meant the recovery of the equilibrium pattern, consequent upon the changes of environment due to [transactions] with the active demands of the organism.[20]

How easily this conception could be misunderstood can be readily seen from the sort of criticism that was evoked when Dewey sought to apply this pattern to epistemology as well as to educational theory. He was accused of blatantly subordinating science to the demands of the "captains of industry" and of cynically advocating the use of the schoolroom to destroy the individuality of children by techniques designed to "adjust" them to the requirements of society. But neither was Dewey a "utilitarian" in the implied sense; nor was he, even unconsciously, advocating a means of submerging the unique qualities of personal individuality in a sea of social conformity.[21]

What Dewey *was* trying to convey in his "need–demand–satisfaction" theory is the plain fact that all change, all action, is transactional in character. To lose sight of this fact, whether one is dealing with elementary physico-chemical processes or with complex psycho-physical ones, is to lose sight of the full range of the causes and consequences of the transactions in question. The point is that both the ancient theory of "self-action" and the Newtonian theory of "interaction" that replaced it place blinders on the inquirer who would understand the processes of nature. The belief that action is basically "self-action" leads inquiry to cease once it arrives at what is conceived of as the permanent "essence" of the active entity; e.g., the stone is said to fall because its essence contains the property of "heaviness," and hot air to rise because of its essential "lightness." The belief that all action is basically "interaction" leads inquiry to seek only antecedent causes and pre-existent design factors; e.g., it is the pre-existent design of material elements that limits their combinatory possibilities, as when Rousseau argues that it is the design of man that he is "born free" and that his "free will" as an individual must be expressed by the "general will."

It is a distinctive feature of Dewey's "need–demand–satisfaction" theory as a transactional account of action that it compels us to see all human activity, including thinking, as inherently axiological.[22] In boldly calling the "recovery of equilibrium" the achievement of "satisfaction," Dewey was calling attention to that aspect of natural processes in which facts are not *merely* facts. The "recovery of equilibrium" is not merely a fact of the natural history of the entity in question, but a fact that is laden with value for that entity. While we may have to stretch our imaginations to see

JOHN DEWEY 139

that such values are inherent in simple physico-chemical processes, we can easily see that when an animal satisfies its hunger by actively searching out its food this search for the "recovery of equilibrium" has axiological meaning. The process of human inquiry, which always presupposes what Dewey called a "problematic situation," is no less axiological than the actions of all those natural entities with which humankind is continuous.

That political inquiry, and action, *are* continuous with the transactions of all natural entities is a central contention of Dewey's major contribution to political theory, his 1927 book *The Public and Its Problems*.[23] There he sets out to put to rest the notion that an adequate political theory can rest on "facts alone"; i.e., that political science can be conducted as a "value-free" discipline. Thus he writes:

The prestige of the mathematical and physical sciences is great, and properly so. But the difference between facts which are what they are independent of human desire and endeavor, and facts which are to some extent what they are because of human interest and purpose, and which alter with alteration in the latter, cannot be got rid of by any methodology. The more sincerely we appeal to facts, the greater is the importance of the distinction between facts which condition human activity and facts which are conditioned by human activity. In the degree which we ignore that difference, social science becomes pseudo-science. Jeffersonian and Hamiltonian political ideas are not merely theories dwelling in the human mind remote from the facts of American political behavior. They are expressions of chosen phrases and factors among those facts, but they are also something more: namely, forces which have shaped those facts and which are still contending to shape them in future this way and that. There is more than a speculative difference between a theory of the state which regards it as an instrument in protecting individuals in the rights they already have, and one which conceives its function to be the effecting of a more equitable distribution of rights among individuals. For theories are held and applied by legislators in congress and by judges on the bench and make a difference in the subsequent facts themselves.[24]

Inherent in this passage are all the germs of Dewey's political thought. When put together with his transactional account of thinking, of the individual and his propensity to association, with his emphasis on the continuity of man's transactional behavior with natural transactions *tout court*, the outlines of Dewey's theory of political action quickly begin to emerge.

IX

The state must be viewed in this same metaphysical perspective. To explain the origin of the state by saying that man is a political animal is to travel in a verbal circle. That human beings are brought into their individual existence in and through association with other individuals is a fact of life on a par with that which characterizes the behavioral habits of the birds and the bees. But man is not merely "*de facto* associated"; as Dewey puts it, "he *becomes* a social animal in the make-up of his ideas, sentiments and deliberate behavior."[25] When the original fact of association is made the object of actions designed more or less consciously to preserve and protect that association, those actions deserve to be called "social" and their product an intentional "community."

But not all communities exist for the purpose of political transactions. Communities are formed for the consequences that follow from associated activity, whether those consequences are as simple as the joys of friendship or as complicated as the products of scientific research. A university may indeed be a great community, but it is not, perforce, a political state, though it may indeed have many a feature of one. It does, for example, constitute a "public" association as distinct from a "private" one, for it has extensive and enduring consequences that affect others beyond those who are immediately associated in its name. (For this reason both our so-called "private" universities and those known as "public" are subject by charter to state regulation.) But, despite its political character, a university is still too narrow a community to qualify as a state. It may have all the earmarks of government—officials charged with specific duties, a constitution and bylaws, a governing body and a chief executive—yet it still falls short of qualification as a state.

Dewey finds four rather rough and ready criteria helpful in identifying the point at which a public association becomes a state.[26] First, the consequences of associated activity must be capable of temporal and geographical location in order that concern *for* them, and some degree of regulation *of* them, are feasible. A second mark of the emergence of a state is the fact that accumulated consequences of conjoint behavior escape private control, thus calling the state into being to restore to the community those conditions of "equilibrium" which have been lost or threatened. This leads to the third trait of the state: that it is concerned with modes of behavior that are sufficiently well established as to constitute an "equilibrium" in fact and not merely in principle. The fourth trait follows from this, and is indicated by the existence of children and others of a dependent nature (the insane, the unemployed) who are understood to be, in a peculiar way, "wards of the state." These are not, Dewey warns, to be understood as hard and fast criteria laid down in order to produce predetermined results. For no mere mechanical criteria, as we saw with respect to Rousseau, can be sufficient to ensure the legitimacy of the state. They are simply and plainly useful criteria for estimating the effectiveness of a state in meeting the needs which call it into being.

There is a very clear sense in which Dewey regards the origins of the modern state in the seventeenth and eighteenth centuries, when it emerged from earlier forms of political association and domination, as justifying an "instrumentalist" approach in political theory despite all the attendant vagueness that is an accompaniment to it. The fact that no sharp lines can be drawn between those transactions between individuals that call for state regulation and those that do not is very basic. It is a fact that portends the need for political experimentation and rules out the possibility of fixed ideology; it is a fact that makes democratic political arrangements both difficult to institute and difficult to maintain in the state. But it is also a fact that accounts for the superiority of democratic institutions over their rivals. For not only can the precise *form* of the state never be fixed in advance; even its precise area of jurisdiction can never be permanently defined. As Dewey himself puts it:

> Transactions between singular persons and groups bring a public into being when their indirect consequences—their effects beyond those immediately engaged in them—are of importance. But at least we have pointed out some of the factors which go to make up importance: namely, the far-reaching character of consequences, whether in space or in time; their settled, uniform and recurrent nature, and their irreparableness. Each one of these matters involves questions of degree. There is no sharp and clear line which draws itself, pointing

out beyond peradventure, like the line left by a receding high tide, just
where a public comes into existence which has interests so significant
that they must be looked after and administered by special agencies,
or government officers. The line of demarcation between actions left
to private initiative and management and those regulated by the state
has to be discovered experimentally.[27]

Thus far the definitions and criteria are such that they are applicable to the relationship between the individual and the public, and
between the public and the state, generically. They show how the
state comes into being as the result of public demand, and how a
public is itself created by the transactions among individuals. But
these factors do not, of themselves, suffice to mark off one or another form of the state as "best" or suffice to justify, in particular,
the difficult tasks of instituting and maintaining the "democratic"
state.

x

It is of paramount importance, at this point, to recall that Dewey
has maintained all along that political inquiry, like all inquiry, is
both transactional and axiological, and, like all inquiry, must be
responsive to the "problematic situation" that calls it forth. It is
also worth notice at the outset that there cannot be expected, in
Dewey's consideration of the justification of democracy, any *a
priori* attachment or ideological fixation either with any particular
form of democracy, or even with the idea of democracy itself.
His philosophy is patently antagonistic to ideological habits of
thought, to ways of justifying some one concept of the state or
system of government by invoking the truth of some particular
idea or historical "law" as of transcendent importance. The view
that is sometimes taken of Dewey as the "ideologist" of democracy is a hopeless blunder, involving as it does an implicit contradiction. His approach to democracy is, by contrast, tentative and
exploratory. Democratic states exist and must be studied in their
de facto forms. Their origins must be examined in detail. The
character of the various publics and their demands that have called
democratic states into existence must be carefully delineated before their success in meeting those demands can even be estimated.
The approach is empirical and descriptive, and objective, but with-

out sacrifice of critical perspective. Not just the origins of the democratic states, but their consequences, both immediate and eventual, must be investigated. The forms of democracy for Dewey are not fixed, but changing, evolving, processive. Democracy adapts and fails to adapt to changes in the publics that it serves, to changes in the economic environment—changes of which the nineteenth-century Industrial Revolution is but a single and unanticipated example. Democracy both responds and fails to respond to dramatic changes in the range and character of communications media, of means of transportation, and of warfare. It responds with evident varying success to changes in the international environment of economics, trade, and political transformations. To choose a word made current since the days in which Dewey wrote: he would subject democracy to operative criteria that are distinctively "ecological" rather than "ideological." [28]

When applied to the specifics of our own American Democracy, this approach yields conclusions that are not wholly sanguine. Dewey's perception of both its successes and its failures is acute. In a remarkable text, Dewey notes that what accounts for success in some areas may amount to the necessity of failure in others:

> The same forces which have brought about the forms of democratic government, general suffrage, executives and legislators chosen by majority vote, have also brought about conditions which halt the social and humane ideals that demand the utilization of government as the genuine instrumentality of an inclusive and fraternally associated public. "The new age of human relationships" (the phrase is Woodrow Wilson's) has no political agencies worthy of it. The democratic public is still largely inchoate and unorganized.[29]

And in another vein and another context Dewey sharply criticizes the failure of our American Democracy to accord sufficient recognition to the paramount moral importance of the individual. For Dewey this failure is not merely a political flaw rooted in the Constitution itself, but a moral flaw perpetuated by decades of narrow Constitutional interpretation by the courts:

> It is moral because [democracy is] based on faith in the ability of human nature to achieve freedom for individuals accompanied by respect and regard for other persons and with social stability built on cohesion instead of coercion. . . . At present, appeal to the individual is dulled by our inability to locate the individual with any assurance. . . . The predicament is that individuality demands association

to develop and sustain it and association requires arrangement and coordination of its elements, or organization—since otherwise it is formless and void of power. But we have now a kind of molluscan organization, soft individuals within and a hard constrictive shell without.[30]

The reasons for these failures in democracy are multiple and varied, but nowhere does Dewey ascribe them to failures *of* democracy. Not less democracy but *more* is called for: more participation by a public that is more aware of itself and its interests, and by individuals who are better informed as to the far-reaching consequences of the public transactions in which they are engaged; and a more tentative and experimental attitude on the part of public officials, executives, and legislators, and, perhaps most of all, on the part of the courts who must interpret the laws and the Constitution. Dewey calls repeatedly for the development of a less ideologically oriented judiciary, one less dominated by a fear of departure from the "intentions of the framers" and one without anxiety at changes in the *status quo*. Reconstruction of the means and the agencies of government is required to soften the "molluscan shell" that so constricts the range and depth of individual contributions to the public welfare.

XI

Although Dewey's political thought was expressed for the most part in the period between the two World Wars, his diagnostic criticism of the flaws in our American Democracy would appear to be as applicable to our contemporary situation now as it was then. The changes that have taken place in the intervening years, not surprisingly, have done nothing to improve the situation, which has, in fact, grown worse. The key to the changes needed to reverse the failures of democracy sketched in the preceding section is, according to Dewey, very plain to see. For the root problem in every case can be traced to the breakdown of communication.

We have the *means* of communication as never before in history. But *what* is communicated too often represents a sharp and tragic contrast between the technical excellence of the media and the intellectual inferiority of its substantive content. The ideas and ideals congruent with the improved means of communication are not communicated. The tools for the formation of an intelligent and organized public are available, but they are not employed. Above all, we have not yet learned how to transform our communications media into the means of conducting transactional relations between individuals, and between the publics which they might then constitute and the agencies which are chosen to represent them. It is this failure, above all else, which presages the eventual foreclosure of democracy. It is not, Dewey argues, because of our choice of "representative" forms of democracy at the outset—a choice determined in the ratification of the Constitution in 1787—rather than the choice of more "classical" forms of participatory democracy that we face this prospect. It is, rather, our failure to transform the instituted means of representation in keeping with the other changes that have taken place in the meantime and, in particular, our failure to link our vastly improved means of communication into the system of representation itself that are at fault.

By the same token, the possibilities of transforming the still embryonic "Great Society" into the "Great Community" that Dewey envisaged have never been so rich and varied as they are at present. Groups and associations are in constant process of formation and re-formation. Individuals are sustained in their individuality by the variety of their associations, a variety that is constantly on the increase in both range and potential quality. Transactions among these associations, and the individuals and groups which sustain them, is likewise capable of indefinite increase. It is true, of course, that the interdependence among them which is a consequence of such transactions is too often ignored and seldom communicated. The formation of publics, consciously aware of themselves as such, requires communication of a kind and a content not now extant. Neighborhoods, localities, and regions can become conscious of themselves as interdependent publics with interests that can be adjusted to compatibility. Professional societies, entreprenurial groups, and labor organizations can likewise shed their "isolationist" attitudes, and will do so as communication among them improves in quality and content. And the same holds true for minority and ethnic groups, religious enclaves, and the most idiosyncratic and isolated of artists, writers, and intellectuals of all sorts. The list is endless. The opportunities enormous.[31]

Dewey was always reminding us of the centrality of communication as a transactional affair and of its fundamental role in accomplishing the purposes of democratic life. But perhaps he nowhere put it more acutely than in this passage from an early essay: "By sufficient preliminary conversation you can avert a catastrophe; . . . apart from conversation, from discourse and communication, there is no thought and no meaning, only just events, dumb, preposterous, destructive." [32] In the end John Dewey rested his faith in democracy on the transactions that occur in dialogue between individuals. He perceived that dialogue must commence in the local community, in interpersonal "face-to-face" relationships, in transactions that are in unbroken continuity with the transactions that his metaphysics ascribes to existences of every kind, "everywhere and everywhen." He closes *The Public and Its Problems* with these thoughts:

> There is no limit to the liberal expansion and confirmation of limited personal intellectual endowment which may proceed from the flow of social intelligence when that circulates by word of mouth from one to another in the communications of the local community. That and that only gives reality to public opinion. We lie, as Emerson said, in the lap of an immense intelligence. But that intelligence is dormant and its communications are broken, inarticulate and faint until it possesses the local community as its medium.[33]

The superiority of democratic political forms lies in their capacity to satisfy this need for the "liberal expansion and confirmation of limited personal intellectual endowment." But that superiority is itself precarious. Viewed in Dewey's metaphysical perspective, the continuous reconstruction of democracy is a condition of its survival, and the understanding of action and change as "transactional" is fundamental to the success of that reconstruction.

NOTES

1. "Introduction," to *Foundations of American Constitutionalism*, ed. Andrew C. McLaughlin (New York: Fawcett, 1961), p. vii.

2. Commager, writing in 1961, obviously did not have the Vietnam War, Watergate, or the Iran–Contra arms affair in mind. However, the apparent ability of the Constitution to survive these events can strengthen his argument only if they are regarded as "aberrations" from what he takes to be the "prosperity of political practice." Another instance of Com-

mager's optimism concerning American political practice is cited by Garry Wills in his "Introduction" to Lillian Hellman's *Scoundrel Time* (New York: Little, Brown, 1976), p. 15: "The record is perhaps unique in the history of power: the organization of the United Nations, the Truman Doctrine, the Marshall Plan, the Berlin airlift, the organization of NATO, the defense of Korea, the development of atomic power for peaceful purposes, Point Four—these prodigious gestures are so wise and so enlightened that they point the way to a new concept of power." It is tempting to add that the potential flaw in each of these instances that Commager cites may come from a failure to appreciate the long-term consequences of power as "transactional" in effect.

3. See the discussion of Aristotle's "essentialism" in Abraham Edel, *Aristotle and His Philosophy* (Chapel Hill: University of North Carolina Press, 1982), pp. 244–46.

4. *Introduction to Aristotle*, ed. Richard McKeon (New York: Modern Library, 1947), p. 16.

5. Jean-Jacques Rousseau, *The Social Contract*, trans. Lester B. Crocker (New York: Washington Square, 1967), p. 7.

6. Ibid., p. 18.

7. Ibid.

8. Sir Isaac Newton, *Opticks, or a Treatise of the Reflections, Refractions, Inflections, and Colours of Light*, 3rd ed. (London: Innys, 1721), pp. 375–76.

9. See also Peter T. Manicas, *The Death of the State* (New York: Putnam, 1974), p. 56; and John B. Noone, Jr., *Rousseau's* SOCIAL CONTRACT: *A Conceptual Analysis* (Athens: University of Georgia Press, 1980), p. 85.

10. Dewey suggested that "Reconstruction *of* Philosophy" might be a more appropriate title for the 1948 reprint, citing the changes that had taken place in the intervening years. He evidently thought that the "continuity" of philosophy with its past *had* been breached in the interim. See *John Dewey: The Middle Works, 1899–1924*. XII. 1920, ed. Bridget A. Walsh (Carbondale and Edwardsville: Southern Illinois University Press, 1982), p. 256.

11. Richard Bernstein has suggested (*John Dewey* [New York: Washington Square, 1966], p. 80) that Dewey first came to use the term "transaction" under stimulus from Arthur F. Bentley in connection with their joint authorship of *Knowing and the Known* in 1946. In a letter to Robert V. Daniels, Dewey referred to this undertaking as a " 'sort of valedictory book' " in which " 'the substitution of "transaction" for "interaction" is the nub of the whole thing.' " The idea had certainly been broached earlier by Hegel and others; Maxwell used it as early as 1876. (See following note.)

12. James Clerk Maxwell, *Matter and Motion* (London: SPCK, 1876), pp. 33–34.

13. See John Herman Randall, Jr.'s brilliant analysis of Dewey's conception of metaphyics in his *Nature and Historical Experience: Essays in Naturalism and the Theory of History* (New York: Columbia University

Press, 1958). See also my discussion in *The Necessity of Pragmatism: John Dewey's Conception of Philosophy* (New Haven: Yale University Press, 1986), chap. 5, "Existence as Problematic."

14. *Experience and Nature*, quoted here and below from *John Dewey: The Later Works, 1925–1953*. I. *1925*, ed. Patricia Baysinger and Barbara Levine (Carbondale and Edwardsville: Southern Illinois University Press, 1981), p. 62.

15. Ibid., p. 172.

16. Ibid., pp. 62–63.

17. (New York: Putnam, 1939; repr. New York: Capricorn, 1963). The 1963 edition is quoted here, pp. 21, 23, 130.

18. (New York: Putnam's, 1934), pp. 16–17.

19. *A Theory of Justice* (Cambridge: The Belknap Press of Harvard University Press, 1971), p. 41.

20. *Experience and Nature*, p. 194.

21. A particularly egregious example of such a misreading of Dewey by an author who should have known better is contained in Thorstein Veblen's *The Higher Learning in America*. See the discussion of this in John P. Diggins, "Point of View," *The Chronicle of Higher Education*, 1 (November 1976), 32.

22. For a more detailed discussion of the "axiological" nature of thinking as Dewey conceived it, see my "Dewey's Metaphysical Perspective," *Journal of Philosophy*, 57 (1960), 100–15.

23. (Chicago: Swallow, 1927).

24. Ibid., p. 7.

25. Ibid., p. 25.

26. Ibid., chap. 2, passim.

27. Ibid., pp. 64–65.

28. See John J. McDermott, *The Culture of Experience: Philosophical Essays in the American Grain* (New York: New York University Press, 1976), pp. 82ff. McDermott suggests here the need for an "aesthetic ecology" and brilliantly succeeds in outlining it in the chapters that follow. He uses the term "ecology" in just the Deweyan sense I have in mind, especially in relation to the distinctive problems of urban "ecosystems."

29. *The Public and Its Problems*, p. 109.

30. *Freedom and Culture*, pp. 162–63 and 166–67.

31. The reference to the "Great Society" at the beginning of this paragraph should be compared with both Josiah Royce's early use of this phrase and the more recent use by President Lyndon Johnson. See Doris Kearns, *Lyndon Johnson and the American Dream* (New York: Harper & Row, 1976), pp. 210–50.

32. *Characters and Events* I, ed. Joseph Ratner (New York: Henry Holt, 1929), p. 129.

33. P. 219.

8

Individuation and Unification in Dewey and Sartre

THELMA Z. LAVINE

George Mason University

INTRODUCTION

THE CHARACTERISTIC OF HUMAN REALITY that the title words "individuation and unification" signify is the source of some of the perennial problems of philosophy. The problem of individuation and unification is perhaps most readily identifiable as (1) the problem of the relation between the individual and the group (or society), and the question that it raises, of course, is the question as to which has primacy, the individual or the group. This is the way the problem may be identified first. But the problem also appears with a familiar face in the Judaeo-Christian frame, in (2) the problems of the individual soul in relationship to divine, transcendent authority, in falling away from God in sin or being unified in obedience. It appears in the form of Christ as Individual, but also as the Son of Man. Individuation receives a powerful and enduring support from the Christian concept of the immortality of the individual soul, as unification does from the concept of the Mystical Body of all believers in Christ.

(3) The problem of individuation and unification likewise appears in the fearful cry of the oppressed and the enslaved in the old Alexandrian Empire, and it produced Gnosticism as a philosophy that condemned the entire physical and social world as evil and as the work of fallen angels, and sought the secret gnosis for one's own escape, as a vessel of light and truth, from a world of horror. (4) The relationship between individuation and unification appears too in philosophical skepticism, with Descartes look-

ing out upon the sum of constituted knowledge and institutional truths—religious, philosophical, scientific, and mathematical—and asking, Of what can I be certain? What can I believe? And the Cogito answer: Only in my own consciousness and its intuitions of my own conscious processes such as thinking, doubting, understanding, affirming, denying, willing, refusing, imagining, and feeling. Individuation appears here as separation and affirmation of the self as independent mental substance. (5) Another and immediately familiar form of the problem is in the antithesis between individualism and statism in political philosophy since the seventeenth century. Here, individualism consists in the superordination of the individual to the state in reality, value, and power; and statism, the reverse, in the subordination of the individual to the state in each of these respects. (6) By the end of the eighteenth century, in part in response to the growth of science and technology and especially to the growth of mass society and nationalistic and imperialistic political power, there appears the individuating protest of early Romanticism with Rousseau and Novalis, and soon thereafter voluntarism in philosophy. Voluntarism in late-eighteenth- and nineteenth-century philosophies from Rousseau to German idealism is the claim of the primacy of will (as against reason or feeling) in reality, knowledge, and morality, and in human nature itself. In voluntaristic philosophies the phenomenon of individuation and unification coincides with the problematic of the individual will in relationship to the authority of a larger or general will. This is the central dialectical problem for Fichte, Hegel, Marx, Kierkegaard, Schopenhauer, and Nietzsche. With respect to Hegel, Max Horkheimer and Theodor Adorno of the Frankfurt School, followers of Marx and Freud and the voluntaristic tradition, offer this sharp comment on Hegel's resolution of the dialectical tension between the individual will and the national will: "Hegel's whole philosophy turns its polemical edge against pure individuality, which the Romantic movement had raised on its banner. . . ." [1]

(7) Out of these psychologizing philosophies of will of the nineteenth century emerged the depth psychologies of the twentieth century, the psychologies of the unconscious personal will, now identified as drive, desire, instinct, imperious needs having primacy in human nature. The individual person has needs for separation

and rebellion, but also exhibits conflicting needs for merger and unification, with the fear of isolation balancing the fear of absorption in a more powerful will. (8) The problematic of individuation and unification is at the forefront, also, in the battle between individualism and holism, as competing methodologies in the social sciences and (9) in the endless controversy between individual psychology and sociology. (10) Literature from the eighteenth century on also reflects the antithesis between individuation and unification in the Romantic vision of the separation of the lonely, tragic conflicted rebel as against the Classical vision of the person who makes an harmonious, unifying reconciliation with universal order or group consensus.

In all these frames—religious, philosophical, political, moral, psychological, social scientific, and literary—what may be observed is that (a) individuation and unification denote processes or tendencies, types of movement or change, and not entities or hypostatized abstractions or names for them. (b) Not only are individuation and unification separate, distinct, identifiable processes; they are counter-processes. They exhibit a paradigm of dyadic dialectic, of thesis and antithesis. Each is called into activity by the other. Each leads ineluctably to the other, the opposite of itself. (c) For any of the frames of reference above, a spectrum can be constructed, a range of positions held or viewpoints expressed, with individuation and unification as the end points of the spectrum. (d) The position occupied on the spectrum by a particular theory or by the work of an individual writer, whether it is on the side of unification or on the side of individuation, can be seen to be a response to a given cultural situation and its perceived stresses and abuses, its balance of conflict and consensus. (e) The position a given theory occupies, again whether on the side of unification or on the side of individuation, will be presented in sharp focus and will attack by explicit condemnation what it perceives to be the opposing viewpoint. But it will also attack the opposing viewpoint by dissociating, by denying its existence, by forgetting about it, and, thus, by obliterating it. (f) Finally, it will be found for any one theory that it defends itself against the excesses of its own position. A consequence of this defense is that the theory will be seen to be invoking ideas, beliefs, and values that are illegitimate within the logical structure of the theory. It will then look as if the theory is cheating. But in fact this must be seen to be a defensive measure taken against the extremities of the position itself.

DEWEY: THE UNIFICATION THESIS

I would now like to bring this conceptual apparatus to bear upon Dewey and Sartre in the hope that it will shed some light on what it is they have to say and how they came to say it in the form they did. Both Dewey and Sartre construct voluntaristic metaphysical systems, i.e., attempts to describe reality in terms of the primacy of will. Each is a moral metaphysics in which the traits of reality are at one and the same time the guideposts for morality. Of these two philosophies, Dewey's is, of course, on the side of unification. To read Dewey as he must appear to Europeans, say to Sartre, is to be struck by the American experience reflected there: the relative absence of conflict; America as the new beginning, as the land of refuge and of opportunity for all, as the social experiment in democracy, as the optimum earthly setting for eighteenth-century Enlightenment optimism, as the center for the fruitfulness of reason, in the form of the development of science and technology, natural rights and democratic institutions—all these providing universal benefits, with Calvinist rewards of prosperity for labor performed. This is in some sense the way in which Dewey presents himself: as a New World, American rebel against the past of Europe, and our own Europe-ridden past. Hence the need for a reconstruction in philosophy, away from absolute certainties (all false, all deceivers, all now obsolete in their time-bound, culture-bound functions, which have no functionality for us). The reconstruction in philosophy which Dewey undertakes is in terms of a unification with nature, in a post-Darwinian naturalism. Nature is the inclusive reality. "Dewey made nature whole again," says one writer, "in a way which philosophers had not known since Aristotle."[2] The real is the natural, exhibiting through enormous complexity of interaction the characteristics of the physical, the biological, and the human. These plateaus are linked by continuity; the human context incorporates, and is continuous with, the physical and the biological. To be a human being in Dewey's world is to be continuous with, unified with, interacting with, having emerged from, the physical processes of nature with the biological capacities and potentialities of the human organism within the social organism in which I discover my language and my meaningful perceptions and values. The whole of human experience has its sources and its consequences in natural processes. As an organic part of nature, human experience has the same traits as nature. It has the plateau traits of the physical, the biological, and the social, and the generic traits of the stable, the precarious, and the qualitatively immediate. No gaps or gulfs separate human experience from the inclusive, all-unifying reality which is nature. Scientific, moral, aesthetic, and religious experiences are differentiated only as distinctive types of contexts, or types of situations, within a common unifying nature. Where a situation in nature poses problems, as in science, or in a moral or political perplexity, in the process of successfully resolving the problem we act as instrumentalities of nature in bringing about unity and a consummation or fulfillment of the originating need. A situation that is consummatory achieves merger with nature in the right way, that is, in bringing about a removal of a disunity. All situations and all experience implicate the natural organism within the environment of nature. Between organism and environment there is interaction, continuity, and unity.

Conspicuous in Dewey's account of his metaphysics, his epistemology, and his social philosophy is the single, dominant theme of the repudiation of gaps, gulfs, divisions, dualisms, dichotomies, separations, discontinuities—all these oppose unification. There are no dualisms, gaps, or gulfs between subject and object, between individual and society, between the is and the ought. There is only the ongoing interaction of organism and environment in problematic situations whose disunities are resolvable into satisfying unifications and consummations within the operations of nature.

Intelligence and morals as well as everyday habits are products of the interaction and continuity of the individual and society. Standards of behavior are those ways that a given society has found useful in bringing about desired and unifying results. Democracy and socialism are means by which society unifies all individuals in the participation toward "the common good." The common good is the only moral good. In direct opposition to the position of political liberalism, Dewey argues that what is best for the individual are the values he shares with others. As Dewey says in the text on *Ethics* which he wrote with James Tufts, "The genuinely moral person is one, then, in whom the habit of regarding all capacities and habits of self from the social standpoint is formed and active. . . . The nature and exercise of this interest constitutes then the distinctively moral quality in all good purposes."[3] It follows from Dewey's naturalistic unification thesis that there is no autonomous self, no independent or substantial self. Personality, individuality, selfhood are themselves natural outcomes, products of the interaction of the organism and specific social environments. The human organism in all its functions, doings, and sufferings is wholly integral with, continuous with, unified with, nature. As Dewey says in *The Public and Its Problems*, "While singular beings in their singularity think, want and decide, what they think and strive for, the content of their beliefs and intentions is a subject matter provided by association."[4] The self is an organization of habits; socially acquired predispositions of response to the environment "constitute the self." Self-development and growth occur when organism and environment interact effectively in situations of increased inclusiveness and complexity. "Life grows," Dewey says, "when a temporary falling out is a transition to a more extensive balance of the energies of the organism with those of the conditions under which it lives."[5] And in *Reconstruction in Philosophy* Dewey says, "Groupings for promoting the diversity of goods that men share have become the real social units. They occupy the place which traditional theory has claimed either for mere isolated individuals or for the supreme and single political organization."[6]

The sense of our links to nature as our supportive, nurturing, fostering, common source excites in Dewey religious sensibilities and a natural piety. Religious feeling, oceanic and unifying, wells up and bursts forth from the final paragraphs of the chapter "Morality is Social" at the end of *Human Nature and Conduct*:

> Within the flickering inconsequential acts of separate selves, dwells a sense of the whole which claims and dignifies them. In its presence we put off mortality and live in the universal. The life of the com-

munity in which we live and have our being is the fit symbol of this relationship. The acts in which we express our perception of the ties which bind us to others are its only rites and ceremonies.[7]

The symbolism of unification with God is scarcely concealed here. For the sacred symbolism of unification with the divine and its worldly manifestations, Dewey has substituted unification with nature and all its ongoing transactions within the life of the community. The steppingstone, the mediation between the Christian and the naturalistic modes of unification, had been provided for Dewey by Hegel's persistent theme of unification with the World Spirit and its historical manifestations in the ongoing life of the social group. From the Christian and the Hegelian language in celebration of unification and community, Dewey seeks to capture, for his own time and in the language of naturalism, the ancient binding aura of the sacred in the feeling of the unity of the self with the modern community and with the processes of nature. And at the same time a new and magnetizing feeling of redemption is offered to the unhappy consciousness of Dewey's generation by his thinly disguised sacred symbolism of a natural and societal unification in place of the older and declining symbolism of unification with God and church.

The feeling of redemption that the naturalistic sacred symbolism offered to Dewey's own generation may be perceived in the life of George Herbert Mead, struggling forlornly with the loss of his own religious faith, and his inability to pursue a career as a Protestant minister, and yet still with the need for wholeness and a sense of vocation, in the face of a growing feeling of isolation. Mead hovered at the edge of a nervous breakdown, depressed by the conflict between supernaturalism and the new science, the conflict between the religious conscience and the new socio-economic transformations of the country, the remoteness of the fashionable Hegelian philosophy from these American problems, and the feeling that the universe is alien and hostile and ultimately unintelligible. In this problematic situation of the generation of Mead and Dewey, Dewey offered the resolving belief system: unification with nature and the community, through shared experience, science, art, and the pursuit of the common good, in place of the now lost possibility of unification with the divine. Mead embraced the Deweyan gospel of nature, a natural and social redemptivism. Mead says of Dewey's philosophy:

"One gets an unshakable faith in a single reality to which all paths lead. . . . For the first time in my life has my thought assumed a definitely positive and cheerful aspect. I don't mean that there has been any break in it, but I have come to consciousness of the meaning of the faith that was in me, faith in the unity and meaning of life, and the absolute completeness of the statement which psychology can give."[8]

So also at about the same time Jane Addams was delivered from a sense of drift and isolation by the Deweyan social gospel. In *Twenty Years at Hull House* she speaks of her struggle with "subjectivity," and her overcoming of inner conflict by work for the community, by redemptive social service.[9] Both Jane Addams and George Herbert Mead expressed for their era its prevailing, anxiety-ridden conflicts between Christianity and science, between private Christian conscience and the changing needs of the public order, between the economy and values of small-town, rural America and the claims of the industrialized urban melting-pots. To both of them, these conflicts now appeared to be resolved (reconciled, transcended, and sublimated) by the symbolism of Dewey's philosophy of unification with the inclusive reality of natural and social processes; while as a personal, redemptive gospel, Dewey's naturalistic resolution of current conflicts lifted guilt, and released and legitimated personal energies for natural and social science, public administration, teaching, social services, and communication media—for the common good.

The gospel of unification with social process that was Dewey's response to the social conflict and alienation of the 1890s remains central in 1930 to his response, now analytically mature and richly informed by the social sciences, to the crisis of the submerging of individuality under corporate domination in the post-World War I period. The task, he argues in *Individualism Old and New*, is "to know where things are going and why" and to redirect and integrate social processes for the common good—"by the social control of industry and the use of governmental agencies for constructive social ends." The task is the transition, made necessary now by industrialization and mass population, to a new socialist society. Unification with the integrated and integrating processes of a socialist society will bring into being a new, "whole," integrated individual. A new concept of individualism, responsive to the new socialist society, will replace the "old individualism" which reflects the lost world of the free, equal, and independent pioneer, farmer, artisan, or merchant. Alienation and disunity will be overcome, and personal energies will be released to direct and sustain the new society.

> The sense of wholeness which is urged as the essence of religion can be built up and sustained only through membership in a society which has attained a degree of unity. The attempt to cultivate it first in individuals and then extend it to form an organically unified society is fantasy. . . .
>
> When the patterns that form individuality of thought and desire are in line with actuating social forces, that individuality will be released for creative effort. Originality and uniqueness are not opposed to social nurture; they are saved by it from eccentricity and escape. . . . A new culture expressing the possibilities immanent in a machine and material civilization will release whatever is distinctive and potentially creative in individuals, and individuals thus freed will be the constant makers of a continuously new society. . . .
>
> A naturalism which perceives that man with his habits, institutions, desires, thoughts, aspirations, ideals and struggles, is within nature, an integral part of it, has the philosophic foundation and the practical inspiration for effort to employ nature as an ally of human ideals and goods such as no dualism could possibly provide.[10]

But the maintenance of the unification type of voluntaristic metaphysics is possible only at a cost—the cost of excluding, by rejecting, or by denying, forgetting, blanking out, dissociating, all those aspects of reality and human experience that threaten the unification thesis. Thus subjectivity, introspection, inner conflict, alienation, dissent, isolation, withdrawal, inner spirtuality, rebellion, self-affirmation, privatism, personal intuitive judgment—all these move toward separation and individuation; all these are threatening; all are repudiated by Dewey. But it was precisely the fear of these—the fear of separation, the loss of community, alienation, dissolution or breakdown of self, the fear of the dangerous Romantic "inward path"—that motivated the unification thesis in Dewey himself. Dewey had healed himself from these fears before offering publicly the social redemptivism that transformed and saved George Herbert Mead.[11] Dewey had had to liberate himself from his guilt-ridden, introspective, conflicted, and unhappy religious consciousness and from the reverberation within it of his mother's voice admonishing him in childhood, "Are you right with Jesus?" He had healed himself and begun his long process of inclusive growth by contributing to the development of the theory and practice of the guilt-lifting, activity-freeing, unblocking, optimistic new moral metaphysics of American naturalism. Thus Dewey himself, like Mead and Jane Addams, had undergone a conversion, literally a turning around of the will from the inner struggles of early commitment to an individualistic Protestant religion to unification with ongoing social processes as these can be directed toward common ends in all human affairs.

What threatens the conversion to unification, what opposes it, is morally anathema. It must be stripped of its significance, rejected, and rebuked, as he rebukes dualisms—the dualisms of mind and matter, experience and nature, mind and body, self and object, individual and society, ends and means, knowledge and action—for their construction of gaps, breaks, and dichotomies that destroy the possibility of consummatory unifications within the inclusive reality of nature. So also he rejects and rebukes all claims to absolute truth, to the immutable, "once-for-all ordered and systematized" that serves to rigidify social processes and to be divisive. He rejects as well transcendent ideals and obsolete political philosophies such as traditional individualism that block ongoing transactions of social change. As John Gouinloch notes, "Fixed ends are hateful to Dewey's view." They do not unify and release the potentialities of a situation; they ignore and fail to utilize the goods within the situation; they are impossible of fulfillment, being separated from intelligent action.[12] Specific attacks are made in almost all Dewey's major works on the notion of an "inner life," on subjective idealism, on privatism, on Romanticism, on self or ego as independent thinking or willing substance.

But in addition to clear and explicit repudiation or rebukes, there is another way in which unification may be protected against danger and that is, simply, by omission, by dissociating, by blanking out. And thus we have all those elements that are simply denied, forgotten, dissociated, left out of the account by Dewey. No one can read the pages of Dewey without finding enormous discomfort with the various circumlocutions by which he avoids the word "consciousness," or the words "mind," "self," "idea." These words do not appear often, and in this way the phenomena they refer to are denied existence. But also blotted out, wiped out, dissociated, are the words that denote realities such as the private self (for example, the private self that happens to be alienated from role-playing and contributing to the scientific and democratic processes); the elements of conflict within the self, between the self and others, and between social groups; the desire many people have for a sense of autonomy; the tragic sense of life; elements of transcendence that one is lured by: an eschaton, the concept of an apocalyptic breakthrough from horrors and suffering into a great day of light; the phenomenon of ecstatic group unity, those rare moments of group unity that transform an entire group from revolt into ecstacy (as in the social movements of the 1960s). All these are absent. Also absent in Dewey's writing is that phenomenon of human life that we must call the demonic, the demonic will that can produce a Holocaust. How can these happen in a Deweyan world? They are dissociated and wiped out.

As for the unhappy consciousness, the conflicted, the solitary person, Dewey does speak of him in order to attack him. He speaks of him as "the lost individual," one of those "who decline to accept . . . the realities of the social estate, and because of this refusal either surrender to the division or seek to save their individuality by escape or sheer emotional revolt."[13] And, he concludes, "If, in the long run, an individual remains lost, it is because he has chosen irresponsibility; and if he remains wholly depressed, it is because he has chosen the course of easy parasitism."[14]

Individuals who are not bound together in association, Dewey says, "are monstrosities." All these characteristics of a lost individual, as well as the other realities rejected or dissociated, are elements making for individuation. They tear away at unification. They exhibit disorder, the negative side of things approved, rather than order. Disorder, for Dewey, is withdrawal from the public world of science, democracy, and social amelioration. In a distinctive formulation of the unification thesis Dewey says, "The sense of the extensive and underlying whole is the context of every experience, and it is the essence of sanity. The mad, the insane thing to us is that which is torn from the common context and which stands alone and isolated."[15] That which dangerously threatens unification with nature and society is, therefore, monstrous, disorderly, and insane, and like all that is detached and withdrawn, it is repugnant. Such phenomena as the lost individual are polluting, not merely threatening and dangerous. They pollute the cooperative endeavors of the healthy-minded in their ongoing efforts at solving competently the problems of an increasingly corporate, industrial mass society.

But the continual barrage of Dewey's attack upon self, consciousness, personal intuitive judgment, conflict, withdrawal, is overdone. The socialization of the self, its integration into nature and community, becomes excessive. The case for unification is so well-established, so excessively established, that Dewey himself may be seen to take protective measures against the dangers and excesses of his own position. In fact, it began to appear that the organicity and the unifying Hegelianism which were his stepping-stone to naturalistic organicity and unity had so triumphed over him that he himself was establishing a block universe, a closed system, now of nature. And thus, to protect himself against falling into these excesses of his own position, he undertakes protective, defensive measures, involving a swing away from the unification side of the spectrum, where his thesis stands, in the direction of individuation. But it is not a total swing, since a total swing would mean a total reconversion. His unification thesis is not extreme; it is susceptible of modification by incorporating some elements of individuation. The modification Dewey undertakes assumes two forms. (*a*) In the first form, deliberate and overt protective measures are taken, such as the introduction of the concept of impulse. Impulse is spontaneous; it yields novelty; it springs from the individual. These traits of impulse are a corrective for the block universe. Plasticity of impulse in childhood is urged as a generational corrective for social stagnation and as a source of habits of independent judgment—another corrective on the side of individuation from the block universe. And again, the qualitative and consummatory, individually felt, aesthetic and immediate aspects of experience fall within the personal context and serve as a protective device on the side of individuation. (*b*) The second form is accomplished tacitly and illicitly. Dewey leans tacitly on traditional values and traditional individualistic virtues by using language evocative of them. Thus he presents his manifesto for a socialist economy and government as "a new individualism." He supports his naturalistic philosophy of unification with societal process by means of language which implicitly carries associations with Christian individualistic virtues of working to build the Christocracy; associations with pioneering individualistic virtues of self-reliance, initiative, and courage; associations with farm and village virtues of independence, hard work, self-respect, and neighborliness; while to a younger generation the Deweyan philosophy evoked associations with personal careerism, entrepreneurial or bureaucratic, in the management of organizational ends.[16] But these various tacit elements are individuating and protective devices which have no legitimate meaning within the natural and social processes of Dewey's system.

SARTRE: THE INDIVIDUATION THESIS

In 1896 John Dewey wrote: "Overemphasis on the personal element in conduct" (signifying for him, as we have seen, the polluting, contaminating, disorderly, threatening, because disunifying) "can end only in useless complications, weariness of the flesh and spirit, and contradictions between our aspirations and our accomplishments." In saying this, Dewey might have been describing Jean-Paul Sartre, who was to be born nine years later. Dewey was speaking in the first flush of his discovery of redemption through natural social activities. As for overemphasizing the personal element and " 'devotion to persons,' " Dewey had found a " 'better way,' " and that was " 'devotion to work, to action, and to persons, whether one's self or others indirectly through their implications in activity.' "[17] The way one should relate to other people is indirectly through work, through their involvement in activity: that is, regard yourself and others from the outside only and as instrumentalities in work to be performed.

Sartre, of course, presents the polar opposite position to unification on the unification–individuation spectrum. He offers us a moral metaphysics wholly centered on the self and on its radical individuation. To read Sartre as an American is to be struck by the subjectivism, by the particularizing, intimate, concrete portrayal of individual human existence, of what it is to be a self hemmed in by mass society, a conflicted consciousness relating to other selves who are also centers of consciousness and conflicted, and threatening to me; and relating also to the world of things, which fill me with horror. And so in contrast to the hard-won, cheerful, pressing on of optimism by Dewey, we have the dark mood of Sartre who says, "We are by nature unhappy creatures without any possibility of escaping from our unhappy state."

The most vivid first impression of an American reading Sartre, especially after having read Dewey, is of his language and his style. As a philosopher of the primacy of will and as a voluntarist, Dewey had conveyed will through the functions of the organism, through organic impulse, need, consummation, and problem-solving in interaction with the ongoing processes of nature. Dewey's language is objectivist, neo-Darwinian; it is the language of the behavior of organisms, of group psychology rather than individual psychology, of scientific and social processes, of problem-solving in cooperative groups. But Sartre as a philosopher of will writes in the language of subjectivism, of the personal will, of conscious desire and frustration, of individual psychology, of feeling and emotion. Sartre's style bristles with technicalities of the phenomenology of consciousness from Descartes (whose Cogito, giving indubitability to the conscious self, is a key resource for him) and from Hegel, Husserl, and Heidegger. Interwoven with these technicalities of the phenomenology of consciousness in the writing of Sartre are his anecdotes and vignettes of the existent self. Each anecdote is an attempt at proof of the philosophy by personalization, by particularization, by the telling case that opens up a crevasse in the frozen sea of human existence. Who can forget the waiter in the café who disappears into his role? Or the woman on her first date who does not notice that he has taken her hand? Or the look on the part of the stranger who catches me peeking through the keyhole?

What, then, is the shape of Sartre's moral metaphysics as a voluntaristic form of individuation? In contrast with the continuum of three plateaus in Dewey's inclusive nature, Sartre describes three modes of being whose significance lies in their separations and discontinuities: Beings-for-themselves, beings conscious of objects as separate from themselves, and conscious of themselves; Beings-in-themselves, the things of which Beings-for-themselves are conscious, and conscious of being separated from; and Beings-for-others, the relations between conscious beings, perceiving one another as Beings-in-themselves, as things, and engaging in endless hostile conflict as Beings-for-themselves. For Sartre, to be human is to be a conscious being, a being-for-itself, a being which is conscious of, for whose consciousness there are, objects. Consciousness is thus intentional; it has an object. It is aware of the object and it is aware of being aware of the object. Consciousness distinguishes between itself and that of which it is conscious, and thus within consciousness there is a gap (distance, emptiness, nothingness) between thought or consciousness and objects.[18] And thus begins the whole series of gaps, of discontinuities that characterize this individuating philosophy, whereas with Dewey we see the closing of all gaps and the absence of all discontinuities.

But these gaps between consciousness and object and my awareness of the gap between them open up the potentiality of my freedom as self. It is this gap that is the very freedom to annihilate, to negate, not to be, the object one is conscious of. Thus the power of the self is the power of the Hegelian principle of negation; this is the principle of my freedom and of my individuation. To be a questioner ("Where is Pierre in the cafe?") is to dissociate myself from the causal laws of being-in-itself, the world of mere things; it is to detach myself from the world of things, and to withdraw from it. By the gap, by the principle of negation, by the power to annihilate, the human self is the being who causes Nothingness to arise in the world, which is the separation of the self from all unification, even within consciousness. Freedom as the freedom of negating, annihilating, is the freedom to reject every project, every ideal, every philosophy. To be a conscious being is to have no fixed essence, but only endlessly to be choosing something to fill up the gap between my self now and my future possibilities, since I seek to negate and transcend myself as I am now.[19] To be free is to discover that I have no foundation, no continuity, no unity, no possibilities of unification to escape from my nihilating freedom. This is the meaning of anguish. Sartre conveys the anguish of freedom most eloquently in *Existentialism and Humanism*: "We have neither behind us nor before us, in a luminous realm of values, any means of justification or excuse. We stand alone, without excuse." Here is the self alone, the individuated self.

I would wish, rather than to live as an empty self, in endless nihilation, to be a being-in-itself, simply a thing, like an inkwell, which is massive and solid and glued to itself. It has no lack; it has no gap. But to try this, to seek to be a thing, to seek to escape from my nothingness, from the gap, is bad faith. Bad faith is the escape from individuation; it is the escape from my consciousness as this nihilating freedom; it is the escape from being-for-itself to try to become simply a being-in-itself. Bad faith is the attempt to escape from individuation, by pretending to be a thing. (As she pretends her hand is a thing.) Bad faith is the attempt to escape from individuation by unifying with thing-like nature. But I am not part of thing-like nature, and thus this unifying defense mechanism is forbidden to me. In complete opposition to Dewey, Sartre is here assailing as bad faith such notions as Dewey's redemptive, therapeutic discovery that relating to oneself and to others indirectly through work and activity is a "better way" than through "the personal element." "We flee anguish," says Sartre bitingly, "by trying to look at ourselves from outside as another [person] or as a thing" (BN 52).

Bad faith is also exhibited by playing a role, as the waiter does who pretends he is nothing but a waiter; he is nothing but his role. His bad faith is an attempt to escape from hideous nihilating feeling, from individuation, by unification with a social role. This is bad faith, because to be a conscious being is to be individuated, to be endlessly negating, to be free in nihilating everything before me. Bad faith is inauthenticity, self-deception, "a lie in the soul."[20] The clear moral implication is that a right act is one in which I acknowledge my freedom of choice as individuating and separating me, totally alone, from things and society.

I exist as a conscious being, in a world of other conscious beings, in a world of Being-for-others. But for others I am a body, a thing, predictable as other things; I am thing-like in the other's eyes and I feel alienated from my world, from the projects I pursue as a conscious being. But in the look of the other I recognize that I am not a thing but a person, yet I also recognize that I am no longer the master of my world. My awareness of the other is not only knowledge of the other, but action, a striving against the other: "While I attempt to free myself from the hold of the Other, the Other is trying to free himself from mine; while I seek to enslave the Other, the Other seeks to enslave me. . . . Conflict is the original meaning of being-for-others" (BN 444–45). The voices of Hobbes and Hegel can be heard as Sartre insists that I want to enslave the other, but I want to enslave him as free; only this will satisfy me. But if he is free, he will escape my absorption of him, and I will lose the satisfaction of mastery over his freedom. And thus all human relations are hopeless. Particularly hopeless is the relationship of love.[21] In a world where I can relate only through enslaving or being enslaved, I myself can be the slave, and a masochistic object for the lover; I can be a sadist and master the loved one by violence; or I can observe the other in indifference. But none of these will satisfy me. "The lover does not desire to possess the beloved (or be possessed) as one possesses a thing; he demands a special type of appropriation. He wants to possess a freedom as freedom" (BN 448). And thus love is conflict and separation.

Far from Dewey's view of a great unifying and supportive (however precarious) nature as the inclusive reality, for Sartre, to be in the world of nature is to perceive it, first of all, as simply there, like the black, knotted root of the horse-chestnut tree in *Nausea*. Things are simply there, contingent, superfluous, and absurd, as the root of the tree is in its rottenness, bloatedness, and obscenity. To Sartre, everything existing is inconsequential, unnecessary, superfluous, "too much," *de trop*. Roquentin's feelings about the world ("The nausea hasn't left me")—nausea, absurdity, and anguish—are shared experiences of the traits of the world.[22]

The most portentous trait Sartre experiences in nature and the world of objects is the viscous. The viscous is a revelation of natural being. It is sticky and slimy, an aspect of the world that fills us with a natural revulsion. Things sink into it and dissolve, although "there is a visible resistance, like the refusal of an individual who does not want to be annihilated in the whole of being" (BN 745). The world of nature may seem docile, but surreptitiously it engulfs one, in a leech-like softness. The viscous symbolizes a sickly sweet feminine revenge, the death of the being-for-itself in the slimy being-in-itself. And the sinking into the sickly sweet viscous substance of nature is like a bee who sinks into the jar of jam or honey and drowns (BN 747). The viscous, symbolizing the whole of nature, is what we hate, but we cannot escape it.

Moreover, I, too, in my facticity as body, am characterized by the contingency and superfluousness of fact, and thus my own life is absurd, as the whole of nature is absurd. My ideal is to unify the gap within myself between Being-in-itself (as a body and as what I have become) and Being-for-itself (as nihilating, transcending consciousness and what I seek to be). My ideal is to become perfect, to overcome my emptiness and lack of foundation by uniting the solidity of Being-in-itself and the nothingness of Being-for-itself. But this perfection, which we traditionally find in God, is an impossible unification. We struggle in vain to close the gap between the in-itself and the for-itself. "Man is a useless passion" (BN 754).

Ethics is impossible for Sartreian existentialism. Extreme individuation has separated me from all suppport for values. I alone in my freedom am the source of value. There is no ground or justification for any moral principle. Moreover, conflict, as the only way in which I can relate to others, removes the possibility of moral consideration of others. Ethics is thus impossible.

If we recognized the hidden symbolism of Dewey's naturalism as the Christian social gospel, Hegelianized and naturalized with its offer of redemption for good works in the social process, so we can also perceive the hidden symbolism of Sartre's world. In Sartre's hidden symbolism, Being-for-itself is this flickering moment of purity, this flickering moment of consciousness in a demonized, Gnostic world. But whereas the Gnostic self learns the secret gnosis by which to escape from the hideousness of nature and the cruelties of government, for Sartre's Being-for-itself there is no exit. Sartre, then, has taken an extreme, radicalized position on the individuation–unification spectrum. I am totally alone, in total despair. There is no support from God. I am as alienated from my own body as it is an alien object for others. I exist in the gap between my consciousness and its object. My freedom is only the power to negate, to sever all links of thought and value. I am repelled by the odor of my own body, by the nauseating qualities of the natural world, by its viscosity. I am in conflict with all other persons, all of whom threaten my freedom and seek to enslave me. I cannot love another; I seek the impossible, to possess the other's freedom, and I end unhappily as a sadist or a masochist. I cannot love myself; I recognize my absurdity in my own contingencies, in my own inability to close the gap between what I am and what I choose to become.

In this desolate landscape, what threatens Sartre's Being-for-itself? What threatens the maintenance of this radically individuating form of voluntaristic metaphysics? All otherness that would possess me, engulf me, include me, limit or destroy my complete freedom, is threatening to me. The determinism of the natural world threatens my absolute freedom as "consciousness through and through—limited only by itself" (BN lxv). As one interpreter of Sartre observes, "He thinks that once one 'fragment' of determinism is admitted into the mind, it will corrupt the whole."[23] Superfluity, contingency, the absurd, the nauseating quality of the thing world, the sticky viscousness of nature—all these threaten to engulf me. My own body, the bodies of others, others as conscious beings are threats to me, as the bad faith of the social order is, flaunting its tailor-made values in the "spirit of seriousness." All these threaten the new philosophy of self to which Sartre sought to convert the French intellectual world, humiliated and exhausted by the "phony war" of 1939–1940 and disgusted by the regimentation of a corrupt government. All these sources of threat are vomited out by the nausea, fear, and sense of absurdity they produce.

Sartre is perfectly explicit in what he rejects in order to support his position. His symbolism is of pollution, dirt, and danger. He speaks of the self-righteous bourgeois world as consisting of *salauds* ("filthy stinkers"); he entitles one of his plays "Dirty Hands"; he speaks of *saleté poissence*, the sticky filth of things; Bouville, the setting of *Nausea*, is Mud Town, a sticky, filthy mire for consciousness. And thus there is a need for a violent cleansing and self-purification. But there is the other mode of defending his position, through dissociation, blanking out, and forgetting, and by denial, circumlocution, and avoidance. Thus Sartre defends his position against threat by omitting the necessary socialization of consciousness. He avoids and leaves out the constructive functions of community, the supportive structures of the natural environment. He leaves out the sense of human competence in facing problems, the American sense of competent problem-solving. Progress in scientific knowledge and technology, melioration in human affairs, are simply not part of the story; they are blanked out.

This extreme position of individuation, far more extreme than Dewey's unification position, is dangerous in its extremity. It plunges the solitary self into nihilism, in which there is no ground for either common or personal ends, and into a life of continual despairing interpersonal conflict. The principle of negation yields a bitter harvest and forces Sartre to take defensive security measures against the excesses of his own position. One of the obviously protective devices he employs is the concept of bad faith. The concept of bad faith leans on the traditional notion of guilt, and signifies a unification with tradition. But there is no legitimate foundation for the guilt of bad faith in his position. In *Existentialism and Humanism* he offers as a protective device the ploy that existentialism is really humanistic so that in choosing freedom for myself, I choose it for others. This, of course, is a false ploy, which he soon regretted.

However, these devices are not sufficient to deal with a position of such extreme individuation. The dangers of the free and solitary will without foundation are so great that only a total conversion away from such dangers to the opposite extreme, to total unification, will do. The violence of individuation necessitates a counter-violence of "totalization," strict unification within the group. And thus occurs the now famous reference to conversion, which appears as a footnote to a passage at the end of his discussion of the circle of sadism and masochism that has laid bare the hopeless, individuating hostilities of Beings-with-others: "Hate does not enable us to get out of the circle. It simply represents the final attempt, the attempt of despair. After the failure of this attempt nothing remains for the for-itself except to re-enter the circle and allow itself to be indefinitely tossed from one to the other of the two fundamental attitudes." The swing toward unification occurs in the footnote to this passage: "These considerations do not exclude the possibility of an ethics of deliverance and salvation. But this can be achieved only after radical conversion which we cannot discuss here" (BN 504).

We now know the meaning of the mysterious reference to radical conversion; it was conversion to Marxism, and to the P.C.F., the French Communist Party, which dominated the intellectual and literary culture of France from the Resistance until the aftermath of the general strike of May 1, 1968. In this conversion, consciousness, the flickering, pure, for-itself, and Existentialism, its philosophy, are both drawn, like the bee to the jam pot, to

Marxism. And in the jam pot, both nearly drowned. But a sticky Sartre finally crawled out ond turned back (in horror at the French Communist Party's role in the uprising of May 1968) to the self and its travails in a study of Flaubert,[24] and to the support of ultra-Left, anti-Communist politics. But when Sartre effected his radical conversion to Marxism philosophically in the *Critique of Dialectical Reason*, it is clear what happened. The despairing will of the individuating philosophy sought out, in the extremities of its position, the stronger will of the Communist Party, with its totalizing philosophy of unification, its organization, its armed power, its press, its network of communication and financial support, its international links, and its unification of the group by violence, which became for the isolated for-itself the unifying whole of deliverance and salvation. The willful negations of Sartrian individuation, a mere series, passes over into the group fused by terror into a single general will. The self becomes massive and thing-like at last by becoming not-self, unified into a single identity in a totalitarian order.

CONCLUSION

Each of these philosophies is a powerful metaphysical system. Each presents a moral, symbolic universe in which human experience and its place in the world are given significance. Each is to the other—the one individuating, the other unifying—as figure is to ground; to perceive one is, not to perceive the other, but to banish the other. Each strips the other of significance. What Sartre overtly repudiates as polluting to pure separated and individuated consciousness, or covertly omits by dissociating it and denying its existence—all these, as functions of unification, are the very strengths of John Dewey. The supportive world of nature, the significance of social fabric in community and nature, the necessary socialization of the self, the significance of human competence in problem-solving, the phenomenon of scientific and technological progress, the potentiality of ameliorating the human condition—these are the strengths of Dewey. On the other hand, what Dewey overtly repudiates as polluting to his pure, unifying naturalistic processes or covertly omits by dissociation and denial—all these, as functions of individuation, are the very strengths of Sartre. The desire for autonomy as a self, for separation from incorporation, "lostness," the infinite dissatisfaction with what I am, the repugnance of body and of things, the sense of inner conflict and that to be is to be an unhappy conscious, conflict with others, the endless sado-masochistic circle, the sense of the oppressiveness of the causal laws of nature, the suspicion of sham and hypocrisy in society's high moral purposes, the human potential for demonic aggression that creates a Holocaust—these are the very strengths that Sartre offers us. Each philosophy robs the other of its moral worth.

But all moral universes are precarious. They are constructed in the face of process, of events that may overtake them and make them superfluous. The fears they sought to overcome in their own time (by unification to cope with fear of isolation or inner conflict or by individuation to cope with fear of being swallowed up) will be imperceptible, lost to a later public, in part precisely because the saving moral universe did indeed overcome them. There will remain visible only the mode of deliverance. Moreover, new, emerging problematic situations may present polar opposite stresses to those a moral universe was created to resolve.

Under these conditions, which have befallen both Dewey and Sartre, each becomes what the opposing position caricatures it to be. So, in a time of need for individuation, Dewey is perceived as Sartre's most damaging caricature of such a philosophy would present it: a Philistine, a mere pragmatist, a "con" man of the Establishment, offering a dehumanized and depersonalized philosophy of adjustment to creeping bureaucratization.[25] And so Sartre has come to be perceived as Dewey might have presented him in a most damaging caricature: a lost individual, now depressed, now rebellious, neurotic, hovering on insanity, alternating between the psychotic withdrawal of Roquentin and the psychopathic antisocial impulse to criminality of Jean Genet, and ending as an apologist for Stalin's concentration camps, before a final withdrawal.

Does any path lie open to us? Surely it is better, while we are cast into this life, to view man as a useful passion rather than as a useless passion. But in response to a telling question which John J. McDermott raised—"Is Dewey now only a museum piece?"—I would like to give two answers. One is that much Dewey revision-ism has been taking place, professing to find central to his thought art, or self-realization, or the consummatory, or a tragic sense of life. But in order to see to it that Dewey is not a museum piece, and that he opens up a path for us, there must be attempts to dis-cover the limitations of this philosophy and how they came about, as the present thematic examination of Dewey has tried to do. Perhaps we can then know how changes are to be made. My sec-ond answer is to suggest that the spirit may now be moving us away from process, and the concern with the processes of nature or consciousness or history, to a new and renewed concern with content and with truth to live by, and that we turn to Dewey to ask whether upon the strength that Dewey gives us we may find our way to content and truth.

NOTES

1. Preface to *Aspects of Sociology*, ed. Frankfurt Institute for Social Research, trans. John Viertel (Boston: Beacon, 1973), p. 42.

2. John Gouinloch, *John Dewey's Philosophy of Value* (New York: Humanities Press, 1972), p. 13.

3. (New York: Holt, 1908), pp. 299–300.

4. Repr. ed. (Chicago: Holt, 1946), p. 25.

5. *Art as Experience* (New York: Minton, Balch, 1934), p. 14.

6. Repr. ed. (Boston: Beacon, 1948), p. 159.

7. (New York: 1922), pp. 331–32.

8. Letters from George Herbert Mead to Henry Northrup Castle and Castle's parents, June–August 1892, Mead Papers, University of Chicago Library; cited in Neil Coughlan, *Young John Dewey* (Chicago: University of Chicago Press, 1973), pp. 146–47. My discussion is indebted to this study.

9. For Jane Addams the liberating force of Dewey's thought was com-municated in such texts as "Christianity and Democracy," his address at the Sunday Morning Services of the Student Christian Association at the University of Michigan, March 27, 1892: " 'The one claim that Christian-ity makes is that God is truth; . . . that man is so one with the truth thus revealed that it is not so much revealed *to* him as *in* him; he is *its* incarnation; that by the appropriation of truth, by identification with it, man is free; free negatively, free from sin, free positively, free to live his own life, free to express himself, free to play without let or limitation upon the instru-ment given him—the environment of natural wants and forces' " (cited in ibid., pp. 89–90).

10. *Individualism Old and New* (New York: Minton, Balch, 1930), pp. 64 (Dewey's specific target here is Waldo Frank), 143, 153.

11. Dewey's role in bringing about wholeness in himself and in others requires reconciliation with his own theory, quoted above, that a sense of wholeness can exist only as a function of societal unity. Dewey does acknowledge that individuals "with special intellectual gifts and equipment" are necessary to provide "at least a first step in a more general reconstruction that will bring integration out of disorder" (ibid., pp. 139–41).

12. *John Dewey's Philosophy of Value*, pp. 179–80.

13. *Individualism Old and New*, p. 82.

14. Ibid., p. 167.

15. *Art as Experience*, p. 194.

16. For an analysis of Randolph Bourne's devastating criticism of Dewey and analysis of his influence, see Coughlan, *Young John Dewey*, pp. 159–62; see also Paul Bourke, "The Status of Politics, 1909–1919: *The New Republic*, Randolph Bourne, and Van Wyck Brooks," *Journal of American Studies*, 8 (1974), pp. 171–202.

17. Dewey's review of S. Bryant's *Studies in Character* in *Psychological Review*, 3 (1896), 218–22 (as cited in Coughlan, *Young John Dewey*, p. 84).

18. Cf. Jean-Paul Sartre, *Being and Nothingness*, trans. Hazel E. Barnes (New York: Washington Square, 1966), pp. 3–19; hereafter cited as BN. Cf. also Mary Warnock, *The Philosophy of Sartre* (London: Hutchinson University Library, 1965), pp. 43–45 ("The Gap Within Consciousness"). My discussion is indebted to this entire study.

19. "In its coming into existence human reality grasps itself as an incomplete being. It apprehends itself as being in so far as it is not, in the presence of the totality which it lacks and which is in the form of not being it and which is what it is. Human reality is a perpetual surpassing toward a coincidence with itself which is never given" (BN 109).

20. A problem frequently raised in criticism of Sartre is whether faith is shown to be possible.

21. BN 447–504 contain Sartre's discussion of love.

22. Sartre here is in agreement with Dewey. Cf.: "Fear, whether an instinct or an acquisition, is a function of the environment. Man fears because he exists in a fearful, an awful world. The world is precarious and perilous" (*Experience and Nature*, 2nd rev. ed. [New York: Dover, 1958], p. 42).

23. Anthony Manser, *Sartre: A Philosophic Study* (New York: Oxford University Press, 1966), p. 57. Cf.: "We are separated from things by nothing except by our freedom" (BN 623).

24. Sartre's commitment to the P.C.F. was incremental, with many vicissitudes, stopping short of joining the Party. For an account of the cat-and-mouse game the P.C.F. played with Sartre, see Mark Poster, *Existential Marxism in Postwar France: From Sartre to Althusser* (Princeton: Prince-

ton University Press, 1975). Sartre declared in 1977 that in fact he was and had always been a political anarchist, thus reclaiming a position of radical individuation.

25. The study by Arthur Vidich and Joseph Bensman, *Small Town in Mass Society* (Princeton: Princeton University Press, 1958), could be offered in evidence of this criticism of Dewey.

9

Josiah Royce: Anticipator of European Existentialism and Phenomenology

JACQUELYN ANN K. KEGLEY

California State University, Bakersfield

IT IS VERY APPROPRIATE, in the context of a bicentennial institute on American philosophy, to return to the work of Josiah Royce. Though best known as the author of a complex and foreboding metaphysical system, Royce was a man with a passionate belief in the practical importance of many of his ideas, and he devoted his philosophical career to stressing those he thought of the greatest practical importance. Among them were: (1) the notion of the fundamental mutuality of the individual and the communal; (2) the belief that authentic selfhood could be achieved through the development of a plan that created new possibilities for the future out of the givenness of the past; and (3) the conviction that in America efforts must be made to build community out of conflicting and pluralistic diversity by means of mediation and interpretation. These ideas have a new relevance in a time when there is increasing alienation of people from each other, dehumanization of individuals, loss of community, and increasing lack of communication of the many "specialists" of our time with each other and with non-specialists.

It is also fitting in this context and at this time to stress Royce's affinities with two supposedly European-born contemporary philosophies that now attract both scholars and laymen: namely, existentialism and phenomenology. I stress these affinities for two reasons: first, to show that American philosophy was not always derivative, as some would claim, but highly originative; and, second, to give emphasis to the interesting continuities of thought—to the wrestling with similar problems and similar solutions by philosophers of seeming radically different national and philosophical backgrounds.

I shall argue that Royce shares with the phenomenologists (a) a belief in the importance of attempting to describe human experience as it is directly experienced; (b) an affirmation of the temporal nature of all experience and the priority of the future in the development of all human meaning; (c) a conviction that human awareness of and contact with the world is initially and fundamentally instrumental and transactional; (d) a belief in knowledge as a "social enterprize" and an insight into the fact that the scientific world of experience is not primordial, but rather represents a modification of primordial experience for the sake of highly specialized interests. I shall also argue that Royce, in contrast to Husserl, but more in accord with Merleau-Ponty, sees that a full Husserlian reduction may not be achievable. As for the existentialists, Royce is in consent with them in (a) holding that self-relatedness is one of the basic structures of human existence; and (b) stressing the role of negativity in the development of self-knowledge and man's development of selfhood as a project he must undertake in freedom and in time. Royce takes important steps beyond the existentialists in emphasizing the essential need of building community, however difficult, and in seeing man not as sole creator of meaning and value in the world.

Edmund Husserl's concern as a phenomenologist was to offer an in-depth description of phenomena as they appear to consciousness, of human experience as it actually occurs. He sought to do this by bracketing (setting aside) all questions concerning the reality or genesis of the objects of consciousness and by screening out all presuppositions so that we could attend to features of experience that we ordinarily fail to notice. In this way, he thought the essential elements of consciousness, rather than the accidental ones, would be revealed. In carrying out this program, Husserl discovered the intentional nature of consciousness: namely, that it is always directed to an object beyond itself. He saw, further, that all experience actually transpires in the "living present" and sought, in his *Phenomenology of Internal Time Consciousness* written in

1904/1905, to work out its essential temporal constitutional structure.

Similarly, Josiah Royce, in his "Thought Diary" of July 21, 1880, spoke of developing "the theory of the world of reality as a projection from the present moment." He envisions a new phenomenology in which the opening contention would be: "Every man lives in the present and contemplates a past and future. . . . the future and the past are shadows both, the present is the only real."[1] In working out his own philosophical system in *The World and the Individual*, Royce begins with the notion of a "specious present," which, he notes, is a characteristically human time-span of consciousness, a time-span that may not be, and probably is not, shared by other beings. Royce also argues for the priority of this lived experienced time to conceptual mathematical time. "The world time is but a generalized and extended image and correspondent of the observed time of our inner experience."[2]

Still further, Royce argues that it is the experience of time that ties the self to the world. In fact, time is the ground of the formation of the self; it is the locus of all human meaning. Our human experience of temporal succession is an experience of a pursuit directed toward a goal. Human experience is essentially temporal, purposive, willful. Thus Royce writes:

> the direction of the flow of time is a character essential to time. And this direction of the flow of time can only be expressed in its true necessity by saying that in the case of the world's time, as in the case of the time of our inner experience, we conceive the past as leading towards, as aiming in the direction of the future, in such wise that the future depends for its meaning only as a process expectant of the future. In brief, only in terms of Will, and only by virtue of the significant relations of the stages of a teleological process, has time, whether in our inner experience, or in the conceived world order as a whole, any meaning. Time is the form of the Will; and the real world is temporal in so far as, in various regions of that world, seeking differs from attainment, pursuit is external to its own goal, the imperfect tends towards its own perfection, or in brief, the internal meanings of finite life gradually win in successive stages, their union with their own External Meaning.

> time . . . as the form of the will is . . . to be viewed as the most pervasive form of all finite experience whether human or extra-human. In pursuing its goals, the Self lives in time [WI II 132–33].

Thus, Royce affirms, with Husserl and Heidegger, the fundamental temporal nature of our consciousness and the priority of the future in the development of coherent meaning. Even more, he affirms the intentionality of consciousness not merely in the Husserlian sense of "consciousness *of* something," but in the sense of "consciousness as essentially *teleological* in character." Man encounters the world in terms of interests and concerns. Ideas, for Royce, are plans of action, proposals about how one intends to act toward the things of which one has ideas. They act as guides in our dealings with the world.

Royce stresses the purposive, teleological nature of human thinking vis-à-vis his notion of the internal and external meaning of ideas. The "internal meaning" of an idea is that which the idea aims to express, and when expressed, is the fulfillment of that idea. Along with the internal meaning, the idea also has an "external meaning," which is the internal meaning's reference beyond itself to an object to which it refers. This external meaning, this object, or "other," which the idea seeks, is only its own greater determination, its fulfillment. Royce writes: "It follows that the finally determinate form of the object of a finite idea is that form which *the idea itself would assume whenever it became individuated, or, in other words, became a completely determined idea, an idea or will fulfilled by a wholly adequate empirical content, for which no other content need to be substituted, or, from the point of view of the satisfied idea, could be substituted*" (WI I 337). It must be noted here, lest Royce be accused of blatant subjectivism, that finite ideas as conceived by humans never have a wholly adequate empirical content. The given always is beyond our ideas. I shall discuss this later in greater detail, for I believe it is an important departure, for example, from the thought of Edmund Husserl.

Royce takes another step in stressing the purposive nature of human thought. He defines truth and reality in terms of the fulfillment of purpose. An idea is true only when it possesses precisely the type of correspondence with its object the idea wants to possess, i.e., when there is complete, determinate, and individual embodiment of its internal meaning. What I achieve when my purpose is fulfilled is not the determinate object I select; I achieve rather the fulfillment, the objectification, of my act of selection. I stand in a meaningful relationship with my object. It is the correspondence, not of a purposive, selective idea to a non-purposive object, but of a not yet completely realized internal meaning to a completely realized one. The implicit meaning of our chosen object becomes explicit. Royce stands firmly, then, with the existentialists and other American philosophers in their rejection of Cartesian dualism, which places a physical object, a mere thing, over against a mental subject, which then has to give human meaning to this mere thing in order for it to be known. Objects can initially appear within our world only as the terminus of some interest. Only when that interest is neutralized or displaced does the object become a mere thing to which meaning must be arbitrarily assigned.

Husserl claimed to be the first to give heed to the way attention alters our consciousness of objects. But fifteen years earlier, Royce discussed how attention selects only a few from the numerous impressions impinging on our sensibilities, letting many slip through our consciousness without being retained or having an effect. Attention, argues Royce, modifies the quality of our impressions— their intensity, for example—and even qualitatively alters our apprehension of the truth. Royce writes: "Attention seems to defeat, in part, its own object. Bringing something into fields of knowledge seems to be a modifying, if not a transforming, process."[3] Knowledge is not merely observation in the sense of traditional empiricism but participation (transactional); it means having an understanding of "being" and being able to relate oneself effectively to being.

Royce's notion of the selective aspects of consciousness not only anticipated Husserl's analysis, but seems also to be an anticipation of Heidegger's notion of the primordiality of Care. Heidegger speaks of man as concerned about his being-in-the world and argues that man seeks to discover the meaning of the things he encounters in order to discover the meaning of his own life. Further, in his insistence on the construction of the future and the use of the past, Royce anticipates Heidegger's notion of the present as a field of activity, continually dynamic in character, and, when authentic, continually constructed out of futural possibility and continually involving selective synthesis with the retrieved past.[4]

But in the emphasis on man as active agent in the knowing process rather than as passive subject, neither Heidegger nor Royce intends to deny the reality of the world. This obviously is so crucial an issue in metaphysics that it must be explored. It is clear that, for Royce, man's encounter with the world is *not* just an encounter with himself. Man encounters a real world. In Heidegger's terminology, although we make the revelation of being possible, *something does reveal itself.* The objects of consciousness must not be confused with the consciousness of objects.

Thus, although truth, for Royce, is complete determination, and the real is *"the complete embodiment in individual form and in final fulfillment of the internal meaning of finite ideas"* (WI I 339), he makes it quite clear that the judger never really *has* Truth, Reality, and Object *qua* Object. At this point, Royce may very well depart from Husserl, who often seems to absorb all into consciousness and who views the phenomenon experienced as fully immanent to consciousness. Royce is clear that internal meaning and external experience fail to give us determinate individualization, the individual fact. Royce writes: *"Neither do our internal meanings ever present to us, nor yet do our external experiences ever produce before us, for our inspection, an object whose individuality we ever really know as such.* Neither internal meanings nor external meanings, in their isolation, are in the least adequate to embody individuality" (WI I 292). This means that the real is always beyond our grasp. "The Real, then, is . . . that which is *immediately beyond* the whole of our series of possible efforts to bring, by any process of finite experience and of merely general conception, our own internal meaning to a complete determination" (WI I 299). Reality, then, for Royce, is a regulative idea of all our judging. It stands for the fact that the internal meaning of a finite subject chooses to know an object beyond its present self-consciousness, which is the external meaning. The judging person "believes that he knows some fact beyond his present consciousness. This involves, as we have seen, the assertion that he believes himself to stand in an actual relationship to the fact yonder, that were it in, instead of out of, his present consciousness, he would recognize it both as the object meant by his present thought, and also in agreement therewith. . . ."[5] The thinking subject selects his object, and thus the internal meaning determines its objects; but this internal meaning is also determined in part by the object, for the thinking subject is not the object and does not completely possess the object. To say that the object sought is the will determinately embodied is not to say that the individual's private will creates the external world.

The notion of "external meaning" refers to our intention to refer beyond ourselves, to our *belief* that we do know and *have* the object as it really is. But, in fact, the object *qua* object is more than we intend and know. Thus, Royce declares: "Neither God nor man faces any fact that has not about it something of the immediacy of a sense datum."[6]

In thus emphasizing the view that reality is determinate and individual, and that human knowledge and experience cannot capture this individuality, Royce focuses on both the transcendence of reality to human consciousness and the relativity and partiality of all human constructions. Because of this focus Royce would probably depart from Husserl and concur with Merleau-Ponty's judgment that "The most important lesson which the reduction teaches us is the impossibility of a complete reduction."[7] Further, because, for Royce, truth is, not a static notion, but a term for an unlimitedly fulfilling process, he clearly stands in the pragmatic tradition established by C. S. Peirce.

Thus, as for Peirce, the "sociality" of human knowledge was a lifelong Roycean conviction. Early in his career Royce recognized the insight of Husserl in *The Crisis*: namely, not only is the mathematization of nature a point of view on the world, with its own historical roots, but indeed it is one that permeates our more immediate experiences of reality—it becomes an integral part of our "life-world." In his *Spirit of Modern Philosophy* he described in detail the world of science, which he calls the World of Description. It is the public, describable world and as such must have two characteristics: (1) reproducibility and permanence, and (2) susceptibility to being categorized. Thus, three central postulates of science are the permanence of substance, the uniformity of nature, and the principle of causation. However, for Royce, these three postulates are not self-evident truths but ideas that are socially very useful. It is our social interests and their demonstrable utility that give the authority to these postulates. He writes: "Hence, in the history of mankind, the discovery of seemingly unvarying laws of Nature has been *the condition for the organization of definite customs*. And just because nature has thus come to be conceived as the socially significant tool, *that aspect of Nature which suggests such unvarying laws has come to be looked upon as the most characteristic of the aspects of the physical world*" (WI II 193).

My point is that Royce, Husserl, and Heidegger can be shown to share a common ground in holding that the objective world, as scientifically described, is not the primordial world of experience but a modification of that world which reflects highly specialized human interests. Science is a humanly important quest. Indeed, Royce holds that all knowledge of the external world has been and is intimately tied to and dependent upon the social context. The social context is crucial first of all for the very distinction between inner and outer. The outer is that to which all observers can refer and on which they can agree. It is essentially "the world whose presence can only be indicated to you by your definable, communicable experience."[8] Because the outer world is public and sharable and thus definite, a characteristic like spatial definiteness is considered important to externality. Royce writes: "Therefore, as only the definably localizable in space can be independently verified and agreed upon by a number of socially communicating beings, and as only what all can agree upon can stand the social test of externality, the principle that what is for all must, if in space at all, occupy a definite place of size and boundaries, becomes a relatively *apriori* principle for all the things of the verifiable external world."[9]

Royce also sees the social grounding of physical knowledge verified in the fact that more reliability is granted to the data of sight and touch than to the data of the other senses. These data and these qualities are the ones most open to social confirmation. Royce writes:

> I can see you touching an object. I can even, in the ordinary social sense, be said, by virtue of familiar interpretations, to see you looking at an object. And, just so, if we grasp a pole or a rope together, or lift a weight together, I feel your grasp of the object, just as truly as I feel the object. But in no corresponding sense can I taste your tasting of an object, nor can I smell your smelling of an object; while I can both see and touch processes which I interpret as your seeing and touching of the object [WI II 179].

Husserl, too, speaks of participating in the manner in which others perceive things. He calls this the functional community of one perception, and by sharing in such a community the self is to get outside of itself.

But there is a crucial difference between Husserl and Royce on this issue of the external, outer, public world. For Royce, objectivity is intersubjectivity: belief in my fellow-men is prior to belief in nature. Man is being-with-others, and man can recognize others like himself in the world and enter into relations with them because his own being is disclosed to him as being-*with*. Here Royce stands firmly with the existentialists who hold that self-relatedness is one of the basic structures of human existence. Husserl, on the other hand, begins with an inarticulate, isolated "I" and attempts to reach others *via* empathy—an attempt which clearly fails. Further, for Royce, not only is our understanding of nature dependent upon the social context; self-knowledge also depends on a social context. My own self as THIS individual comes into view only as I find myself in some contrasting relationship involving another who listens to me, who contradicts me, or who interrupts me and who approves or disapproves of what I have done. Royce writes:

> I affirm that our empirical self-consciousness, from moment to moment, depends upon a series of contrast-effects, whose psychological origin lies in our literal social life, and whose continuance in our present conscious life, whenever we are alone, is due to habit, to our memory of literal social relations, and to an imaginative idealization of these relations [WI II 260].

> [T]ake all this other experience out of my conception, and forthwith I lose all means of becoming conscious of my experience as mind, of knowing what I mean either by my whole individuality or by my present ego.[10]

Furthermore, other selves add to my fragmentary life; without them I would be incomplete.

> They answer our questions; they tell us news; they make comments; they pass judgments; they express novel combinations of feelings; they relate to us stories; they argue with us, and take counsel with us. . . . [O]ur fellows furnish us the constantly needed supplement to our own fragmentary meanings. Hence, since Reality is through and through what completes our incompleteness, our fellows are indeed real [WI II 171–72].

Royce places great stress on the role of negativity and the *no-consciousness* in the development of self-knowledge. Here his affinities with existentialism are again apparent. Thus, Sartre distinguishes being-in-itself (en soi), undifferentiated self-identity, from being-for-itself (être-pour-soi), the being that distinguishes and differentiates, which is fundamentally negative.

Because of this need to distinguish and differentiate, Sartre, for example, sees that man is always confronted with the task of having to be himself. Man's life is a task, a project; he confronts himself always as engaged in projects to realize himself in the future. Man must accept the facticity of experience: namely, that he is in the world already—thrown into existence—but that now he must do something about it. He must decide how he is going to live in the world. For Sartre he must even create his own values and live by them. For Heidegger there is resoluteness, full recognition and acceptance of the past, of the historical context that is indeed beyond control, together with the freedom of new possibility within the past for the active and imaginative construction of an emerging future. Royce, we recall, also speaks of creating the past out of the present for the future. And in his "Berkeley Lectures on Logic" he writes: "this is a phenomenon of knowledge, namely, that whenever we know, we always know by and through comparison with some former knowledge. . . . Cognition is invariably Recognition."[11] To know is to relate new and always partial truths to our previous fund of knowledge.

Not only is Royce related to the existentialists in terms of their emphasis on negation and on creating the future out of the past, but his understanding of selfhood bears striking affinities to the existentialist analyses of Sartre and Heidegger. First of all, if one recalls Royce's analysis of individuality in terms of love, one comes close to Heidegger's notion of man as the being who "cares." Royce writes, "the principle of Individuation, in us, as in reality, is identical with the principle that has sometimes been called Will, and sometimes Love. Our human love is a good name for what first individuates for us our universe of known objects."[12] Love is a form of exclusive interest, which we devote to a being or an object. The love we have for it makes us declare it unique, of its kind, irreplaceable, and without any possible equivalent. Royce uses the example of a child whose toy soldier is broken and who is not consoled by the promise of another similar or better toy. This demonstrates, says Royce, that the root of love is a spontaneous affirmation: namely, "There shall be no other." Royce also sees individuality as a matter of will, of a plan of action. Ego is not given from the outside; ego must confer unity on itself. Individuality can be defined only in terms of willed or chosen order. "The true or metaphysically real Ego of a man . . . is simply the totality of his experience *in so far as* he consciously views this experience as, in its meaning, the struggling but never completed expression of his coherent plan in life, the changing but never completed partial embodiment of his one ideal."[13]

To be somebody is to have a plan, to give unity to your aims, to intend something definite by your life, that is, to set before yourself one overriding ideal. The task of an individual is to be an individual and unique self in contrast both to other selves and to the Absolute. It is to be a Self who is nobody else just precisely insofar as my life has this purpose and no other. In other words, it is not a question of having; but of *being*, i.e., of *making ourselves*. "*By this meaning of my life-plan, by this possession of an ideal, by this intent always to remain another than my fellows despite my divinely planned unity with them,—by this, and not by the possession of any Soul-Substance, I am defined and created a self*" (WI II 276).

Individuality is a free act of will. In a sense, then, individuals add a teleology of their own to the overall teleology of the universe, for they can deliberately will their own ends and aim at a harmony—of ends. For the individual to be a reality, an *act* is required or, in Roycean terms, a *free* fact. "Whatever is unique, is as such not causally explicable. The individual as such is never the mere result of law" (WI I 467).

Royce, like Sartre and Heidegger, also sees the self in terms of temporality, history, and future. For him, the self is a complex unity of life extended over a temporal interval and unified by a purpose that distinguishes it from all others. The self, as internal meaning seeking embodiment, traverses time. Thus, in any present we can become aware of some portion of ourselves—thoughts, hopes, feelings, plans, deeds—and in so doing, we become further aware of a past through which we have lived and of a future through which we expect to live. In The Problem of Christianity, Royce sees the "self" in terms of interpretation, which is essentially both a temporal and an historical process. "In brief," he writes, "my idea of myself is an interpretation of my hopes and my intentions as to my future."[14] In this connection, we recall the authentic historicity of Heidigger's *Dasein*; Heidegger writes:

Anticipatory resoluteness brings this Being-towards-death into authentic existence. The historizing of this resoluteness, however, is the repetition of the heritage of possibilities by handing these down to oneself in anticipation; and we have interpreted this historizing as authentic historicality. . . . The Self's resoluteness against the inconstancy of distraction, is in itself a *steadiness which has been stretched along*—the steadiness with which Dasein as fate "incorporates" into its existence birth and death and their "between", and holds them as thus "incorporated", so that in such constancy Dasein is indeed a moment of vision for what is world-historical in its current Situation.[15]

Royce, in fact, describes interpretation in terms of an achievement of a vision of a realm of conscious unity that gives one determinateness and self-control. Further, interpretation creates community, which is a unity of past, present, and future. Community, at whatever level, is basically temporal and historical. Royce writes: "[The community] . . . is essentially a product of a time-process. A community has a past and will have a future. Its more or less conscious history, real or ideal, is part of its very essence. A community requires for its existence a history and is greatly aided in its consciousness by a memory."[16] It is also interesting that the will to interpret, which brings about a community of interpretation, is a form of love, of care, of concern.

There is missing in Royce, however, the stress of Sartre and Heidegger on inauthenticity, on the danger of becoming an *en soi* or of self-forgetfulness, of surrendering self to the everyday *Dasein*, the nobody. Because of their rightful fear of collectivism, the existentialists stress the individual standing alone in the world—a lonely self-maker. For Royce, self can be achieved only in community, and community is essential, however difficult it is to achieve.

Royce attempts to achieve a community, a harmonization of many different and opposing wills, without resorting to a collectivism in which all individuals, *qua* individuals, are lost. He begins with tension, struggle, opposing forces, differences of opinion, and then seeks to mitigate the destructive consequences of these by containing them in a wider, more inclusive unity.

Further, though Royce, like Husserl and the existentialists, generally asserted the intentional, temporal, and historical nature of consciousness—the essentially human nature of consciousness and knowledge—and stressed man's encounter with reality as one of doing, of freedom, purpose, care—a responsible making of self and world in the context of a given past with others—he takes a step which Husserl and most existentialists do not take: namely, *he does not see man as sole creator of meaning and value in the world.*

For Royce, total, complete fulfillment, complete individualization, is presumably beyond our human reach, but fulfillment is achieved in the Absolute, in the self-representation system. Man's "self" is not exhausted in the present or passing existence. Royce writes:

> The world forms a Whole because it is as if the Absolute said (or, in our former terms, attentively observed) that, since the absolute system of ideas is once fulfilled in this world, "There shall be no other world but this," i.e., no other case of fulfillment; and therefore other abstractly possible fulfillments remain not genuinely possible. It is this aspect of the ultimate situation which defines the world as a whole, and which without introducing an external cause, or a mere force, does as it were colour the whole unity of the Absolute Consciousness with a new character, namely, the character of will.[17]

Intentionality, then, for Royce, is a characteristic of Being itself. In our human conscious act, we, by attention, sharply select from the field of possible objects only one and bring it into focus. In an analogous way, the Absolute, by its attention, rejects many possibilities, freely chooses its world, by its "idea"; internal meaning determines the experience (external meaning) in which it finds perfect and rational fulfillment. "The Divine Will is simply that aspect of the Absolute which is expressed in the concrete and differentiated individuality of the world."[18] Royce is asserting that just as the near future fulfills our present projected field of action, so the future fulfillment of experience in the Absolute grounds the value and meaning of temporal future experience.

Thus, though Royce is firm about the active role of man in creating meaning, world, and self, man does not do it alone. There is a transcendent ground of meaning and truth. The community, the world, has an actual interpreter encompassing all with one eternal vision and value.

I conclude with a few comments on the relevance of Royce's thought. To affirm the necessity for each man to carve out his own niche in the world is to remind man of his responsibility to resist the tendency of modern society to turn man into the "nobody." With the existentialists, Royce was concerned to point to the intentional, temporal, and historical nature of human consciousness and to man's capacity to organize his world and to see it from a human point of view. Once again, in an age in which we speak of the dangers of technology and of the mass media, we need to be reminded that man creates the world in which he lives; technology and mass media are his products and his responsibility. Man must control what he makes, not vice versa, and he must do this with *care*!

With the existentialists in their anti-Cartesianism, Royce begins with concrete-being-in-the world, and out of this initial complex he sees the self and the world arise as equiprimordial realities. With Heidegger, Royce affirms that science is essentially a social process, a humanly important quest. First, scientific research is a social process, a community endeavor. Truth is achieved through the cooperative and imaginative work of many; Einstein, for example, reflected on how he "stood upon the shoulders of many men," his work made possible only by their previous work. Because of its social nature Royce, as well as many other American philosophers, saw it as a model of "community"—the overall commitment to a common ideal and a common method. Secondly, as a human endeavor, science can never claim to have the Truth, but only to be working toward ever-broadening the horizons of human knowledge. Finally, as a human process, science should serve its creator, man, and never man science—an affirmation sorely needed in a day when the word "science" has such an "authoritative and godly" ring.

Finally, I have argued that Royce takes a step that many existentialists fail to take for fear of deadly "collectivism": namely, he affirms the fundamental role of the *community* in the achievement of authentic selfhood. Royce is perhaps the finest spokesman for the American discovery of the fundamental mutuality of the individual and the communal. In *The Problem of Christianity,*

Royce provides a powerful antidote to both existentialist and American individualism with his analysis of what constitutes a community and what it can accomplish. Communities are not mere collections of individuals like piles of rocks; rather, they constitute a set of bonds, relations, and linkages between individuals, however diverse their goals, personalities, and backgrounds. Community brings men out of isolation and into cooperative endeavor. Community is not mass collectivism, because individuals retain their identity and distinctness though they sacrifice their isolation in coming together to work for the realization of some worthwhile purpose, which could never have been realized through separate and uncoordinated endeavor.

In *The Problem of Christianity*, Royce also provides a theory of interpretation and mediation that addresses itself to a major problem of our variegated society: namely, to find ways of harmonizing conflicting claims and interests. Fundamental to this theory is the notion that we both *love* and *hate* our neighbors: whenever people are related *only in pairs*, they constitute a dangerous community precisely because they are bound to conflict. And this psychological tension, which exists at the most intimate level, foreshadows the social conflicts that stem from all the dyadic relations forced upon us by a highly organized society—buyer and seller, producer and consumer, management and labor. Further, Royce saw that these social conflicts cannot be overcome merely by the overcoming of individual-to-individual hate relations. We must ascend to another level at which individuals are taken out of themselves and have opened to them the opportunity for a higher commitment that goes beyond the love–hate relationships. What is needed is a third party, an interpreter, who is willing to interpret the parties to each other and to build a common community of understanding between them. All persons then can become committed to a higher ideal and engage in a cooperative effort. In a day when there is increasing alienation among individuals and increasing lack of communication, Royce's call to community, to interpretation, to moral commitment to community and his wrestling with community are a highly relevant message to which all of us who seek authentic individuality should return, for these are "wellsprings" from which refreshing and healing water can be drawn.

NOTES

1. "Thought Diary," *Fugitive Essays*, ed. J. Lowenberg (Cambridge: Harvard University Press, 1920), pp. 35, 31. These comments are dated April 3, 1879.

2. *The World and the Individual*, 2 vols. (New York: Macmillan, 1899, 1901; repr. New York: Dover, 1959), II 129. Hereafter referred to as WI.

3. *The Religious Aspect of Philosophy* (Boston: Houghton Mifflin, 1885), p. 314.

4. See Martin Heidegger, "The Priority of Time," in *The Human Experience of Time: The Development of Its Philosophic Meaning*, ed. Charles M. Sherover (New York: New York University Press, 1975), pp. 519–47.

5. *The Spirit of Modern Philosophy: An Essay in the Form of Lectures* (Boston: Houghton Mifflin, 1892), p. 375.

6. "A Critical Study of Reality," Unpublished Papers, Folio 81 (1897), p. 34.

7. M. Merleau-Ponty, *Phenomenology of Perception*, trans. Colin Smith (New York: Humanities Press, 1962), p. xiv.

8. "The External World and the Social Consciousness," *The Philosophical Review*, 3, No. 5 (September 1904), 520.

9. Ibid., 519.

10. *Studies of Good and Evil* (New York: Appleton, 1898), p. 215.

11. Royce Papers, Harvard Archives, Vol. 58, Lec. II, 30.

12. *The Conception of God* (New York: Macmillan, 1897), p. 259.

13. Ibid., p. 291.

14. *The Problem of Christianity*, 2 vols. (New York: Macmillan, 1913; repr. Chicago: The University of Chicago Press, 1968), II 243.

15. *Being and Time*, trans. John Macquarrie and Edward Robinson (New York and Evanston: Harper & Row, 1962), p. 442.

16. *Problem of Christianity*, II 324–25.

17. *Conception of God*, p. 212.

18. Ibid., p. 202.

10

The Transcendence
of Materialism and Idealism
in American Thought

JOHN LACHS
Vanderbilt University

WHAT IS UNIQUE about American philosophy? Is there anything beyond the nationality of the authors that justifies us in grouping a broad range of philosophical books as works of "American philosophy"? We shy away from talking about Afghanistani philosophy, Armenian philosophy, and even Spanish philosophy. Many would argue that, similarly, it is appropriate to talk of philosophy in America or philosophy done by Americans, but not of philosophy that is in any important way American in character.

Yet we do not hesitate to speak of German philosophy, and when we do our minds are not empty. We understand in some general but important way what would be "Germanic" in philosophy, just as we understand what is usually meant by Catholic philosophy or medieval philosophy or even Platonic thought. It would, for instance, be clearly Platonic to look for *the essence* of Catholic philosophy or of American thought. And whatever American thought may be, it is clearly not Platonic. So let me begin with the reassurance that I am not interested in finding the one generic feature all American philosophy has that is not shared by anything else. The search for such essences is the work of tight, tidy minds that welcome conceptual games and invite frustration by reality.

The special character of American philosophy is, like all real things, a messy and difficult affair. There is a complex set of features many of which are shared by a goodly number of the works in American thought. The features are there to differing extents in different philosophers. Some may be altogether absent in one or another, yet that does not take away from the American character of the work any more than the failure to have a four-chambered heart destroys the mammalian character of an animal. For no *one* feature is unique to American thought; none is a necessary and sufficient condition of its Americanness. It is the configuration of the characteristics, the total shape of the philosophy that makes it usefully classifiable as American. This is what I suspect Santayana meant when he spoke of the smell of philosophies.

I wish to focus on one member of the complex set of characteristics which defines American philosophy. It is, I think, one of the more interesting ones. Rightly understood, it shows the continuity of American and Continental thought, while it distinguishes the two by the intriguing, if not radical, twist in American thought on Continental themes. It would be rash to say that this difference in continuity has been altogether overlooked. Yet it has not received the critical attention it deserves.

Perhaps the best way to focus on the feature I have in mind is by reference to a standard though ill-defined distinction in much of modern philosophy. From Lucretius or before, philosophers have proudly declared themselves to belong to one or the other of two broad groupings. Some claimed to be materialists, while others announced their allegiance to idealism. These views were frequently conceived to be not only mutually exclusive but also conjointly exhaustive. All philosophical theories were to be classified *either* as materialistic *or* as idealistic, on an "if you are not with us, you are against us" mentality. Admittedly, conceptually there is little to be said for such an exclusive disjunction, yet intermediate dualisms have tended, on the whole, to be unstable and to revert quickly to one or the other of the fundamental monistic positions.

I take materialism to be the view according to which the ultimate ingredients of reality are spatio-temporal units that exist independently of mind, ideas, or will. The specific details of the conception of matter are relatively unimportant: whether we think that the ultimate units are indivisible atoms or charges of energy or minute vortices is irrelevant so long as we all agree that they are to be found in a single, continuous space, arrange themselves in a single, continuous time, and operate as a total system governed by autonomous laws.

I take idealism to be the view according to which the ultimate constituents of existence are ideas or minds or expressions of will or fragments of consciousness or moments of sentience. It is not that idealists deny the existence of a space–time world with all its apparently independent and apparently insensate furniture. But they are convinced a closer examination of this world shows the surprising result that what seems lifeless in fact quivers with sensitivity or, at least, that the spatial world is an eternally dependent product of creative minds.

It is evidently impossible to catch all the conceptual subtleties that have been developed in 2,500 years of defending the two positions. There are foolishly strong versions of materialism, such as that of Lucretius, who maintains that only atoms exist and then finds himself having to admit the reality of the empty space in which they move. And there are utterly implausible versions of idealism, such as that of Leibniz, according to whom each finite physical shape hides an infinite set of dull, minuscule minds. There are also methodologically cagey, weaker versions of each view. Thus some materialists maintain simply that the ultimate ingredients of the world are more like the unconscious, purely spatial parts of our bodies than anything else. By contrast, sophisticated and careful idealists asseverate that the ultimate units of existence are more like our experienced sensings, cognizings, or desirings than anything else. I do not hesitate to lump all these views together because, however bold or however cautious, they all profess to give us information about the ultimate nature of reality, they all claim that it is of one sort and not another, and they all agree that, at least on the surface of it, the human body paradigmatically belongs in one sphere and the human mind in another.

The important thing about both materialism and idealism is that, however phrased or modulated, they are efforts on the part of theoretical reason to understand the world. Their very rivalry presupposes their agreement on the starting point, on the task and on the method of philosophy: both claim that a purely cognitive grasp of the world is possible and necessary.

The moment we put the matter in this way, we are reminded of Kant's revolution in philosophy. The point of that radical reversal is not so much what it is frequently conceived to be—viz., the assignment of a central role to human cognitive faculties in the creation of reality—as the ultimate shift away from the primacy of theoretical reason. I suspect that Kant himself did not fully grasp the revolutionary significance of placing human creative activity at the center of reality. This, at least, is suggested by his disavowal of Fichte's philosophy, in which many of the radical consequences of Kant's departure are boldly displayed.

The primacy of practical reason, of *action* in the end, permits the development of a novel metaphysics, which undercuts the distinctions and categories of much earlier thought. It is remarkable that it took generations to draw the full implications of an activity-centered metaphysics. Fichte himself, even though he bravely declared that "in the beginning was the deed," failed to see that that insight, if adequately developed, would render obsolete the previous metaphysical distinction between materialism and idealism. It was this failure that made it possible for him to declare himself a "critical idealist" and to maintain that each philosopher belonged to one or the other of these warring camps.[1] He attempted to deduce all of reality from a primordial activity. But he failed to see that such a predeterminate burst of energy can be neither physical nor mental and that therefore his attempt to distinguish his own view from the similarly conceived but presumably materialistic theory of Spinoza was altogether without hope and merit.

The movement from the metaphysics of ultimate ingredients to a metaphysics of activity was essentially completed in the work of Fichte. Yet, amazingly enough, the self-understanding of the new philosophy was altogether inadequate, making the full development of its consequences impossible. Fichte still drew a sharp distinction between idealism and the conviction of the people he called "dogmatists." Idealists, he thought, attempted to explain human experience from the starting point of a self-like, free activity. Dogmatists, by contrast, undertook the same task by reference to independently existing, inanimate things. There were then, as there are today, philosophers of both kinds. But what Fichte overlooked was the way in which insistence on the primacy of the act destroyed the contrast between the two views and made room for the development of a new sort of philosophy.

The metaphysics of activity was present also in Hegel and in Marx, and it is their agreement on the primacy of creative act that makes the usual contrast drawn between them as idealist and materialist, respectively, so difficult to understand. This contrast is frequently conceived in the philosophically feeble-minded fashion popularized by Engels. "Those who asserted the primacy of spirit to nature and, therefore, in the last instance, assume world creation in some form or another . . . comprised the camp of idealism," he says. "The others, who regarded nature as primary, belong to the various schools of materialism."[2] Engels specifically focuses on Hegel in this context and characterizes the contrast between him and Marx, who supposedly "stood him on his head," as the simple one that the former believed thought creates nature while the latter denied this.

Engels' idea is, of course, a simplistic misreading of both Hegel and Marx. In fact, the fundamental metaphysical contrast between them is vastly more subtle and not at all easily drawn. If Lukács is right that the primary category of Marxism is that of totality, perhaps there is no such difference at all. Nevertheless, some maintain that there is one centered in a disagreement as to the *sort* of activity supposed primary. For Marx believed, and Hegel presumably denied, that the economically productive activities of the human race enjoy a special primacy in human life and that only by studying them can we understand the course of history. This view helpfully focuses on the fact that Marx was not interested in the ultimate constituents of the universe; his efforts were concentrated on understanding the human world, viz., the world that human activity creates. Yet why should insistence on the primacy of economic relations render him a "materialist"? It is futile to argue for this by reference to the fact that economic activities always involve the physical interaction of man and his environment. There is indeed an element of crude physicality in growing food and in eating, but Marx believed that in the end thinking was no less physical than mastication. And he also thought that social and legal relations which are, in this rudimentary sense, not physical were no less real and causally efficacious than the production and distribution of goods.

If there is a contrast between Marx and Hegel, it must be conceived as a function of divergent views of the nature of man. The primacy of "material" production in Marx can be justified only by a special theory of primary human needs which focus human energies on their satisfaction. Yet even this contrast tends to fade, if we take seriously the hints in the young Marx that the source of our world is the species-being, species-powers, or species-activity of the race. For these relatively undeveloped ideas of Marx take us back to the metaphysics of activity in its purest form. An indeterminate, all-creative, and primordial activity is then seen to beget a determinate, multi-faceted world. The generation occurs with a necessity based on the freedom of the initial act; the act and its infinitely varied products stand in the relation of dialectical identity. Viewed in this light, the differences in detail and emphasis between Marx and Hegel do not disappear. But there emerges an overwhelming similarity in their patterns of thought, and we can see how both of them transcend the materialist–idealist dichotomy.

I have given but the barest sketch of the tradition of activity-metaphysics from which a fundamental trait of American philosophy hails. The primacy of action is at once the primacy of will and is paralleled in ontological theory by the primacy of the concept of activity. One way to put the matter is by saying that, for such a metaphysics, substance itself is an ultimate outcome of activity. This does not mean that activity is analyzed into substantial constituents or substance into portions of activity. The entire idea of analysis into elements is rejected, to be supplanted by a study of the dynamics by which creative activity fashions a real world. Engels' notion of creation by thought or matter is also transcended; the starting point of reality is taken to be an activity that is neutral with respect to such later or special determinations as materiality and mentality.

In William James and even in Josiah Royce there is a fundamental insistence on creative activity which derives directly from this metaphysical heritage. The view is of course pre-eminently clear in John Dewey. His entire philosophy presupposes the centrality of human purposive activity in the reconstruction of the world. Primary experience itself is a primordial activity in which subject and object, matter and mind, agent, action and deed, individual and society are not distinguished. His emphasis on human desires and purposes as undergirding our life is but his version of the thesis of the primacy of will. "Man," he says, "is the tool of tools," suggesting that we are essentially creatures of interactive transformation. And we are creatures of it in two important senses: first, in that we are beings who engage in such continued activity, and, second, in that we ourselves are products of our own activity and the activity of others. This fundamental activity-emphasis in Dewey is, in effect, the hallmark of his thought. Admittedly, he shies away from high metaphysics. Yet the philosophical task he sets himself is clearly metaphysical: he attempts to develop a general characterization of human experience in terms primarily of the purposes we have and the activities in which we engage.

Dewey was perhaps the first philosopher who understood that such a metaphysics of activity undercuts the distinction between materialists and idealists. Not all in the American tradition of philosophizing have reached this level of self-understanding. Some have altogether misread their alignment. A prime example of such a philosopher is George Santayana, who, contrary to popular opinion, fits squarely in the American tradition. He thought that he was in fact a materialist, "perhaps the only one living." What could have occasioned as shrewd a thinker as Santayana to misunderstand his own philosophy? This is a difficult matter to explain, and it may be instructive for my greater purpose to explore it in detail. If I can show that materialism is transcended even in Santayana, I will have gone a long way toward demonstrating my thesis.

Santayana draws a sharp contrast from the first between consciousness or spirit, consisting of what he calls intuitions, and the material world. Intuition, he thinks, is cognitive and synthetic. It is a unitary act focused upon a more or less complex object. He views unity as somehow central to consciousness: each intuition is unified as act and presents a unitary vista. By contrast, the material realm is necessarily granular; it is spread out through space and diversified in time. The reasons why Santayana feels compelled to draw this sharp distinction between body and mind are not of any significance to us here. We must begin with the fact that such a contrast looms large in his thought.

The moment the distinction is introduced, Santayana faces the task of giving an account of the two realms. His description of consciousness is specific, sensitive, and successful. Part of the reason for this success is the fact that instead of the futile task of describing the nature or constituents of mind, he focuses on the description of spirit's activities. He gives an eloquent account of the work of mind in art and religion, in social customs and in natural science. Even the later accounts of consciousness, such as those in *The Realm of Spirit* and in *The Idea of Christ in the Gospels*, focus on the work of mind in purified experience and in symbolic structures, with bold disregard for his self-confessed view of the impotence of consciousness.

The shift from the analysis of mind to description of its activities and products is natural for Santayana. Even on his own account, there is nothing in the act of intuition, which is the foundational and the only unqualifiedly mental thing, to describe. It is but an activity in Aristotle's sense, an evanescent union of doing and deed. By nature it is, in G. E. Moore's famous phrase, diaphanous: as with light or a pane of window glass, when we look at it, we see only what it reveals. To describe it to any extent, therefore, is to describe its objects or products, the vistas of imaged reality it reveals. We understand mind, then, only by developing a phenomenology of the world it lights up or creates.

By contrast with his confidence in the sphere of spirit, Santayana approaches his account of matter with caution and diffidence. He is quick to limit the task of the natural philosopher to identifying ontological realms. The nature of matter is something for scientists to determine, he insists again and again. Yet he himself knows that this easy disclaimer is simply not enough. If philosophers are to distinguish matter from other sorts of beings, they must have some specific notion of what it is. Perhaps they can afford to remain ignorant of the subtler laws of its behavior, but they cannot leave matter as a mere cipher or as the referent of a purely designative name.

With characteristic stubbornness, Santayana's first tendency is, not to develop a theory of the nature of matter, but to try to explain why we can know nothing of it. According to this account, matter is the formless other of essence. It is simply that which is responsible for the introduction of external relations, for existence, for the instantiation of any essence. This faceless force, frequently declared by Santayana to be a surd, can have no form. Any essence of it would still be only an unexemplified form intrinsically; even *that* form would have to be instantiated by something beyond itself, by some formless, natureless power. In one place, Santayana compares matter as it picks essences for instantiation with the shapeless wind that whips sand into a howling vortex.

Yet this account will obviously not do for at least two reasons. First of all, it is unintelligible how the formless or the natureless can be thought. Yet Santayana is clearly thinking it. The affair is best put in terms of a dilemma. If matter is natureless, it cannot be thought. And if it cannot be thought, it can be no part of a philosophy. If, however, matter can be thought, it is not without form after all. And if so, it is neither radically distinct from essence nor unknowable.

The second reason why this account fails to satisfy is that it makes a mockery of Santayana's own account of his materialism. He does not claim to be a materialist in the simple-minded Lucretian sense of maintaining the sole reality or sole existence of matter. He gladly admits the *existence* of both matter and mind and the *reality* of no less than four factors, namely, matter, mind, essence, and truth. At a dramatic juncture in *The Realm of Matter* he announces that his materialism amounts merely to the claim that material reality alone has creative or generative power. Yet the force of this assertion is destroyed the moment we add to it the confession that this single source of generative power is, in the end, unknowable. There are philosophers who maintain that God is the ultimate or immediate source of all causation while they piously add that inquiries into God's nature reveal only contradictions, for He outstrips the power of our minds. How are we to distinguish such a view from Santayana's "materialism"? Admittedly, to call such ultimate unintelligible power "God" or "Providence" is unjustified and is but the expression of the hope or optimism of these philosophers. But is it any less unjustified to call the faceless power "uncaring matter"? This may well be no more than the expression of Santayana's pessimism about our place in nature and our ultimate prospects in the world. If we follow out the implications of this move, the difference between materialism and theism becomes but a difference in our attitude toward the unintelligible source of our being. What we then have is not ontological views, but expressions of our unjustified faith.

There are few philosophical problems about which Santayana is as ambivalent as he is about the nature of matter. He appears to have struggled with the problem over a span of sixty years, even though most of his changes of thought and reversals are hidden by a confident façade. He gives the appearance of having but one view about matter; in reality, however, a careful reading of the texts suggests three or four divergent and incompatible approaches. Santayana clearly sensed that leaving matter as an unintelligible, unthinkable surd is simply inadequate. The sense that he must do better and say more is surely what underlies the systematic confusion that exists in *The Realm of Matter* and elsewhere between the notions of matter and of substance.

There is a perfectly obvious distinction between these two concepts in Santayana's thought, a distinction echoing in some important ways Aristotle's original ideas on the subject. Substance consists of both matter and form: for Santayana, it is an ontological hybrid constituted of a "parcel" of creative energy and some essence harnessed to give it specificity. Essences do not exist on their own and even matter is only a necessary condition of the possibility of existence. The two combined form individual substances or enduring existents. In a more extended sense, Santayana allows that there is but one substance and that is the sum total of the universe. The form of this substance is the staggeringly complex one that is displayed little by little in the total history of the world.

Given Santayana's contrast between intuition and the external world, it is easy to see why he can comfortably slide from matter to substance without even noticing the shift. For the world of substance is what we normally call the physical world. It has a reality that appears independent of our will and serves as the medium in which we live and in which our fortunes are made. If anything is "material," tables and dogs and fried liver with onions are, so if we want to study "matter," it is these things we must analyze. Yet these substances or modes of material substance are not "matter" in the technical, ontological sense in which Santayana uses the term. Matter stands related to them not very differently from the way in which Spinoza's *natura naturans* is related to elements of his *natura naturata*: such physical things are the products of the creative activity of an indeterminate, infinitely fertile force. If we think of matter, therefore, as indeterminately infinite activity, we can think of the entirety of the world-substance as the infinitely determinate product of this act. Santayana himself approximates this language at the end of *The Realm of Spirit*, where he calls matter the self-actualizing indefinite potentiality of all things and says that in existence the "infinity of essence is determined to a particular complex . . . of forms."

It is interesting to note that this shift from the attempt to describe simple, unitary, faceless matter to giving an account of its works parallels Santayana's move, noted earlier, from describing the act of intuition to giving a phenomenology of the works of spirit. This change is perfectly evident by the second chapter of *The Realm of Matter*. There Santayana sets himself the task of explicating the indispensable properties of substance. He proceeds under the assumption that he is detailing the generic features of the physical world, as these may appear to an animal engaged in the pursuit of its own purposes. Viewed in this light, it turns out that substance is diversified in space and time; its units, though unevenly distributed, compose a single field. The field is continuous with our bodies; it is, in fact, nothing but the dynamic domain in which we act and are affected, in which we move, seek, and respond. This idea is expressed by Santayana again and again throughout the volume, but nowhere as eloquently as when he says that substance is universal food. He means by this that the real world is a sphere of perpetual interaction which both presupposes and takes the primary form of the continued incorporation of agents into one another.

"There is no occasion for positing any substance save as an agent in the field of action," Santayana declares. Substance itself is but the dynamic continuum in which we live. The primary reality, therefore, is not a thing or a set of things, nor even a process or set of processes with some ontologically definite nature. It is, instead, the actions in which we and others engage. Whatever things there may be acquire significance and reality for us only as agents whose actions might affect us. The field itself is not a container in which transactions occur; to call it a single arena is but a summary way of describing the continuity that exists between all the beings that act and react.

Santayana is quite explicit in maintaining that there is nothing to be known about the real world beyond what our doings and sufferings reveal. What sense does it make to call this dynamic world "material"? Analysis of it reveals nothing but change, action, motion, energy. This is a world in which desires and purposes ride supreme, in which our psyches live only by the selective rejection or incorporation of alien beings and alien goods. The primary categories here must be purpose and action, not matter and mind. That everything belongs in a single sphere of interaction is no justification for calling that sphere material or mental. That action occurs in space and time is once again inadequate to show its materiality. On the contrary, Santayana himself insists that space and time are but properties of action or categories derivative from the primary one of activity.

I suspect that what happened at this stage in Santayana's philosophy is that the notion of the causally active has been collapsed with or has taken the place of the concept of the material. And as if to adduce evidence for this identification, Santayana again and again reminds us that the mental, the immaterial, is at once also the causally impotent. Epiphenomenalism thus becomes an analytic consequence of this new version of his "materialist" view.

I think we have come far enough to show that, in spite of his own protestations, even Santayana transcended the materialism/idealism dichotomy. For we have seen how he moved by insensible degrees from what he declared to be an outright materialism to a view in which the notions of action and interaction hold primacy. The entire philosophy of animal faith is in reality a shift away from the traditional mind–matter conceptual framework to an activity-metaphysics whose consequences Santayana worked out only in part and whose presence in his thought he never fully recognized. He reached only the stage of suspecting the collapse or coincidence of materialism and idealism. In the eloquent last chapter of *The Realm of Matter*, he argues that in accepting all the evidence and all the distinctions presented in our daily life of action, idealists have in effect shown themselves to be but materialists in disguise. The real world in which we live, he correctly remarks, is seen no differently by the one group of philosophers than by the other; the only difference between them is that of terminology. Berkeley, for instance, simply renamed the ultimate source of brute contingency "God," and the same elaborate project of renaming may be discerned in other idealists.

In his famous review of *The Realm of Matter,* John Herman Randall retaliated against this charge of the latent materialism of idealists by accusing Santayana, the materialist, of latent idealism. This mad exchange of labels in fact reveals a deeper truth than the parties to the conflict supposed. The insight that certain materialists can be viewed as idealists and certain idealists as materialists is at once the first step toward grasping that both sides have transcended the matter–mind dichotomy and are operating with categories that are neutral with respect to it. Santayana has clearly reached this stage, even though for reasons that might have been at least partly sentimental, he clung to the label "materialist."

I leave unexplored for the moment the radical impact this reading of Santayana has on the rest of his philosophy. One thing is clear. Had Santayana himself taken his philosophy of animal faith and the primacy of action seriously, he would have laid less emphasis on essence and would have altogether eliminated his view of the impotence of mind. The discovery of essence is the only positive outcome of the skeptical phase of *Scepticism and Animal Faith.* This phase leads to the rejection of the rationalist criterion of knowledge, of subjectivism, and of the whole skeptical enterprise. It is altogether surprising that in rejecting the method of seeking certainty by reversion into the mind, Santayana did not at once also reject whatever meager results the method yields. The introduction of animal faith is a new beginning: it might have been appropriate for Santayana to make a clean sweep of it and to develop the philosophy of animal activity without a doctrine of essence encumbering it. The pure intuition of essence itself is postulated only because the skeptical reduction left Santayana with unembodied forms; if the ontology of essence were removed, mind would no longer be the impotent observer of nature Santayana supposed it to be.

I also leave unexplored the outlines of a metaphysics of activity. Part of the reason for this is that there is no single, compelling metaphysics of this sort. There is a variety of ways in which the basic ideas have been developed; some of these constitute the gems of American philosophy. The differences among the various versions of activity-metaphysics are instructive and important, but they presuppose similarities of starting point and of certain developmental patterns. This is not the time to study any of them in detail; it should be sufficient to call attention to the presence of a primary activity-orientation in much of American thought.

The stress on activity is clearly there in Santayana. This shows, in contradiction to the usual appraisal of him as a Platonic or Scholastic metaphysician, that he is much closer to American pragmatism than is normally believed. Pragmatism itself is an interesting American development of activity themes which pervade post-Kantian German metaphysics. The notions that social activity is world-creative and that human nature itself is a human product had been widely present in philosophy since Kant. But it was in pragmatist thought that the mad metaphysical excesses of this idea were first eliminated. One might say that in much of American philosophy human world-creative activity was naturalized: the focus here fell not so much on some ontologically primordial, indeterminate creative act as on the continuing, piecemeal, animal, and cultural creativity of the species. And the object of the activity was at last conceived not as an alien and hateful medium to be subjugated or overcome, but as a tractable world continuous with our life and energy.

The notion of this fundamental activity undercuts the subject–object, process–product, mind–matter, individual–society, will–intellect distinctions. Such discriminations may have their point and usefulness. But they are derivative and partial, and they command no ontological prerogatives. For much if not all American thought, philosophy begins and ends with the examination of daily human practice. This is perfectly evident in Dewey, but elements of it may be found in all major American thinkers. I have tried to show that these ideas are there in more than trace form in Santayana, who is supposed to be paradigmatically a non-American non-pragmatist. I maintain boldly, without proof here, that they are there also in Chauncey Wright, in Peirce, in James and in Royce, not even to mention Mead and Perry and C. I. Lewis. The presence of these ideas or ideas like them is one of the great enduring traits of American thought.

An adequate philosophy of human values and of daily life seems systematically to elude us. Many among us have altogether surrendered the task of speaking to the human estate and feel fulfilled if we can clarify a stray, insignificant thought. Others continue to voice worn fallacies, as if we could lay siege to the truth and by repeating falsehoods make it capitulate. Many proceed in the old ways, trying to subjectivize the world or objectivize human nature, pretending to see little replicas of their minds all over nature or patches of inanimate nature in themselves. All these false starts and frustrations can be avoided by taking social activity in nature as our starting point. The development of a philosophy upon such a foundation is not without its pitfalls. But it offers our best chance for understanding human nature and human society.

In the American philosophical tradition we have ready at hand the starting point, many of the tools, and the proper aim of a full philosophy of life. A creative rediscovery of this tradition, along with its further development, would meet our intellectual needs. An adequate philosophy of life would, in turn, serve not only to enhance our understanding but also to guide our practice. To take human activity as our starting point, therefore, is in the end to render that activity more intelligent, more fulfilling, and more humane.

NOTES

1. *The Science of Knowledge*, edd. and trans. P. Heath and J. Lachs (Cambridge: Cambridge University Press, 1982), pp. 9ff.
2. *Ludwig Feuerbach* (New York: International, 1941), p. 21.

11

C. I. Lewis
and the Pragmatic Tradition
in American Philosophy

SANDRA B. ROSENTHAL
Loyola University, New Orleans

THE HISTORICAL PATH leading to the present condition of American pragmatism is not irrelevant to what is probably the central issue in Lewis scholarship today. Pragmatism is, of course, the philosophical movement that is most distinctively American. Yet the distinctively American flavor of pragmatism has been the very factor that has tarnished its respectability in many philosophical circles. The language of American practicalism, in which its philosophic ideas have frequently been couched, has too often hidden from view the depth and breadth of its insights as a response to enduring and deep-rooted philosophic problems. The systematic import of pragmatism has been further hidden from view by the fact that neither the founders of pragmatism nor their critics were in agreement concerning either the origins or the doctrines of pragmatism. Thus, there was held to be not one "pragmatism" but many pragmatisms embodying various doctrines and ideas.[1] Further, though there was a variety of doctrines and ideas, such variety was seen as quite limited in scope. Discussions of pragmatism usually centered mainly on problems of meaning, problems of truth, and problems of method, while other vital philosophic issues discussed by the pragmatists were seen as extraneous to, at times contradictory of, their pragmatic assertions. Gradually, amid the confusions of the meaning and import of pragmatism, interest in it began to wane, and the position came to be viewed as outmoded.

Indeed, it is perhaps symptomatic of the status given to pragmatism within the philosophic community in the not too distant past that the author of two major books on the pragmatic movement thought it necessary "in these days when pragmatism is unfashionable" to justify his putting it "in the company of the great philosophies of the past." [2] As he goes on to observe in offering such a justification:

> In matters of intelligence and art, fashions are less to be trusted than feared. Few virtues and many vices may be fashionable. One difference between good and bad philosophic thought is that the former has a way of enduring in pertinence and effect despite fashions, while the latter, if not fashionable, is nothing. Pragmatism, I think, has achieved permanence and has a future, though as a suggestive body of ideas rather than as a school of thought.[3]

The assessment of the philosophic role of pragmatism, expressed in the last phrase of the above quotation, is an accurate statement of the status to which pragmatism has been relegated in the past and explains, to some extent, the recurring role that has been foisted upon it throughout its philosophic history. That role has been, by and large, to serve as the bearer of an unsystematic welter of philosophic insights from which varying movements could draw in showing that the pragmatists, in their more sensible or more philosophical moments, were really idealists or realists or logical positivists or language analysts, or, most recently, budding phenomenologists.

Yet, though the statement is an accurate reflection of the role relegated to pragmatism in the not too distant past, it is perhaps a bit premature concerning the future. Pragmatism in this country bloomed, grew old, and was laid to rest before it had the opportunity to come to full fruition. It is, however, in more recent times, showing signs of new and vigorous life. The title of the April, 1973 issue of the *Monist*, "Pragmatism Reconsidered," well portended the tenor of much pragmatic scholarship during the ensuing years. Pragmatism is indeed undergoing a philosophic reconsideration. What is slowly but surely being laid bare in the literature today is a unique philosophic complexity and richness that has just begun to assert its real philosophic worth. Thus, though pragmatism has been identified with the American scene since its birth, it is asserting a new and invigorating force in this country and is, at this moment, standing at a crucial crossroad. It can choose that path that allows it to continue to emerge as a growing philosophic force that defies assimilation, or it can again allow itself to be dismembered and its parts—inadequate precisely because dismembered from the systematic whole that gives them life—examined within the context of assimilation to some alien movement and shown inadequate. If the first road is to be chosen, then pragmatism, in asserting the strength of its newly found vitality on the contemporary American scene, must pass from a loosely knit "body of suggestive ideas" to a united system displaying the depth and breadth adequate to present a strongly interwoven and unique response to enduring and broadly ranging philosophic issues.[4]

The outlines of this crossroad are reflected most strongly in the critical endeavors directed toward Lewis' philosophy, all of which, either implicitly or explicitly, conceptually situate Lewis' thought on one of the above two paths. And in Lewis' case, far more than in the case of the other pragmatists, the path of assimilation is chosen. In Lewis' case this path leads most directly to the framework of analytic philosophy. Lewis' writings, more than those of any other of the major American pragmatists, have been assimilated by his critics into the framework of analytic philosophy— either into the Vienna Circle type of positivism and constructionalism or into the British ordinary language analysis of post-Wittgensteinian variety.[5] Indeed, Lewis has at times been considered to be a turning point in American philosophy, to represent the beginning of that turn of American philosophy away from classical American pragmatism and toward the analytic tradition.[6] True, he is a pragmatist of sorts—a pragmatic analyst.

The position of the present essay is that Lewis' position in the history of American thought lies down another road, that he, like Peirce, James, Dewey, and Mead before him, is traveling the path that, when properly illuminated, can be seen to culminate in a comprehensive and tightly interlaced, though delicately elusive, whole that forms a unique pragmatic system. It is perhaps not an overstatement to say that the significance and endurance of Lewis' thought, and the estimate of his stature as a philosopher, hinge on the path in which he is placed. Indeed, it has been fashionable in

Lewis scholarship to present various aspects of his philosophy within the framework of the analytic tradition in some sense, and then to show that there is "something wrong" with Lewis' thought: his distinction between the analytic and synthetic is untenable; his concept of the *a priori* is empty; his construction of objectivities out of sense data does not work; his depiction of the verification of empirical beliefs is self-defeating; and on it goes.[7] And, indeed, the critics are, in a certain sense, quite right. Lewis' "analytic philosophy" is open to all sorts of reasonable objections by reasonable critics. Lewis' position yields such inadequate analytic philosophy precisely because Lewis is not an analytic philosopher. He is a pragmatist—a classical American pragmatist. And, indeed, those same key elements within his philosophy, so inadequate when viewed from the analytic perspective, when placed within the framework of classical American pragmatism and examined for their significance, both offer insights into the unity and adequacy of Lewis' own position and add significantly to the refinement of the systematic depth and breadth of the American pragmatism from which it has emerged.

There is, of course, a reason for the almost constant assimilation of Lewis' thought to the analytic framework. Lewis is perhaps the most technical of the pragmatists. Where Dewey could call upon his fellow philosophers to look less to the technical problems of technical philosophers and more to the concrete problems of mankind and society, and where James's philosophical writings could elicit assertions that he wrote philosophy like a novelist, Lewis concentrated on the technical aspects of epistemology and logic. His technically detailed Carus Lectures, published in book form as *An Analysis of Knowledge and Valuation*, stimulated much discussion, came to have much influence, and is today far and away his best-known book. Yet there is no one work that is definitive of Lewis' position, and *An Analysis of Knowledge and Valuation*, taken in isolation from *Mind and the World Order*, or from his many journal articles, or even from the context of his work in intensional logic, is again a dismembering of something the functional adequacy of which relates to a whole body of thought. Various technical aspects of Lewis' epistemology, when taken in isolation, do lend themselves to assimilation by analytic philosophy—frequently to be shown inadequate in the end. But, when placed within the context of his overall philosophic thought, and within the even larger context of the pragmatic tradition, such aspects both reflect and further develop the similar but perhaps less technically developed insights of the other classical American pragmatists. It is said that Lewis' pragmatism is more narrow than that of other pragmatists. It is more narrowly technical at its heart, but such concerns fan ever outward in Lewis' writings and provide a needed technical strength for the delicate fabric of an emerging system of American pragmatism.[8]

The following discussion will focus on the three aspects of Lewis' philosophy which have, as indicated above,[9] been considered fundamental to pragmatism from the start. They have been again and again interpreted, within Lewis' philosophy, from the framework of the analytic tradition and have been shown wanting by his critics, but, in fact, they root him firmly within the tradition of classical American pragmatism in all its emerging uniqueness and systematic complexity. These areas are: his theory of meaning, his focus on method, and his theory of truth. An adequate development of the systematic pragmatic implications emerging from these three aspects of Lewis' philosophy is, of course, beyond the limits of space available here. The following discussion can only hope to trace the outlines of such implications in an attempt to provide some understanding of the general "feel" for the spirit of American pragmatism that dominates Lewis' epistemological outlook, guides his groping thoughts in the area of related metaphysical issues, and provides the key for the systematic synthesis of the diverse strands of his thought—even in those areas of his philosophy that at first glance are impervious to the infiltrations of the spirit of American pragmatism. It is to Lewis' theory of meaning, then, that we now turn.

Lewis' theory of meaning is usually approached from the framework of either linguistic analysis or phenomenalistic reductionism, and it is then shown to be inadequate to handle the function that Lewis gives it within his philosophy. The first of these two approaches—and what is probably the most widely held approach to his position—attempts to analyze his theory of meaning exclusively at the level of language.[10] Yet Lewis stresses in many places and in many ways that meaning is not limited to language or linguistic meaning. Rather, the basic sense of meaning for

Lewis is sense meaning. He stresses that meaning "cannot be literally put into words, or exhibited by exhibiting words and the
relations of words."[11] Lewis does not consider this a required
function of language, for he holds that "Patterns of linguistic
relation can only serve as a kind of map for the location of the
empirical item meant in terms of sense experience" (AKV 140–
41). Such an inability to express meanings exactly produces the
result, recognized by Lewis, that an examination of linguistic entities can give us no exact conception of meanings and their relationships and hence of the necessary relationships among meanings on which Lewis' position so strongly relies.[12]

Here it becomes important to note that for Lewis linguistic
meaning and sense meaning are supplementary rather than alternative. They are separable in analysis rather than factually separated (AKV 133). Though language is not the most basic level
of meaning, Lewis does not deny that language is indispensable
to articulate thought. Language serves the positive function of
providing precision for our sense meanings, but only by abstracting from a meaning too concrete to be captured by words. Language, by its selective and abstractive nature, makes precise that
which "spills over" its verbal containers (AKV 403).[13] It is here
that one can see the supplementary role of linguistic meaning and
sense meaning. Linguistic meaning does allow for more precision,
but it is not self-sufficient. It can only symbolize sense meaning,
not capture it. It makes our concrete meanings not only communicable but also more precise, yet only at the price of abstracting
from the concreteness of meaning. Such separation of sense meaning and linguistic meaning serves a useful function for purposes of
analysis, for it is helpful to consider meaning in both its linguistic
and its sense aspects. Lewis, however, considers it disastrous for
epistemological theory when one makes the distinction absolute
and posits linguistic meaning as the focal point for epistemological investigations. Such a procedure, by omitting the underlying
relations of sense meanings, leads to the linguistic conventionalism
that Lewis firmly rejects. If the search for the fullness of meaning
as it functions in Lewis' philosophy is transferred to the linguistic
level, then it will indeed be unsuccessful—as so many analytic
interpreters of Lewis have been quick to point out.

It is precisely this focus on sense meaning, however, which leads to the interpretation of Lewis as putting forth a phenomenal-istic reductionism that views meanings as reducible to the sense data out of which they are built. This interpretation again misses the role of sense meaning in Lewis' philosophy, for sense meaning is not reducible to the sensory data of expe-rience. Though meaning is derivative from the sensuous, and though meanings themselves can be termed sensuous insofar as they refer to experience, meaning, even in its sensory aspect, cannot be reduced to the content of experience. The difference can best be clarified by stating that the sensory aspect of meaning provides, literally, the *"sense"* or principle or form by which hu-mans interpret and organize the sensory aspect of experience. In-deed, for Lewis, it is only within the context of such an interpretive principle that the sensory comes to awareness. An implicit sense meaning, for Lewis, is a disposition or habit by which humans in-teract with the environment, while an explicit sense meaning is a precise "inspectable" schema or criterion by which they grasp the presence of that to which a particular type of response is appro-priate, in order to gain a certain type of result.[14] In brief, sense meaning incorporates not just the data of our environment, but also our response to our environment, a response that in turn enters into the very character of the data. Sense meaning is not reducible to data as existing apart from this response. For Lewis, as for the pragmatists in general, perceptual experience emerges within the context of our habits of response to our world. Humans, for Lewis, are basically acting beings, and only through their responses to the world do meaningful data emerge. As Lewis states, a meaning is "a sort of purposive attitude."[15] This, however, brings us more precisely to the issue of the pragmatic concept of meaning as it relates to our dispositional modes of responding to our environ-ment and to our particular activities.

A disposition, for Lewis, cannot be reduced to any limited series of acts in relation to any limited number of specific data; nor can it be constituted from such a series. For Lewis the most adequate model to indicate the relationship is that of a "mathematical rule generating a number series" (AKV 110). Such a mathematical rule cannot be reduced to the number series; nor can it be con-structed out of the series, for it is necessary for the formation of the series. It is the rule for the generation of the number series with its capacity for indefinite expansion. And as for the rule for the generation of the number series, so with the disposition for the generation of particular acts of response in relation to particular types of data. Further, like a mathematical rule, such a dispositional rule of generation cannot be separated from that which it generates, for that which is generated represents an aspect of the structural order by which it is generated. In understanding the relational structure of that which is generated, we understand, to that extent, the rule which generates it. Similarly, the disposition or basis of meaning cannot, it is true, be inspected exhaustively, but it is inspectable in any aspect. That the total concrete sense meaning as a disposition or mode of responding cannot be made fully explicit, according to Lewis, is clear. Indeed, he emphasizes that a meaning is something that is determinate beyond what any number of observed occasions can assure with theoretical certainty (AKV 144). In brief, a habit or disposition is a "living meaning" that generates acts of response in relation to criteria for grasping situations in terms of which such activity is appropriate. Such a "living meaning" is inspectable in any aspect through its possible particular applications, but can never be exhaustively examined, since it can never be reduced to any series of such applications.[16] In light of this very brief overview of Lewis' theory of meaning, how relevant is it for coming to grips with the pragmatic concept of the human as an "active being"?

The concept of the human as active agent is used by pragmatism in two senses. First, it is used at the level of the human use of knowledge actively to change society or the environment. This is a level frequently intended in pragmatism. Yet this level, if erroneously taken as the sole sense of active agent, leads to the often-heard condemnation of pragmatism as overly concerned with action, as indicating an anti-theoretical attitude that makes knowing only for the sake of doing. The second, and more technically important, aspect of humans as active agents indicates the manner in which they know the world through the structures of the meanings created by their responses to their environment. Here the focus on the role of the human as active is a concern, not with what one should do with knowledge, but with what knowledge is. It is a concern with human activity or response as built into the very structure of perceptual awareness. Lewis, in his theory of sense meaning, has provided a technical tool for dealing with the latter aspect of the human as active. He has provided a precise theoretical tool for coming to grips with the pragmatic concept of meaning as embodied in our habits of responding to our world. Further, in his concept of meaning as incorporating an interactional element between humans and their environment in terms of a reciprocal relation among data, response, and anticipated results, Lewis has in fact incorporated the first aspect of the human as an active, goal-oriented being into the very heart of a technical theory of meaning. The first sense of active agent is incorporated into the very internal dynamics of the meanings by which we come to perceive our world. If ever there is a definitive rebuttal within pragmatism to the condemnation of its focus on human action as embodying an anti-theoretical over-practicalism, it is here, within Lewis' theory of sense meaning, that it may well be found. What, then, are some of the systematic implications of Lewis' dispositional theory of meaning?

First, it puts Lewis in that mainstream of pragmatism which is gradually emerging as process philosophy. Lewis' dispositional theory of meaning requires the concept of time as process. What occurs within the present awareness is not the apprehension of a discrete datum in a moment of time, but rather the time-extended experiential "feel" within the passing present of a readiness to respond to more than can ever be specified. As Lewis observes, "It is not the time-extended cognition but the chopping of it up into unextended instants which is fictitious" (AKV 330). Or, as he states elsewhere, "There is only one given, the Bergsonian real duration. . . . The absolutely given is a specious present, fading into the past and growing into the future with no genuine boundaries . . ." (MWO 58).

Second, Lewis' dispositional theory of meaning leads to a realism as opposed to nominalism, not a realism of eternal essences but a "process realism" in which there are real modes of behavior that govern what occurs. Laws cannot be understood as some shorthand for what occurs. Laws, which outrun any number of actualities are, as modes of behavior, the source of the structures emerging in what occurs. Human dispositional responses are precisely one such type of lawfulness operative within nature.[17]

It is frequently claimed, in attempting to keep pragmatism

within the limits of problems of meaning, method, and truth, that the pragmatic theory of meaning, which roots meaning in experience, makes its assertions of realism as opposed to nominalism meaningless. As the question goes, "How can any experience of what occurs provide a meaningful experiential content for the concept of unactualized possibilities, of a reality of potentialities which outruns any experienced actualities?" It is here, in Lewis' technical, pragmatic theory of meaning as dispositional, that the answer to the problem of the meaningfulness of real potentiality is to be found, for a disposition or habit as a rule of generation is something whose possibilities of determination no multitude of actually generated instances can exhaust. It is the awareness of habit as a disposition or readiness to respond to more than can be specified that gives a concrete meaning to the concept of a "process realism," of a real lawfulness that governs unactualized possibilities. Thus, the meaning of the potentiality, and hence of the real relations of which Lewis speaks and for which he is so frequently criticized, is to be found in the awareness of the actuality of habit as that which can never be exhausted by any number of exemplifications. Further, that readiness to respond to more than can ever be made explicit, which is "there" in the functioning of habit, is immediately experienced in the passing present and gives experiential content to the concept of the "more than" of objectivities which can never be exhaustively experienced, to the concept of unactualized possibilities of being experienced which pervade every grasp of the world around us and which belie any attempt at phenomenalistic reductionism.

Finally, meaning as dispositional brings a sense of real alternatives—the "could do otherwise"—into the heart of perceptual awareness and leads away from deterministic hypotheses and toward a recognition of what Lewis refers to as a "primordial sense of probable events" (AKV 320). It may be argued that such broad ranging implications seem somewhat strange for a position that focuses so much on scientific methodology. Thus, at this point it may be well to turn to the problem of methodology as espoused by pragmatism, and, more particularly, as such an espousal shapes certain key aspects of Lewis' philosophy. Indeed, a lack of understanding of the significance of the pragmatic use of the model of scientific methodology is one of the basic sources of misinterpretation not only of Lewis' philosophy but of pragmatism in general. Where it is often misinterpreted as implying within pragmatism an over concern with technology and a narrowly focused view of the human and of nature, it is, in fact, the key to the humanism and the broadly encompassing naturalism of pragmatism.

Perhaps the most crucial aspect of the cognitive situation that is found by an examination of scientific methodology is human creativity. The creation of scientific meanings requires a noetic creativity that goes beyond what is directly observed. Without such meaning structures there is no scientific world and there are no scientific objects. Further, scientists do not build their objects out of their data and then their world out of their scientific objects. Rather, their scientific data emerge as meaningful data only within the context of their scientific objects, and their scientific objects emerge as meaningful only within the context of their scientific world, a world partially dependent upon the scientist's own ability to structure a situation creatively. In brief, scientific methodology, not as a formalized deductive model, not as indicating any particular content, but as the lived experimental activity of the scientist, reveals an interactional unity between knowers or perceivers and the world they know. Thus, the focus on the model of scientific methodology itself indicates that knowledge is not "finding what is there" but creatively interacting with what is there through the bringing of meanings. And, again, such meanings cannot be understood in terms of reductionism or phenomenalism. Such meanings are not built from the data, for without the meanings there are no meaningful data. Thus, the import, within Lewis' philosophy, of the *a priori* element that runs through all experience, that element of meaning that we bring to experience through human creativity to make experience meaningful, that element of experience that is rooted, at its most basic level, in humans' bringing to experience dispositional modes of response to their environment.[18] In brief, a look at scientific methodology shows Lewis that "We cannot capture the truth of experience if we have no net to catch it in" (MWO 307). The net is, of course, provided by us.

Second, within scientific methodology, there is directed or goal-oriented activity that is guided by the possibilities of experience contained within the meaning structures that have been created.

The system of meanings both sets the context for the activity of the scientist and limits the directions which such activity takes. This aspect, again, is well reflected, at its most basic level, in the dispositional meanings that direct our responses to the environment.

Third, the adequacy of such meaning structures in grasping what is there, or in allowing what is there to reveal itself in a significant way, must be tested by consequences in experience. Only if the experiences anticipated by the possibilities of experience contained within the meaning structures are progressively fulfilled—though never completely and finally fulfilled—can truth be claimed for the assertions made. Initial feelings of assurance, initial insights, initial common assent, or any other origins of an hypothesis do not determine truth. This, of course, leads directly to the issue of truth, which is best put aside for the moment.

Finally, within scientific methodology, though the contents of an abstract scientific theory may be far removed from the qualitative aspects of lived experience, such contents are, not the found structures of some "ultimate reality," but abstractions from the richness of nature, the very possibility of which require and are founded upon the lived qualitative experience of the scientist. Scientific methodology, when properly understood, belies *by its very nature* any attempt to project the findings of science as the ultimate building blocks of reality. Thus, Lewis can allow, at the level of lived experience, that element of spontaneity which belies determinism or physiological explanation and which, in the human, allows both for that noetic creativity which makes scientific knowledge as well as common sense knowledge possible and for that freedom which grounds "the ethical" as developed by Lewis.

Lewis' understanding of scientific method prevents his falling into the trap of projecting the contents of physics as the ultimate building blocks of physical reality, and the contents of psychophysics as the ultimate building blocks of our awareness of our world. For Lewis, the reaction of humans to their environment is to be understood, not in terms of physiological responses to external stimuli, not in terms of sense data as the postulated correlate of brain states, not in terms of the reduction of our perceptions to the collection of brute data, but rather as the creative interaction of humans with their environment through purposive, goal-oriented modes of response.[19] In brief, an examination of scientific methodology itself reveals that the pervasive textures of lived experience need not be made to conform to the contents of science. If Lewis' statements are forced into the very scientism which his focus on scientific methodology leads him to reject so radically, then the setting for some form of reductionism is established, but the significance of Lewis' position has, in turn, been lost. The implications of those pervasive textures of lived experience—which need not be made to conform to the contents of science—will be discussed further in connection with one aspect of Lewis' theory of truth. It is to the general issue of truth that we will now turn.

There are three different types or aspects of truth in Lewis' philosophy, each of which is relevant for the present discussion. There is, first, what Lewis calls *a priori* truth. Such truth is formal truth; it is truth that implies a correct elaboration or drawing out of what is implicit in the meanings that we bring to experience. Such *a priori* truth cannot be affected by experience, for it is, not descriptive of what future experience may bring, but prescriptive of the way in which we will interpret or interact with future experience. Nor can such *a priori* truth be affected by linguistic convention, for, as discussed above, what is contained in a meaning is something the truth of which cannot be altered by any decision about symbols or about the use of language. Such a truth underlies language, for such a truth is the truth embodied in the consistency of the responses through which we interact with the world. The *a priori* at all levels rests upon the ability of humans to formulate meanings and to reject from classification and interpretation under these meanings any datum that does not conform to the criteria they have established.

Past pragmatists, Lewis holds, are vulnerable to the charge of capriciousness in which "they seem to put all truth at once at the mercy of experience and within the power of human decision" (MWO 266). Our meaning structures or conceptual schemes prescribe the character of reality, and any conceptual scheme has a truth that neither experience nor convention can touch—a truth that is formal, a truth that indicates that the meanings have been consistently and correctly explicated, though experience may indicate that such a context for interpreting experience is pragmatically useless (it does not work well enough) and so should be replaced by one that is more useful. Thus, contexts of interpretation are not proven false; nor does empirical truth literally change. Rather, holds Lewis, when the pragmatic factor in experience is properly located, it is seen that contexts within which any empirical truth can be determined are replaced. The truth of any empirical generalization is determined by the relationship of an interpretative context to given experience, and remains true relative to that context. Apart from some context of interpretative structures that prescribe types of realities, the search for empirical truth is literally senseless, for as scientific methodology has so well pointed out, all truth is truth relative to an interpretative context.

Lewis' own illustration brings home his point here as well as any that could be given. As he observes:

> In the case of the Copernican revolution, it was the invention of the telescope and the increasing accuracy of observation which mainly provided the impetus to reinterpretation. But these new data, though practically decisive, were decisive of simplicity and comprehensiveness only. As we have seen, celestial motions are theoretically as capable of interpretation with respect to axes through the earth as by reference to the fixed stars. Now suppose that mathematicians and astronomers had so much spare time that both these systems had been worked out, for all the data, with some completeness. Which would be the truth about the heavens? Obviously, both. The laws of celestial motion in the two cases would be quite different, and the divergence would extend beyond astronomy to physics. But both would be absolutely and eternally true in their own terms. The one would be better truth, the other worse, from the point of view of workability. But except in the practical sense that we must stick to the one or the other all through and cannot apply them piecemeal, they could not contradict one another.[20]

The sense, then, in which truth is "made by the mind" and is "relative to human interest and purpose" is the sense in which we choose the interpretative structures by which we prescribe the outlines of realities of particular types and in so doing set the context for the discovery of empirical truth. As Lewis states, "Mind makes classifications and determines meanings: in so doing it creates that truth without which there could be no other truth" (MWO 240). Such a priori or conceptual truth "represents the activity of mind itself; it represents an attitude in some sense freely taken" (MWO 196–97). Further, such truth underlies all empirical knowledge, for "We cannot capture the truth of experience if we have no net to catch it in" (MWO 307). Such a net, shown above to be evinced by scientific methodology, is precisely the analytic or *a priori* truth contained in the interrelationship of the interpretative structures through which we interact with the environment. Here, then, within his analysis of *a priori* interpretative contexts, Lewis has attempted both to accentuate in a precise manner the pragmatic factor in knowledge, the aspect of truth that *is* determined by human interest and purpose, and to correct any tendencies toward subjectivism that may be implicit in past pragmatic assertions of the relation of truth to human interest and purpose.

The above discussion has focused on the relation between *a priori* interpretative contexts and empirical truths, on the way in which truths of experience must always be relative to our chosen conceptual systems. It is now time to turn more directly to empirical truth, and Lewis' focus on such truth in terms of verification in sense experience. We have seen that it is through sense meanings that man grasps and responds to his environment. And it is Lewis' emphasis on interpretation as providing sense meaning in advance of verification that prevents his verification theory of empirical knowledge from being assimilated to that of the logical positivists or the operationalists. Sense meaning becomes the tool by which Lewis, throughout his theory of empirical truth in terms of verification in sense experience, avoids the extensionalist confusion of meaning and evidence.[21] Lewis does not hold that meanings are reducible to the instances that verify, for as indicated by his dispositional theory of meaning, meanings outrun in principle any number of instances, and in fact help give structures to the instances. What is important here concerning the structure of sense meaning is the fact that a habit of response is not a collection of possible responses to particular types of data but rather the rule for relating responses and data which, in its very being as a rule, contains the possibility of generating more than can ever be specified. Thus, though our statements about the world are confirmable by verifying experience, they are not reducible to those experiences. There is always the possibility of more and other experiences. As Lewis so well emphasizes: "Any theory of the meaningfulness of empirical statements plus the validity of empirical knowledge requires the assumption of a relationship of items which is not sense observable—though particular instances of it become sense confirmable." [22] Meanings for Lewis are rooted in experience, and verified by experience, but not reducible to experience.

Further, though meaning applications are verified by experience, there remains the significant issue as to the nature of the experiences that verify. For Lewis, as for the pragmatists in general, experience is that rich ongoing transactional unity between humans and their environment. Only within the context of such an interactional unity does what is given emerge for conscious awareness. Indeed, one of the most distinctive, most crucial, but most often ignored aspects of Lewis' position in relation to pragmatism is the concept of experience as having the character of an interaction between humans and their environment, a transactional character that takes the form of experience as experimental. The concept of experience as experimental, of course, reflects the focus on scientific method. Indeed, by focusing on scientific method, the pragmatists can be said to have, in their own way, followed the example of Plato in the *Republic* and turned to a model "writ large." At the level of science, the dynamics of our interaction with our world are more explicit, and hence easier to distinguish. As such, the methodology of science serves as a model by which to understand the nature of the human transactional experience at the more basic level of everyday lived experience. Even at its most rudimentary level, lived experience, according to the pragmatist, reflects the ongoing dynamics of experimentalism, with all the features of experience that experimentalism, by its very dynamics, incorporates. The philosophic attempt to view experience in terms of a reduction to any type of atomic elements loses the very nature of experience, for its loses the ongoing dynamic process of our interaction with our world. Hence it loses the characteristic features of lived experience which such a dynamic incorporates, characteristics which are "there," which are experienced, but which are lost to the philosophic awareness which tries to understand experience in terms of what remains after the reductionist axe has murderously chopped it to bits. But this statement brings us precisely to the systematic significance of those pervasive textures of experience as lived before interpreted by science, textures of experience implied in the discussion both of scientific methodology and of meaning as dispositional. It is to these pervasive textures of experience, and to the systematic significance of a type of "truth" which is the foundation for, rather than partially determined by, the alternative meanings which we bring to experience, that we will now turn.

The stress on alternative conceptual schemes for interpreting experience may seem to harken back to the conventionalism rejected above. Indeed, later analytic philosophers have rejected much reductive analysis and are concerned instead with identifying, classifying, and describing the most general features of our conceptual structures. Yet even those who focus on the aspect of alternative conceptual schemes in Lewis' philosophy as the basis for viewing him as an analytic philosopher, even they at times have been led to note a "nonconformity" in Lewis' thought. The reason is that, for Lewis, certain fundamental principles, such as the if–then order of potentialities and real connections, and the serial order of time, are not partially determined by alternative conceptual schemes, but rather are necessary for the very possibility of the applicability of any conceptual scheme to experience. Such a view, it has been observed, is not "something the pragmatic analysts are in the habit of saying,"[23] and hardly conforms "to the typical positivistic model of a relativistic theory of categories."[24] And, indeed, this "puzzlement" from the framework of analytic philosophy points indirectly toward one of the critically important aspects of Lewis' own position. For Lewis, as for all the pragmatists, humans are natural organisms in interaction with a natural environment. It is from such a backdrop that issues of meaning, method, and truth must be located. And if experience is an interaction of human responses with an environment, then the nature of experience reflects both the responses and the pervasive textures of that independent reality or surrounding natural environment. There is, thus, for the pragmatist in general, and for Lewis in particular, a "two directional openness" within experience. What appears opens, in one direction, toward the structures of the independently real or the surrounding natural environment and, in the other, toward the structures of our modes of grasping that independently real, since what is experienced is, in fact, a unity formed by each in interaction with the other. There is, for Lewis, an ontological dimension of what appears which reveals itself in experience and which forms a limit on our interpretations. The pervasive textures of experience which are exemplified in every experience and without which our responses to the world could not be as they are are at the same time indications of the pervasive textures of that independent universe which, in every experience, gives itself for our responses and provides the touchstone for the workability of our meanings. The basic textures of experience thus lead to the outlines of the categories of metaphysics. The categories of metaphysics, for Lewis, are the categories of a philosophy of nature, but not the nature of the natural scientist. Rather, it is the sense of nature before natural science, the level of nature to which I, in my lived experience, am fundamentally bound. It is that nature which is one with my body in that it is accessible only through the commerce and union which my body has with it.

Pragmatism, perhaps more successfully than other philosophic positions, brings together the being of humans in the world and the knowing by humans of the world. If one focuses on Lewis' philosophy as offering an exclusive concern with the knowing by humans of the world, as is usually done, then the full significance of his pragmatic naturalism, and, hence, the broad scope of his philosophy, are lost to view.[25] And indeed, if one misinterprets his focus on scientific methodology, then one *must* miss the significance of his pragmatic naturalism. For were he to make the mistake of focusing on the contents of science and projecting them as ultimates in any way, then his pragmatic naturalism, which focuses on those pervasive aspects of experience which are lost by such scientific abstractions, becomes impossible.[26] Further, if one misinterprets his theory of meaning, forcing it into some kind of reductionism or into some kind of linguistic framework, then his pragmatic theory of meaning cannot allow for the grasp of precisely those pervasive textures of experience which his philosophy asserts, and hence such assertions do become meaningless within his position. Indeed, as was indicated earlier in this paper, it is the dispositional theory of meaning, which itself is lost if one imposes on Lewis' theory of meaning any type of reductionist framework, which allows (a) for the grasp, at its most basic level, of process, continuity, real relations, and real potentialities; (b) for a sense of an anti-deterministic world in which one grasps real alternative possibilities, a sense of the "could be otherwise" without which real value orientation becomes meaningless; and (c) for the "feel" of the surd, the brute, the otherness of the environment to which we must successfully respond.[27] And these subtle tones of experiencing are at once the subtle tones, or modes of being, of that which enters into all experience, for experience opens, in one direction, toward the structures of the independently real and, in the other direction, toward the structures of our modes of grasping or responding to the independently real. Or, in other terms, what we experience is a function of both in interaction and thus "mirrors" neither exactly, though it reflects characteristics of each.[28]

Such an emerging position has elements of idealism. What we grasp reflects the structures of our modes of grasping. Yet such an emerging position has elements of realism as well, for that which is the object of knowledge is ontologically independent of human knowing.[29] It is that independent, brutely there, real universe within which humans find themselves, within which they have their being, and with which they must successfully interact, if they are to survive. We have already seen that phenomenalistic or linguistic interpretations of Lewis are inadequate conceptual nets for capturing the significance of his position. At this point, one may ask, what label remains? The answer provided by this essay, of course, is contained in the opening paragraphs. Lewis is a pragmatist. Neither Lewis' position nor the positions of the other classical American pragmatists can be adequately grasped if one tries to understand what is emerging today as a rich, complex, yet delicately elusive system of philosophy by assimilating it to the frameworks of other positions, or by forcing it into the "either–or" alternatives of the traditional labels of traditional dichotomies. This essay maintains that it is in both reflecting and further developing through a much needed, painstakingly technical, nurturing of its root ideas, the rich complexity of an emerging pragmatic system of philosophy, that the real significance and endurance of Lewis' thought, and his full stature as an American philosopher, will be found.

NOTES

1. A. O. Lovejoy, *The Thirteen Pragmatisms* (Baltimore: The Johns Hopkins University Press, 1963), distinguishes thirteen types, while F. C. S. Schiller, "William James and the Making of Pragmatism" (*The Personalist*, 8 [1927], 81–93), holds that there are as many pragmatisms as there are pragmatists.

2. H. S. Thayer, *Meaning and Action* (New York: Bobbs-Merrill, 1968), pp. ix–x.

3. Ibid.

4. The scope and significance of pragmatism, as implied in this essay, is taken in a broad sense that some will dispute.

5. In *The Philosophy of C. I. Lewis* (ed. Paul A. Schilpp [La Salle, Ill.; Open Court, 1968]) interpretations of Lewis as some type of analytic philosopher abound.

6. His influence on analytic philosophy is not denied. But there is a difference between what a philosophy is asserting and how it influences those who assimilate it within their own framework.

7. Almost without exception, the interpretations of Lewis' position in terms of analytic philosophy of some variety wind up by showing the inadequacy of his basic concepts.

8. Thayer notes, concerning pragmatism, that "the future may well be with Dewey, Mead, and Lewis" (*Meaning and Action*, p. 456).

9. See above, p. 205.

10. This is one of the relatively few areas in which Thayer assimilates a basic tenet of pragmatism to the view of another position. As he notes, in speaking of Lewis' notion of the *a priori*, "Lewis' discussion of the a priori in knowing could be recast into an account of analyticity in languages" (*Meaning and Action*, pp. 230–31).

11. C. I. Lewis, *An Analysis of Knowledge and Valuation* (La Salle, Ill.: Open Court, 1946; repr. 1962) p. 140. Hereafter referred to as AKV.

12. Such necessary relationships are, of course, the foundation for Lewis' analytic, *a priori* structures which underlie and make possible all empirical knowledge.

13. Lewis here is explicitly referring to the epistemological level of brute givenness, but at all levels of awareness the function of language, according to Lewis, is to provide clarity and precision by abstracting from the more concrete, not to capture the concreteness.

14. Although Lewis usually speaks of sense meaning as a precise, explicit schema, sense meaning is, for him, intensional or conceptual meaning, and this he frequently identifies as a disposition or habit. He clarifies this dual aspect of sense meaning when he observes that "a sense meaning *when precise and explicit* is a schema" (AKV 134). Furthermore, though he speaks of sense meanings as being "in mind," he observes that though "we have thought it well judged to take sense meaning as criterion in mind," "the important character connoted by 'in mind' here is 'entertained in

advance of instances of application which are pertinent.' . . . One may consider such criteria of application, as meanings entertained in advance, in terms of incipient behavior or behavior attitudes if one choose" (AKV 143–44).

15. C. I. Lewis, *Mind and the World Order* (New York: Scribner's, 1929; repr. New York: Dover, 1956), p. 229. Hereafter referred to as MWO.

16. For Lewis, the *a priori* is a meaning or purposive attitude in terms of which we approach experience. Such meanings or *a priori* structures are justified on pragmatic grounds—their usefulness in the organization and integration of experience. The analysis earlier of the relation between implicit and explicit sense meaning shows the way in which *a priori* relations are analytic, for a habit or implicit sense meaning contains within itself the power to generate the relationships that have been creatively fixated by it. The dispositional rule or implicit sense meaning contains analytically all that it has creatively fixated, or, conversely, all that it now has the power or potential to generate. A *priori* truths are analytic truths expressing containment relations among sense meanings.

17. Lewis, in his metaphysics, rejects substance in favor of lawful modes of process. The manner in which such a metaphysical position develops from his analysis of the "textures" of perceptual awareness will be seen in the later discussion of his naturalism.

18. This *a priori* element is embodied in the meanings in terms of which man interacts with his world. See note 16.

19. Though Lewis states that qualia are characterized by their "sensuous feel," such qualia cannot be reduced to sensations or defined by correlation with nervous processes. Feeling, sensuous feel, or quality of feeling is intended by Lewis to indicate a rudimentary epistemic level, not a "state of" an organism. Feeling refers to the epistemically more immediate, not to sensation. (See especially MWO 57, 127n; AKV 444.) Further, Lewis holds that his position does not deny that "the content of the presentation is an authentic part or aspect or perspective which is ingredient in the objective reality known" or that "the content of presentation may be 'numerically identical' with a part of the objective reality . . ." (AKV 187–88). Thus, Lewis is in no way making the qualitative richness of perception a psychical content that is set over against a "barren" mechanistic nature or that cuts off from direct knowledge of a qualitatively rich external world.

The relation of scientific explanation to lived experience is well exemplified by Lewis in his discussion of the scientific view of man as compelled by causes—either internal or external. As he observes, "The denial of 'self-determination' on account of universal motivation by psychological causes, would be the absurdity of first setting up this animistic metaphor and then turning it against that kind of fact which alone gives it any content. . . . Assimilation of motivations by reason to self-determination, merely reports a patent fact of experience, however that fact should be scientifically formulated" (AKV 484n).

20. "The Pragmatic Element in Knowledge," *Collected Papers of C. I. Lewis*, edd. John Goheen and John Mothershead, Jr., (Stanford: Stanford University Press, 1970), p. 256.

21. As a related point, it should be noted that knowledge, for Lewis, must be not only verified as true, but justified as rationally credible. Lewis rejects what he considers the overemphasis on future experience contained in empiricistic theories and, more specifically, in much of the writings of the pragmatists, which put forth an account of the verification of knowledge as if it were the whole story. It is precisely the function of empirical judgment to save the hazards of action without foresight. In this fact lies the significance, for Lewis, of the justification of knowledge as distinguished from its verification. Lewis is thus led to define empirical knowledge not as verified belief but as justified belief.

22. "A Comment on 'The Verification Theory of Meaning,' " *Collected Papers of C. I. Lewis*, edd. Goheen & Mothershead, p. 334.

23. Lewis White Beck, "The Kantianism of Lewis," *Philosophy of C. I. Lewis*, ed. Schillp, pp. 283–84.

24. Ibid., p. 274.

25. Lewis makes the distinction between the "order of being" and the "order of knowing," and stresses that an epistemological analysis does not make superfluous analyses of other sorts. He stresses that the mistake of too much philosophy "since Kant, and perhaps particularly amongst the idealists," is the tendency to "attach to epistemological analyses a kind of *exclusive* truth." As he further observes, "In some one of the innumerable meanings of the word 'is' it must be true that a thing is what it is 'known as,' identifiable with its *ratio cognoscendi*; but it is also the effect of its causes, the cause of its effects, the organized whole of its physical or other constituents, and a hundred other significant things besides" (MWO 149–50). Though Lewis' main emphasis is usually on the epistemological aspect, the other senses of "is" are always there in the background providing the context for his discussion.

26. Lewis' theory of knowledge is usually analyzed by his critics in complete oblivion to any tendency toward naturalism which may direct his thoughts in epistemology. If such a tendency is recognized, it is sometimes dismissed by taking note of Lewis' statement that "To make it clear that *empiricism* in epistemology and naturalism in ethics do not imply such relativism and cynicism has been one main objective in the writing of this book" (AKV viii). Precisely what is at issue, however, is the nature of the experience in which knowledge is rooted for Lewis, and hence the nature of the empiricism Lewis espouses. Pragmatism can claim to be a "radical empiricism" precisely because it returns to the richness of lived experience which has been lost by past empiricism's erroneous focus on scientific contents as opposed to scientific methodology as lived experimental activity.

27. It is precisely because the "hereness and nowness" of events and the real connections which they display are independent of our concep-

tualizations and of the possibilities which they allow that there must be a pragmatic interplay between our concepts and actual experience.

28. As Lewis states, "Empirical reality does not need to be assumed nor to be proved, but only to be acknowledged" (AKV 361).

29. This realism which is opposed to idealism should, of course, not be confused with the type of realism which is opposed to nominalism, a realism which was indicated above to be held by Lewis—with modifications appropriate to process metaphysics.

12

The Social Philosophy of George Herbert Mead

DAVID L. MILLER
Late of the
University of Texas at Austin

GEORGE HERBERT MEAD was born in South Hadley, Massachusetts, in 1863 and died in Chicago, Illinois, in 1931. He taught at the University of Chicago from 1894 until his death, a period of thirty-seven years. He studied at Oberlin College and Harvard, and at Leipzig and Berlin. He considered Josiah Royce to be one of his best teachers, though Mead moved away from idealism and became a pragmatist mainly under the influence of Peirce, James, and Dewey. More impersonal intellectual influences on Mead were Darwin's theory of evolution and Wilhelm Wundt's notion of the gesture. Both Darwin and Wundt studied the gestures of lower animals, and both conceived of gestures in social terms. Mead's great insight consists in understanding that the vocal gesture resulted in language or in language gestures, notably words, which have the same meaning to both the speaker and the other to whom words are addressed. Words (or speech) are the instruments by which concepts or meanings are communicated from one person to another. Only by language can meanings or concepts be shared and communicated from one organism to another. How does it come about that we can share meanings with others? How is it that the individual can share the attitudes of other members of the community? How is it that there is what we call public opinion, or a *mit Welt*, as Max Scheler calls it, or a *Weltanschauung*? Also, what does it mean to put oneself in the place of another, or what precisely does it mean to take the role of the other? Although many sociologists, anthropologists, psychologists, and philosophers use the expression "taking the role of the other," I find that they explain neither what it consists in nor how it is possible. Mead did explain it and by doing so solved several problems of great concern to people today—namely, the problem of solipsism, the problem about the possibility of a private language, the problem of how it is possible for an individual to have a new idea, and the problem of the functional relationship between the individual and society.

Let me begin cautiously by explaining gestures of lower animals, gestures whose meanings are not shared by these animals but which, nevertheless, have one of the essential features of language gestures in that they evoke action in the animals that sense them. (Mead calls a language gesture a significant symbol.) The word "gesture" can be clearly defined. (1) A gesture is an act or a part of the behavior of an animal. For example, the bark or snarl of a dog, the song of a bird, the roar of a lion, may be gestures. Shrugging one's shoulders, raising one's eyebrows, smiling, winking, etc., may be gestures. Shaking hands, saying "good morning," are gestures. There are literally thousands of different kinds of gestures. (2) For an act to be a gesture it must be sensed by a second animal; it must be heard, seen, or felt by another. (3) It must evoke a response by the other in order to be a gesture. We see offhand that all gestures are social in that they involve at least two animals. The behavior or any part of the behavior of an animal in isolation from other animals cannot serve as a gesture. The function of every gesture is to evoke action by another animal. If the growl of a dog is a gesture, it must be sensed by another animal and elicit a response by the other. In that case, as in all cases, the gesture is a stimulus to another, and it evokes a response by that other. If we ask what the growl of the big dog meant to the little dog, we say the meaning is what the little dog did, say, it ran away. Running away was the response aroused by the stimulus, the bark. In general, a gesture is a stimulus, and the meaning of the gesture is the response it evokes. It should be made clear that the response is not to the stimulus. Rather, the stimulus or the gesture evokes a response to a later phase of the social act, even as the buzzer evokes a response by the dog not to the buzzer, but to the meat. Every sign, stimulus, gesture, or symbol evokes a response toward something other than itself. Hence, every such response is directed toward something in a future, and thus every social act has a teleological factor. This, of course, is not true of the interaction among physical objects. Here we see that the meaning of the gesture is not in the mind of the dog. It is not something subjective. Rather, it is the act of running away or of eating meat. It can be sensed by anyone who observes the behavior of the dogs. Mead wanted to relieve all meanings of subjectivity and privacy. He wanted to get meanings out in the open. He held that neither meaning nor mind can be separated from action, from social behavior. His task was to show that all meanings arise out of social behavior, that there can be no meaning, that nothing can have meaning for us, apart from conduct. Finally, as I will show, neither mind nor thinking, or cognition, can be separated from conduct. Mind and thinking are functionally related to overt actions, though not reducible to such actions. Mind and all cognition emerge from behavior, notably social behavior, and it in turn is instrumental in facilitating the human social process. Cartesian dualism is evaded completely by Mead. But I am getting ahead of the reasons for this.

Now, let me consider the gestures of lower animals and show why they are not language gestures, or what Mead calls significant gestures, that is, why they are not gestures whose meanings are shared by both the animal making the gesture and the animal stimulated by it. The growl of a dog may be heard by a second dog, and it may evoke the response by the second dog of baring its teeth. The first dog may see the teeth and respond by raising its fur, etc., and so the conversation of gestures may result, finally, in a dogfight that was not planned. It is just a conversation of gestures at the non-cognitive level. Here we should understand that the growl made by the first dog has meaning to the second dog only, and the meaning is the response of baring its teeth, which is a preparation for the oncoming attack. The meaning of the growl is simply the response it evokes in the other dog; it is confined to the other dog. The growling dog does not anticipate the response its growl will evoke in the other; it does not intend to elicit that response; it is not aware of the meaning of its gesture, the growl. If the growling dog were aware of the kind of response it will arouse in the other, it would share that meaning with the other. If the growling dog could anticipate the response its growl will provoke in the other dog, then it would be aware of what is to happen later; it would be conscious of a future happening. It would be responding implicitly or vicariously as the other will actually respond later. Which is to say, the growling dog would be responding to its own behavior, its gesture, as the other responds to it. This it cannot do. It cannot take the role of the other. It cannot respond to stimuli in their absence. To respond to stimuli in their absence, one would need a symbol for that response, and the response would be mental and cognitive. A universal would be involved. Nietzsche says of lower animals that "They live, they eat, they procreate, they die in an eternal present." That is, lower animals, having no language, have no conception of either a past or a future, and are not conscious of time.

How does the human being break out of a present? How does it come about that humans can become aware of possible future events and can remember other events as past? This is made possible, Mead explains, because one is able to take the role of the other; and this could not happen without language, or without gestures whose meanings are shared by the participants in a social process, without gestures whose meanings are universal with respect to the group using that language. Mead's great discovery was that language gestures are different from all other gestures in that they enable us to share meanings and to convey meanings to each other. The child at birth has no language, no mind, no self, and it does not know the meaning its crying has for the mother or nurse. If the mother would not talk to the child in conjunction with caring for it, the child would never be aware of the meaning its behavior has for the mother. But through behavioral transactions with others, there comes a time when the child is able to make a request, when it is able to say the word "bottle" in the presence of the mother and in the absence of a bottle. Also, it anticipates the response the mother will make to the word "bottle." Which is to say, the child is able to respond to its own behavior, its gesture or word, as the mother will respond. It knows the meaning of the word and it shares that meaning with the mother. By anticipating the response the mother will make because of the gesture, the child is taking the role of another, namely, its mother. In that case, not only is the child responding to its own bodily pangs of hunger; it is responding to its own responses. In saying that by a language symbol one responds to one's own response, I mean that the anticipation of the response one evokes in the other (by that symbol) is itself a response, though covert, evoked by the symbol, which is a stimulus evoking the overt response of the other. Lower animals do not use significant symbols. Thus the child takes the attitude of the other toward its behavior before it is aware of itself as a subject. It is first an object to itself before it has what we call self-consciousness. Or it is in the perspective of the other, or it takes the attitude of the community, before it develops a personal perspective, before it is an "I." The great Immanuel Kant said more than two hundred years ago that the child is aware of itself first as a "me," as "baby," and later as an "I," though by his system he could not explain why. Josiah Royce understood that apart from social relations with others there could be no self. He says: " 'For a man's self has no contents, no plans, no purposes, except those which are, in one way or another, defined for him by his social relations.' "[1] Royce again says:

> As a matter of psychology, *i.e.*, of the natural history of our beliefs, a vague belief in the existence of our fellows seems to antedate, to a considerable extent, the definite formation of any consciousness of ourselves. . . . It is nearer the truth to say that we first learn about ourselves from and through our fellows, than that we learn about our fellows by using the analogy of ourselves.[2]

Max Scheler writes: " 'Man is a member of a community before he is conscious of his own self as an *I*. I know myself to be a member of a *we* before I know myself as an individual I.' "[3]

Similarly Mead holds:

> It is the implication of this undertaking that only selves have minds, that is, that cognition only belongs to selves, even in the simplest expression of awareness. . . . It is further implied that this development has taken place only in a social group, for selves exist only in relation to other selves, as the organism as a physical object exists only in relation to other physical objects.[4]

Clearly Mead does not commit the phenomenological fallacy of believing that the individual experiences inner perceptions that are private or that the individual has direct knowledge of events existing in his own mind on a sort of internal cinema.

I may have belabored the point that the social perspective precedes the personal perspective, but this is crucial in understanding the nature of the self and the nature of mind. Until very recently most philosophers, psychologists, and theologians assumed that every child has a self and a mind at birth, apart from social transactions. In fact, such men as Hobbes and Rousseau, in advocating the social contract theory, held that originally men lived apart from each other and later they held a conference and agreed to live together. Locke held that the individual first has ideas and then develops a language by which to express them. I am reminded of the story about a baby who didn't like its nurse. It said to itself, "when I get old enough to talk, I will have her dismissed." On the contrary, as Mead explains, selves and minds emerge out of social behavior, and a social perspective antedates self-consciousness or the emergence of the I. Every self has this social component in its makeup. The social component of the self is called, by James and Mead, the "me." Every normal person has an I and a me. The me consists of what is shared or sharable with others plus one's special skills. Thus the me includes the attitudes and customary, habitual ways of behaving that are shared by other members of the community. We all have the same attitude toward a red stop light, toward paying just debts, toward the privilege of voting, toward many customs. Many of these habits have been socialized or institutionalized, and they are incorporated in either the written or the unwritten civil code of law or in customs and in etiquette. The me consists of what Max Scheler calls the *mit Welt*, what some have called the Superego, and what Mead calls the generalized other, the voice of the rational other, the voice of the community.

If it is true that the child must first share a community perspective before it can be aware of itself as an I or as a subject, it follows that solipsism and a private language are impossible. It also follows that one can become self-conscious or be aware of oneself as an I only by taking the attitude of the other toward one's own conduct, only by responding to one's behavior as the other or an other does. Many sociologists and anthropologists recognize that group attitudes condition the behavior of members of the group, and many go so far as to claim, erroneously, that the individual's thinking and acting are determined by mores, folkways, and taboos. They want to assimilate the "I" to the "me," and make a person all "me," all social, all other. Although we fight major wars under the banner of freedom and self-determination, students are often taught in the classroom that thinking and the behavior of the individual are completely determined by such things as culture, environment, heredity, and technology. One of the greatest responsibilities of educators today is to explain how an individual member of society can help change and redirect the social process, or how the individual can help reshape our institutions so that the actualization of individual selves and personal achievement can be effected. It is our responsibility to make clear to students the conditions necessary for the development of healthy persons in a healthy open society.

Members of a tribal society believe that the mores and folkways are fixed and adequate for the good life, and the individual has no desire to deviate from tradition and custom. There is no room in such societies, in theory at least, for the expression of individuality. Even many persons outside tribal societies, living in our own country, are conformists who want to adhere strictly to custom. They have what Nietzsche called a slave morality. But in Western culture, especially during the Renaissance, the theory emerged that institutions should exist for the sake of persons, that governments should be for and by the people. Nevertheless there are many today who erroneously believe and teach that man is born into a prestructured natural and moral order. Others claim that they have discovered that fixed order and that it is our duty to conform to it. That is, they believe the individual can save himself only by entering into an institution whose structure was there prior to the existence of man.

At the other extreme, there are those who believe that a person can be himself, can have self-identity, only if he is free from all institutions, and that each individual, insofar as he is authentic, is alone in deciding what he should do. To put it in Mead's terms: the determinists want to assimilate the "I" component of the self to the "me," whereas others want to make a person all "I." They seem to think that freedom requires the denial of all social restraints and controls, the doing of one's thing by oneself. If the other had no influence on one's behavior, a person would act, not from intelligence, but from sheer biological impulses. He would revert to the sub-human animal level. Mead believes both these views are wrong: that is, we do not think and act in isolation from others; nor is our thinking completely determined by others. It is not despite the fact that each of us in our thinking and acting is conditioned by our mores and institutions that we are free, but because of them. It is not despite the fact that one's habits and one's past have a claim on one that one is free, but because of it. In other words, freedom and creativity of the individual are made possible by the fact that he is a member of society, because he shares attitudes with others, or because he can listen to the voice of the community. The individual can have a new kind of experience only if that experience is recognized as one that is unintelligible in terms of the attitude of the community. It should be noted that it is only by virtue of exceptional experiences that reflective intelligence is possible. Thinking or reflective intelligence is carried on only by individuals. Thinking is not, as Plato would have it, a conversation of the I with the I, but a conversation of the I with the other, the generalized other, the rational other, or with the voice of the community. Every person who uses a language carries with him this social component of the self; every self must share certain customs and habits, as well as meanings, with other members of the group. Mead calls this the "me" component of the self, or the generalized other. Another component is the "I," the active, choosing, thinking, creative component. If one thinks, the I must converse with the other component of the self, the me. These two parts of the self are involved in reflective intelligence. The other is literally a part of the self; no one can have a self without it. Royce says, "We are as dust, save as this social order gives us life." Mead would say it is in this great social sea that we live and move and have our being.

When does the "I" act and what does it do? Under what conditions does the "I" have an opportunity to have new ideas leading to new ways of behaving and to changes in our institutions? Peirce explained that a belief is a readiness to act or a commitment to act under certain conditions according to a rule, and that doubt is the opposite of belief. Mead agrees with that, but according to John Dewey,[5] Mead was the first to point out that doubt arises in the individual and in society when action is obstructed and when, as a consequence, some item in the environment or situation has conflicting meanings, or when we tend to react to something in incompatible ways. Thinking takes place when action is inhibited due to conflicting tendencies to respond or to conflicting meanings. All you are doing when you think is indicating to yourself, in their absence, stimuli that will release desired responses that are at present inhibited. Mead spent much time in considering what he called exceptional or conflicting experiences that arise within conduct. Exceptional experiences are those that cannot be understood in terms of customary or traditional ways of thinking; old laws and indeed old habits of action break down at this point, and new interpretations are called for. An exceptional experience is always had by an individual member of society, and it is in conflict with the attitudes of the community. It gives rise to a conflict between the I and the generalized other, or the attitude of the individual and the voice of the community, or between the "I" and the "me." Reflective intelligence or what we call thinking and reasoning amounts to an internalization of the conflict, or an attempt to resolve the conflict by use of symbols and the symbolic or mental process. This conflict is easily recognized in the case of a scientist who experiences some phenomenon that is unintelligible in terms of accepted laws or theories. For example, Benjamin Thompson discovered that an unlimited amount of heat could be generated by boring cannons with dull bits. This experience, first by an individual, was in conflict with the caloric theory of heat, and the conflict was resolved by instituting the kinetic theory, which was also first proposed by an individual.

The symbolic process, or thinking, is due to a conflict, and thinking is a dialectic process. But the conflict is not between classes or concepts and ideas or between universals, as Hegel and Marx would have it. Rather, the conflict is between an individual and the group, between the I and the generalized other, between old attitudes the person shares with the community and the experience and perspective of that particular person. Objects or situations can have conflicting meanings to the individual only if he already has a "me," that is, the perspective of the group. Private perspectives emerge out of a universal perspective. We cannot build up the community perspective out of a set of isolated private perspectives. The universal perspective is there first. The social component of the self, the "me," precedes the "I," the personal component. Again, a strictly private language and solipsism are impossible in principle and in fact.

Now, by reflective intelligence, by the use of the symbolic process, a conflict between the attitude of the individual and the generalized other may be resolved. When a person offers a statement of an exceptional experience, that person is stating what we call the brute facts or the data that constitute the problem at hand. At first these experiences belong to the biography of an individual, and they may be called private experiences. But the solution of the problem consists in offering an intelligible account of the brute facts, that is, in conceiving of hypotheses, new laws, or theories that will make the exceptional, the novel, understandable to all members of the group. If and when a solution is found, some old attitudes and beliefs must be given up, and new ones will take their place. Which is to say, the generalized other, the community perspective, must be changed. The individual and the data have been saved, but the "me" component of the self, the old universal perspective, has been modified and enriched. We understand the datum, the brute fact, an exceptional experience, only if we can fit it into a system, only if we can formulate the lawful way in which it interacts with other items in the system, only if we can formulate it in terms of what Peirce called generality or *Thirdness*, or by showing how it functions in a process. This involves changing shared beliefs, thus modifying the generalized other. Mead substitutes the generalized other for the Hegelian Absolute. For Mead, the generalized other is open, subject to change, modifiable. A mentally healthy society is an open society, and it is kept open because of open selves having new ideas that change the attitudes, the habits, the institutions, of the group. If the individual is that which must ever transcend itself, it can do so only by enlarging its social perspective or by modifying the voice of the community. And only if society continually transcends itself can the individual do so. The great philosopher Nietzsche did not understand the functional relationship between the "I" and the "me," the person and society. When Nietzsche said "Do not follow me, follow yourself," and implied that we cannot follow God because He is dead, it is clear that he overlooked a primary component of the self, the social. (Nietzsche, though probably unwittingly, accepted Descartes' antisocial theory of the self.) After all, the individual finds his greatest security in attitudes shared by others, and these basic attitudes give rise to the birth of meaning. Attempting a retreat into one's self or trying to become all "I" is a form of narcissism

leading to what William James called sick souls. Louis Pasteur is
dead, but his attitudes live in us every time we drink from a cup.
Aristotle, Plato, Augustine, Thomas Aquinas, Mendelssohn, Darwin, Newton—all are dead but some of their basic ideas are deeply
interwoven in our attitudes, in the social component of the self of
each of us. These attitudes are handed down from parent to child,
from teacher to pupil, like an heirloom throughout generations.
When the individual first realizes that he is sharing the ideas and
attitudes of great persons, both dead and living, then he will have
an intellectual aesthetic experience, for then he will understand
that he is a member of the human race, a member of what Royce
called the community of mankind, the Beloved Community.

If an individual ever doubts his own sanity, he can be reassured
if he knows that he shares opinions, beliefs, and basic attitudes
with others. One who cannot hold onto or share concepts and
beliefs with others has lost a part of the me component of the self
and is partially insane. But I want to emphasize once more that a
healthy self is not one who is satisfied with the status quo and who
conforms to the present attitudes of society. A healthy mind cannot be all "me." Rather, she or he is one who, like Pasteur, Mendelssohn, Darwin, and many, many others, exercises the creative
component of the self, the "I," one who has new ideas that feed
into, modify, and enlarge the generalized other, the social component of the self. The "me" is enhanced when the individual
makes a contribution to society. In every case when the individual
contributes to the growth of the generalized other, that person
recognizes that there is an incompatibility, a conflict, between a
present situation and traditional concepts; the individual under-
stands that present experiences cannot be adequately interpreted
by resorting to currently accepted beliefs or customs. At such times
the community needs help, and the individual, a self, is that phase
of the social process which serves as mediator. The self in creative
action is that phase of the process which lies (temporally) between
that overt phase of the social process which has been obstructed or
frustrated and a later phase in which the process continues in an
obstructed way. The creative self, then, often internalizes an overt
obstructed social process, and it mediates between the old and
the new, between the traditional and the newly initiated, between
the past and the demands of a future, or between an ideology and

a utopia. Whenever the "I," the subject, functions, it acts as arbiter in a present between an estopped social process and its future continuation. The self emerges out of a social process but functions within that social process as mediator when conflicts arise.

If we remember that the locus of human dignity and worth is in individuals and that self-actualization and personal achievement are the highest values, we can understand that our customs, our institutions, the generalized other should be the servant to the "I." This is analogous to a situation in which a mechanic's tools serve him both in achieving his goals and in making new tools when old ones are inadequate for the task at hand. Our habits, our past, our basic thought structure, our institutions, should all serve us as individuals as each of us in our own creative way helps direct and control the social process. Each of us finds his identity when he finds his place in the social process and performs a role approved by the group. Anyone who is fully committed to performing a social role thinks of that work as a calling in Calvin's sense of the term.

In support of his theory that healthy societies are open societies supported by open selves, Mead held that man is not born into either a prestructured social or physical order. Rather, in accordance with those who support the sociology of knowledge claim, Mead believes the world will lend itself to being structured in various ways, many of which will be adequate and no one of which is absolute and closed. Just as organisms with chromatic vision confer colors on objects, so human minds confer new meanings on items in our social and physical environments. "Language does not simply symbolize a situation or object that is already there in advance; it makes possible the existence or appearance of that situation or object, for it is part of the mechanism whereby that situation or object, is created" (MSS p. 78).

This is to say, all our common sense objects, such as chairs, tables, and cathedrals, are objects or things only in relation to human communication. As Dewey explained, through communication by language, "Events turn into objects, things with a meaning." [6] This means literally that what is real for us, or for a society of any culture, is a social construction. The meanings objects have for a person must be shared or sharable. The word "chair" has the same meaning to each of us; it means something to sit on. By symbols we can indicate these objects to ourselves in their absence. We can, by symbols, both remember and anticipate, both regret and plan. Lower animals cannot do that. You will never see a dog off by itself practicing for the circus. You will never see chimpanzees playing baseball, say, according to rules. Many lower animals play, but none plays games. Only man can play according to rules. Rules are not discovered, but freely formulated. Only man can control his present behavior by a conception of future consequences. What we call the meaning of life or of living emerges in connection with rules, customs, morality, all of which are social. Only human beings make tools, knowing in advance how they are to be used. Peter Berger and Thomas Luckman,[7] under the influence of Alfred Schutz, James, Dewey, and Mead, are able to show that everything said by a society to be real is due to a social construction. It must be something that is namable, a concept of which can be communicated from one individual to another by language gestures. All classifications, all definitions, all meanings, arise out of social interactions. Would there be gasoline as fuel apart from human inventions? Would there be natural resources apart from symbols and shared ideas? The meaning of whatever is real passes over into a generalized other. A football game is a social object; a heart transplant is a social object. Queens College and Fordham University are social objects. You cannot get your hands on them but they are real.

Apparently Mead was the first to offer a behavioristic social account of the origin of mind and the self. He believed there is a difference between the human organism and all lower animals, and this difference is found basically in three factors: namely, (a) the structure of the nervous system, notably the brain and especially the cortex; (b) the fact that the eyes focus on objects we handle; and (c) the structure of the human hand. Without these, minds could not emerge and language would be surplus baggage. It is known that a disproportionately large area of the cortex is devoted to controlling the hands. By the hands and tools and instruments, which amount to an extension of the hand, we dissect objects and reassemble them in multifarious ways. What we call culture and civilization is due to what hands have wrought under the control of significant symbols. Mead claims that reflective intelligence is concerned primarily with what he calls the manipulatory phase of the social act, that is, with handling *things*, physical objects, which serve as means to ends having intrinsic value. Intelligence operates on what lies between the impulsive or perceptual phase of the act and the consummatory or final phase of the act. The wolf both kills and devours with the same teeth. Practically this is one and the same act, or the manipulatory phase of the act amounts to very little and is integral to consummation, whereas human beings put a long series of acts between the killing and the consumption of beef. What lies between, including knives and forks, is what we call civilization. The Germans have two different words for this: animals devour, *fressen*; human beings dine, *essen*.

Also, with the same hands a person can be a pianist, a surgeon, a barber, a typist, a ballplayer, a dentist, etc., and this facilitates taking the role of the other. Our highly complex social community is made possible by virtue of the hand. If we consider a society of bees, ants, or termites, we easily understand that the division of labor among its members and the complexity of their social organization is due, not to language, but to basic physiological differences. The queen bee cannot gather nectar; nor can the drone. And although the working bee can make a dance after depositing nectar, a dance that is a gesture, it is not a language gesture for the reason that the dancer does not share the meaning its gesture has for the other. It does not mean to tell the other bees anything. The ways of the bees have been relatively fixed for the past fifty thousand years, most of their behavior being predetermined in the form of inherited behavioral patterns. But lower animals, including bees, have no cultures, no civilization, no institutions, no language, no common or personal perspectives.

Indeed there are basic physiological differences between men and women, and their correspondingly different functions are essential to propagation and the survival of the human species. But, in contrast with the social organization of lower animals, human physiological differences are not the basis for our institutions or for the continuation of civilizations.

To be human the individual must first have within its self the perspective of the other, the generalized other. Often we speak as if a person can at will choose to or choose not to take the attitude of the other. We often speak as if one can look at things from one's own personal perspective alone. This is impossible. The "me" is there first; the perspective of the group is prior to the operation of the "I." A personal perspective emerges from a shared perspective as a necessary background. To lose the perspective of the community is to lose one's mind. We can give a definition of what it means for a person to be normal, a definition that will apply to any and every culture. A normal person is one who can utilize the generalized other, who can use the "me" effectively for the solution of problems at hand and who can, thereby, contribute to keeping the social process going satisfactorily.

Saying that human beings are different from all other animals in that they have a language and use symbols whose meanings are shared is identical with saying that selves can take the role of the other. This can be translated into another statement equivalent in meaning: namely, a person can respond to his own behavior (his language gesture) as another does, or, as Mead says, a person, by his gesture, can evoke in himself the *same* response as he evokes in another. Here I want to explain the sense in which the word "same" is used, inasmuch as it is quite often and legitimately used in two different senses which are at times conflated. A lower animal cannot by its gestures or by any means evoke in itself the same response as it evokes in another in the sense in which human beings do. Of course, a person's response cannot be numerically identical (or the same in that sense) with another person's response. After all, your overt response, your observable behavior, must be carried out by you and mine must be carried out by me; they must be existentially or numerically different and they usually take place at different places and times. In this sense they cannot be the same. But when Mead uses the word "same" in this context he does not mean the two responses are numerically or existentially identical (or substantially the same). Rather, he means they are functionally identical; their identity or sameness consists in the universal form of the act, the habitual, customary, general form of the act, or in what Peirce called *Thirdness*. It is a kind of act one anticipates from another when one opens a door and yells "Fire." It is the general form of the act one anticipates, not its particularity. Two acts or any two or more things are necessarily existentially different and not the same in that sense. But they can be and are functionally identical or the same if they function alike or, more precisely, if they can be subsumed under the same concept, or the same habit, or the same law. Which is to say, any two or more acts or any two or more entities are functionally identical if a given concept applies to each. The word "dog" applies to several absolutely existentially different dogs, and since it does, these different dogs are the same in the sense of functional identity. When we share meanings with others, what we share are concepts, the general, the universal, and not particular responses. A concept, though shared by different people, is numerically identical, the same in both persons, even as the law of gravity is the same from day to day, though it applies to existentially different bodies. When an individual by his gesture evokes the *same* response in himself as he evokes in another, what is evoked is a concept that is the same in each, and the meaning the concept has is indeed applicable to the particular response made by the other, the response evoked by the gesture after the meaning of the concept is had. I submit that any two things, though necessarily existentially different, are the same or functionally identical if the same law (habit, custom, universal, concept) applies to each. (A given habit applies to an indefinite number of particulars, say cigarettes, and these particulars are, consequently, said to be functionally identical or the same.) This distinction between the sameness of numerical identity and the sameness of functional identity is essential to understanding Mead's claim that self-consciousness arises in the individual when he is able to elicit the same response in himself, by his gesture, as he evokes in the other. We can also understand by this distinction why it is that when one sheep simply follows another into, say, a barn, the leader is not evoking in itself the same response as it evokes in the other. Their separate acts are numerically different, and we can say they are functionally identical because we have the concept of "going into a barn," something a sheep cannot have. It is the meaning that is shared, and it is the same (numerically identical) when we communicate by use of significant symbols, but particular responses are not shared, even as pains, such as a toothache, cannot be shared.

Language may be used to describe, to evaluate, and to incite action. Mead has shown that the primary function of language is what John L. Austin called its perlocutionary force. Description and evaluation are parasitic on the perlocutionary force of language gestures. Language is a phase of the social behavioral process, and its primary function is to incite action. Recently problems in epistemology have been approached from the standpoint of what is called the sociology of knowledge—namely, from the supposition that the way the individual thinks and what is called knowledge are conditioned by the attitudes and the language of the society or the culture in which that individual lives. Also, the exponents of the sociology of knowledge view hold that knowledge cannot be separated from cultural or societal interests. Karl Marx, Max Scheler, Max Weber, Karl Manheim, Alfred Schutz, and Jürgen Habermas have this new approach to the problems of objectivity and knowledge. But it is more than obvious that the American pragmatists, Peirce, James, Dewey, Mead, and C. I. Lewis, as well as Royce, were dealing with epistemology from the point of view of the sociology of knowledge. C. Wright Mills, when he was a student at the University of Texas, studied the philosophy of the American pragmatists. All his publications pertaining to the sociology of knowledge are influenced directly by Peirce, James, Dewey, and Mead. Before he read Karl Manheim's works he wrote a master's thesis at Texas, the subtitle of which is "An Essay in the Sociology of Knowledge." I submit that Peirce, Dewey, James, Mead, and Lewis will furnish students with a much more systematic approach to these problems than the Europeans will.[8]

I do not have space here to explain that communication by use of language symbols always requires universals or concepts, and that universality is found in what Peirce called *Thirdness*. When we communicate, we communicate the customary form of responses, of habits shared by others. Universals, like meanings, are to be found in transactions, in process, in the lawful, habitual, or customary manner in which particulars interact with each other. A new universal emerges where the individual restructures a part of the world by incorporating an exceptional experience in a system of laws, thereby changing a part of the generalized other or enriching it. If Mead is correct in his claim that minds and selves emerge out of social interaction and that each self is of necessity sustained by virtue of its social relationship to other selves, it follows that what we ordinarily think of as a selfish person is one who does not understand that the highest of values is found in interpersonal, social relations. As a consequence, the selfish person often places a higher value on *things* than on persons and, as Kant suggests, such a person will sometimes use another person as a means only, or as a thing. If that is the case, a selfish person is also one who reverts to the biological level and cherishes, above all else, the fulfillment of biological needs (and impulses) and thereby fails to contribute, to the fullest extent, to social action essential for the achievement of shared ends and values. No person can develop his self without also contributing to the welfare of the group. Of course we know there is selfishness in our midst, that there is skulduggery, malice, cheating, stealing, murder, and major crimes of various sorts. We know, too, that malicious criminal behavior is antisocial and irrational in that the impulses prompting such conduct spring solely from the biological man. Still we must continue to hope that people will understand that their effort should be directed toward the attainment of shared ends. The highest of shared values is found in the "me" component of the self, in the social component, or in what cannot exist apart from the community. The "I" component of each healthy individual self is sustained by the "me," and its creative activity is always directed toward enriching the "me."

In conclusion, we know that no one can develop a self or attain personal achievement without performing a social role, without being an integral phase of an ongoing thriving open social process. Thus it behooves us to fashion our social, our educational, our religious, our economic, and our political institutions so as to permit every self, every person, to exercise the "I" component of the self in order to modify the generalized other and, consequently, in order to help direct and redirect the social process toward an ever newly promised future. Every healthy self must be a participant in the social process.

The understanding that the healthy self is one in which the ego is continually motivated by a "promised land" was not born in Athens, but in a wilderness between an enslaving land and a land promised. And although many present-day critics are worried about the "human condition," we must give up our hankering after the flesh pots of an enslaving past.

All men cry out for freedom, but unless we put self-actualization and the dignity of man at the core of our social role performances, we will likely find ourselves worshipping a golden calf, symbolic of a fictitious age beyond recall.

Without hope of a better future no person can be mentally healthy, and short of the death of meaning and the negation of self-actualization, we must continue to believe that a bird in the bush is worth two in the hand.

NOTES

1. Quoted in *The Social Philosophy of Josiah Royce*, ed. Stuart Jerry Brown (Syracuse: Syracuse University Press, 1950), p. 105.
2. *The World and the Individual*, 2 vols. (New York: Dover, 1959), II 170–71.
3. Quoted in W. Ranly Ernest, *Scheler's Phenomenology of Community* (The Hague: Nijhoff, 1966), p. 72.
4. *The Philosophy of the Present*, ed. Arthur E. Murphy (Chicago: Open Court, 1932), p. 178.
5. See *The Philosophy of John Dewey*, ed. Paul A. Schillp (LaSalle, Ill.: Open Court, 1939), pp. 25, 26.
6. *Experience and Nature*. (Chicago and London: Open Court, 1926), p. 166.
7. *The Social Construction of Reality* (Garden City, N.Y.: Doubleday, 1967).
8. Peirce's article "The Fixation of Belief" and Mead's essay "The Objective Reality of Perspectives" are excellent in this area. James's definition of the real in *Principles of Psychology* (2 vols. [New York: Holt, 1890], II 295) is also quite relevant, Jürgen Habermas' *Knowledge and Human Interest* shows definite influences especially of Peirce.

13

Existence as Transaction:
A Whiteheadian Study of Causality

Elizabeth M. Kraus

Fordham University

Introduction

If any theme can be said to run through classic American Philosophy as a unifying thread, it is the conception of human experience as an encounter, an interaction, a coming-to-terms with and a reflective transformation of the divine, human, biological, and physical environment out of which it emerges, against which it is set, and within which it must work out its weal or woe. Between the Puritan dream of the City on the Hill and John Dewey's Call for a U. S. A. Inc. stretches a series of strangely analogous philosophical visions, each interpreted in the varying textures of different philosophical schemes, each focused on different problematics, but all proclaiming in their own accents that the foundational experience of being human is that of being an organism creatively responding to its environment.

The thesis of this essay is that Alfred North Whitehead, although British by birth,[1] can be interpreted as standing squarely in the philosophical tradition of his adopted homeland. It is not my intention to make my point by demonstrating the influence of American philosophers on Whitehead. His praise of James, his expressed admiration of Peirce and Dewey, are sufficient evidence of the congruence of his thought with the American tradition to make such demonstrations corrolarial. What this essay attempts is

An earlier version of this chapter appeared in *International Philosophical Quarterly*, 25, No. 4 (December 1985), 349–66.

something more substantive: to come to grips with a fundamental issue in process philosophy, one which has resulted in the hesitancy of many Whiteheadians to attribute a doctrine of genuine causal interaction to Whitehead. This hesitancy springs from their perception of the implications of his epochal theory of time. If it is the case, as Whitehead maintains, that the "concrete time system" which common sense would call a chain of causes and effects is in reality a series of discrete, atomic events each of which is an active and self-directed synthesis of the events in its past (a synthesis which when completed becomes part of the factual past for a new synthetic activity), then how can the traditional interpretation of causation as an active modification of the existence of a subsequent other be maintained, since it would involve the persistence of the activity of a fact—a *former* event, a "being"—in the process constitutive of a present event? If genuine causal agency is postulated between atomic events, it would seem to imply an "overlap" of events (and a consequent violation of the autonomy of a present event), a collapse of the distinction between factuality and actuality (between past and present), and a reduction of being to becoming—all of which implications are not consistent with the expressed tenets of the Whiteheadian system.

As a result of this apparent inconsistency, it is customary for Whiteheadian scholars to interpret past facts as an inert given which provides the context and the resources for the present, and to root all activity in the present event, thereby safeguarding its autonomy. The theses to be developed in this essay are (*a*) that such a reading results from a failure to read Whitehead's accounts of what goes on at the present in a Whiteheadian manner, i.e., as perspectival accounts revealing what is significant from the standpoint of the perspective; and (*b*) that a genuinely Whiteheadian approach to the texts can demonstrate that the classic doctrine of causality is not inconsistent with an epochal theory of time.

In the language of the philosophy of organism, if this essay is to accomplish its objective, it must concern itself with "transition," with that modality of process wherein that which has been aimed at and achieved in the self-creative process of an actual entity transcends its subject to become a datum demanding to be taken into account by future acts of self-creation. I deal, therefore, with the interface between causes and their effects, with the boundary between subjects and objects, with the borderline joining and at the same time separating past and present, and I ask the Hume-provoked question: What goes on at this boundary to guarantee that the past genuinely *acts in* the present, that environment and organism genuinely *interact*, that causality is not simply invariable sequence?

Both the subjective and the objective functioning of an actual entity must be examined if the theoretical possibility of the coherence of a doctrine of efficient causality within the Whiteheadian system is to be established, for the two modes of functioning are so interdependent that neither can be understood in abstraction from the other. To demonstrate that Whitehead *could* have held to a classically interpreted doctrine of causality is not to demonstrate that he in fact did. My theoretical analyses, therefore, must be complemented by further examinations of the texts in search of overt affirmations of a genuine causal relation existing among actual entities. Through this twofold examination, I hope to show not only that Whitehead's understanding of the organism–environment interrelation is consistent with the mainstream of American thought, but also that it provides the metaphysical framework needed to support the more pragmatically oriented theories of Peirce and Dewey.

THE CAUSE–EFFECT INTERFACE: FOUR PERSPECTIVES

A Whiteheadian analysis of the cause–effect interface must be multifaceted and highly complex since, as an interface between two entities, the face it reveals is a function both of the entity from within which it is viewed and of the analytic perspective chosen by the viewer. The Principle of Relativity (see SMW 25)[2] precludes the possibility of an external, privileged vantage point from which "causality-as-such" could be surveyed. As an internal relation binding causes and effects, causality can be examined only from *within* a cause or from *within* an effect. From within each vantage point, the dynamic relation displays different aspects of itself as a function of whether what is conceptually isolated is the activity of the cause (constituting itself as cause by deciding its future effects in its present subjectivity) or the activity of the effect (building the causality of the past into its emerging subjectivity so that it can *be* and be an effect). I interpret these perspectives as intimately related to, if not identifiable with, the four stages in the becoming of an actual entity which Whitehead enumerates in PR 149: datum, process, satisfaction, and decision.

Following Whitehead in affirming that these stages detail features of the growth (i.e., abstractions from an organic unity) and not the growth of the features (i.e., a linear sequence of events within a subject), this study takes the stages as analytic perspectives, as conceptual filters adopted to reveal the complex of aspects factually interfused in the process of prehensive unification whereby an actual entity creates itself as both subject and superject of its experiences. This essay therefore takes Whitehead's account of each stage and isolates how the cause–effect relation appears from the perspective of that stage. Through the use of this device, a metaphysical interpretation of causality can be developed which is more adequate because it is not subject to the limitations imposed by a single perspective.

The Actual Entity as an Effect of the Past: The "Datum" Stage

The root metaphor which colors all aspects of Whitehead's theories regarding actual entities is experience, which he views, not as something which "happens to" a subject, but as that activity which processively constitutes the subject. No connotations of consciousness are to be appended to this basal image. Quite obviously, the conscious experience *is* Whitehead's empirical model; but he is careful to generalize the model so that it interprets all varieties of events, each of which he sees as displaying the same complex interrelations among its elements as the conscious experience does.

Just as a perceptual experience can be examined from the standpoint of the complex of objects perceived, so also the analytic perspective taken in the following pages focuses on the objective content of the more fundamental mode of experience constitutive of an actual entity—on its "given," i.e., the settled past world of accomplished fact. Whitehead describes this given as "irrational, ... brute, ... to be accepted as given" (PR 42), as the "provoker of subsequent experience" (AI 176), as "the definiteness to which our experience has to conform" (PR 215), as "the stubborn fact which at once limits and provides opportunity for the actual entity" (PR 129), as "passing on" (PR 213), and "intervening in processes transcending itself" (PR 220), as "not [allowing] us to think at haphazard" (PR 215) but rather "[laying] a compulsion on the mind, constraining us to think about [it] in a certain way" (PR 215). Yet at the same time he speaks of it as "dead" (PR viii), "passive" (AI 179), "dry bones" (PR 85), maintaining that its "*esse* . . . is *sentiri*" (PR 220). A resolution of the apparent contradiction between these two sets of characterizations of the datum of experience is essential if any case is to be made for the possibility of genuine agency within the framework of the Whiteheadian system; for if the given basis of experience is merely the sort of given which initiates a mathematical demonstration, then causality becomes merely a logical relation of material implication.[3]

The resolution I propose attempts to go between the horns of the dilemma by showing that no single account of the given is to be taken as absolute, that the contradictory descriptions are perspectival accounts relative to the analytic perspective assumed (hence revealing the given *as it appears from that standpoint*), and that the descriptions must therefore be treated as complementary, each remedying the partiality imposed on the other by the limitations of its perspective.

There are several abstractions under which it is entirely correct to style the datum of experience as inert.

1. A datum is rightly to be considered "dead" insofar as it has been "divested of its own *living* immediacy" (PR viii; emphasis added). "Its own process, which is its own *internal existence*, has evaporated, worn out and satisfied" (PR 220; emphasis added). The absolute "for itselfness" with which the entity sought its own identity indeed perishes when that identity is attained; but such an account is abstract unless it is also seen that this "death to self" or "death of self-functioning" is at the same time a resurrection into objective immortality. A subject does not perish into the impotent vacuity of non-existence. Rather, its death marks its transition into a new mode of functioning: the stubbornness of fact which, as a new characterization of the creativity, necessarily conditions all subsequent creatures. Having overcome the private isolation of the moment of self-creation, it can pervade the universe, demanding entrance into all subsequent self-creative experiences, functioning as an "objector" whose "objection" must be heard.

2. From another abstract vantage point, one isolating the formal structure of an individual fact, the inertia of the datum appears again, but under a different guise. Any entity, any act of experience, is the togetherness of the universe from its perspective, a togetherness which is not *mere* conjunction but a complex, aesthetic, fully determinate, graded configuration—a togetherness in the unity of an intricate pattern which can be conceptually isolated. This pattern—a form or eternal object—is truly passive: a pure potential incapable of exercising anything other than final causality, a possible having no genuine agency inasmuch as only actual entities can be causes. That Whitehead intends this position to be viewed as an abstraction is obvious. He maintains that "each fact is more than its forms. . . . The definiteness of fact is due to its forms; but the individual fact is a creature, and creativity is the ultimate behind all forms, inexplicable by forms and conditioned by its creatures" (PR 20). A fact is a complex configuration in which the élan of the universe takes form. As a *configuration*, it is inert; but as a creature of the creativity, it bears the dynamism of creative activity.

3. When the datum is considered as an individual fact in isolation from the nexus of facts constituting the past of any self-creative process, it again appears inert. When the self-functioning of an actual entity evaporates, "worn out and satisfied" (PR 220), the creative activity passes over to the situation, to the complex of data which is at the same time the actual world *for*, and the dative phase *of*, a newly emerging creature and is, hence, the creativity of and for the new creature.

> This basic situation, this actual world, this primary phase, this real potentiality—however you characterize it—is as a whole active with its inherent creativity, but in its details, it provides the passive objects which derive their activity from the creativity of the whole. . . .

> Thus viewed in abstraction, objects are passive, but viewed in conjunction they carry the creativity which drives the world [AI 179].

Thus again the passivity of objects, of the dative content of experience, results from the abstractness of a viewpoint which perforce "murders" so that it can "dissect." In the concrete, objects never *are* other than "in conjunction," and hence are foundationally active.

Whitehead himself warns the reader that although "datum" and "object" etymologically imply "being given to" and "lying in the way of," "both words suffer from the defect of suggesting that an occasion of experiencing arises out of a *passive* situation which is a mere welter of data" (AI 179; emphasis added). He remedies that defect by his more concrete, alternative formulations of the mode of being of an object, all of which imply that that mode of being is, to borrow a term from Charles Sanders Peirce, "insistence." When only the objective content of the experience is under scrutiny, the source of the insistence is not revealed. Hence it is characterizable only as stubborn, brute, intervening, constraining, as an irrational provoker demanding that experience conform to it. It is this action, coupled with the subject's initial conformation to the demand, which is "essentially the primary phase of a new occasion" (AI 179).

The Actual Entity as Self-Causing Creature: The Stage of "Process"

When "process" becomes the perspective from which the cause–effect relation is analyzed, the self-functioning of an actual entity—its subjective activity of structuring an objective content (its data) into the unity of an experience—assumes the foreground position in the discussion. The full details of the self-creative "transition from datum to issue" (MT 131) are irrelevant to the purposes of this essay. It is of central importance, however, to a discussion of causality that the discussion include a thorough examination: (*a*) of the initial phase[4] of the process—the phase in which each item in the objective content of an experience becomes a private, subjectively formed aspect involved in the unity of that experience; and (*b*) of the process of "feeling" through which this subjectification of objects is accomplished, which feelings stand to their objects as effect to cause.

The problem to be solved via subjective functioning is the transformation of each public datum, fully determinate in itself (but indeterminate as to the mode of its incorporation into the emerging subject), into an internal relation between the subject and that datum, a relation which is determinate, private, and coordinated with all other internal relations established with all other items in the data. The determinacy, the haecceity, of an individual datum is precisely the obstacle which must be overcome if an object is to be capable of functioning in subjective process. It is the "this-ness" of an object in terms of which it ob-jects, i.e., throws itself in the way of a subsequent subject as a stubborn, obstructive fact provoking that subject to take its factuality into account. The subject's response is the activity whereby an aspect of the "this" becomes the mode under which the object will function in the growing determinacy of the subject.

Thus, a highly complex, "doubled" activity lies at the root of the object–subject relation: (1) on the side of the past subject, a transcendent decision of what it shall be for the future, a "cutting out" of those aspects of its unitary self (aspects or "objectifications" whose unity is that unitary self) through which it will function in the future; and (2) on the side of the emerging subject, an immanent decision whereby (a) one of those intertwined aspects is selected as the functioning objectification in the emerging subject, and (b) the other possible objectifications are "eliminated." Corresponding to each activity is a passivity to be distinguished in the other pole. The active, anticipatory decision of the past subject (its "giving," its super-jection) finds a correlative passivity in an emerging subject: its "subjection," its receptivity, its responsivity, its passive conformation to what is given. The active selection–elimination decision of the emerging subject (its subjectification) finds a correlative passivity in each datum: its real potentiality for transcendent functioning in a new subject (its objectivity, its given-ness). Each activity takes place in the immediacy of the subjective process of the correlative subject.

Each activity—and from a certain perspective, each passivity— is a feeling, an emotional grasp, a concrete fact of relatedness among subjects each of which is the synthetic unity of its own feelings. The nature of objectification and feeling vis-à-vis a subject's transcendent decision will be discussed later. My concern here is with the role these activities play in the immanent decisions whereby a subject binds itself to its past by feeling that past into its emerging subjectivity.[5]

From the viewpoint of these initial bonding activities—of these initial "physical" feelings—the data to be bonded are grasped as a "multiplicity of private centres of feeling" (PR 212), as subjects each of which is a "feeler" (i.e., the synthetic unity of its own feelings) to be felt not in its private unity but under an abstraction from that unity—*one* of its feelings. "The feelings are felt as belonging to the external centres, and are not absorbed into the private immediacy" (PR 212). What it means to feel a feeling as alien, as belonging to "another," to an "external centre," becomes, therefore, the central interpretative issue.

The adjectives Whitehead uses to characterize these initial feelings point the way toward the meaning sought: "vector," "conformal," "repetitive," "reenactive." The feelings are vectors in the physical science sense of the term: they bear as part of their character in the here–now the fact of their origination in the there–then. Only through subsequent "mental" feelings which "value" the initial feelings with respect to the importance they will have in the experience of the emerging subject does the scalar overwhelm the vector. Until that point has been reached, feelings conform to, re-enact, and repeat their vector origins, thereby bearing the past into the present.

But to what do they conform? What do they re-enact? What do they repeat? Whitehead responds: the subjective form of the feeling felt, that which stamped it as a feeling *belonging* to its subject, "*how* that subject [felt] that objective datum" (PR 221). But does to conform, to re-enact, to repeat a subjective form mean merely to abstract the form from the past feeling and to use it to structure a present feeling? If it does, then an actual entity is merely a stage play about the world and not its "cumulation." Discovering the appropriate significance of re-enaction demands further examination of the concrete fact of relatedness called physical feeling, and likewise requires a more detailed account of the nature of a subjective form and of the manner of its entry into processes transcending its subject.

In its general sense, physical feeling is "the term used for the basic generic operation of passing from the objectivity of the data to the subjectivity of the actual entity in question" (PR 40). Feelings are "variously specialized operations effecting a transition into subjectivity" (PR 40–41). They are, therefore, relational activities caught in their activity of relating. Furthermore, as dynamic relations, they exhibit a complex constitution analyzable into the five factors Whitehead details in PR 224.[6] Of these, the fifth—the subjective form—is the critical factor vis-à-vis the issue under discussion. As its name implies, the subjective form of a feeling has to do with the feeling's private, personalizing aspect. It denotes an emerging entity's reaction to the influence of the data, the reaction through which the scalar begins to overwhelm the vector, through which the immediacy of the here–now begins to assume dominance over the there–then, through which novelty initiates its conquest of repetition, through which final causality gradually wrests primacy from efficient causality. A subjectively formed feeling may have "reproductive reference to the data" but is "not wholly structured by them" (PR 223). The private aspect of the structuring is induced by the subject's aim to achieve the fully determinate unity of its identity; hence no subjective form can be torn from the unity of its subject, since that unity pervades it. "The datum is felt with that subjective form in order that the subject may be the superject which it is" (PR 233). As the multiple feelings initiating the emergence of the subjective feeler progressively grow together into the final unity of a determinate feeler, the subjective forms become richer, more personal, more inextricable from each other, until they are intertwined fully and determinately in the emotional complex which is the subjective form of the "satisfied" subject.

In abstraction from a feeling which it subjectively structures, a subjective form is merely that—a form, a complex pattern of interrelated patterns: (1) a pattern of qualities, (2) a pattern of intensities, (3) a reproductive pattern, and (4) a valuation. When a feeling is re-enacted, conformed to, repeated, it is this complex of patterns, as already *realized* in the feeling felt, which is repeated in the emerging subject, which structures its physical feeling of the objective datum. The feeling reproduces not merely the qualitative and quantitative patterns in the feeling felt but its valuation as well, i.e., the importance of the feeling in the determinacy of the past subject.

The interpretive problem alluded to earlier opens up at this juncture: the temptation to conceptualize the re-enaction in terms of an emerging subject "abstracting" a universal from a particular and "entertaining" that universal in its own subjectivity. The thesis of this essay is that an emerging subject's activity of feeling a past feeling, of admitting it as a concrete relational fact re-enacted in its present, is to be interpreted, not as "copying" a pattern separable from the feeling it patterned, but as allowing that relational activity to act again. The difference between the two interpretations is the difference between conceptualizing the impact of a falling brick in the equations of Newtonian mechanics and reeling from it. The former experience yields only the quantitative and qualitative patterns of the action and reaction and is equally applicable to all analogous events. The latter experience testifies both to the causal efficacy of the brick re-enacted in its effect (the feeling subject) and to the subject's appropriation of that causality (the pain). Whitehead himself maintains that "this transference of feeling effects a partial identification of cause and effect, and no mere *representation* of the cause. . . . It is a feeling *from* the cause which acquires the subjectivity of the new effect without loss of its original subjectivity in the cause" (PR 237–38). The feeling felt is genuinely re-enacted, not "entertained"; through the partial identification (partial because it is an *aspect* of the alien subject which functions in the emerging subject), the alien subject "acts again" in the immediacy of the emerging subject.

The second part of the temptation is more subtle: the temptation to view a subjective form as a universal. Although what is felt and re-enacted in a conformal feeling is another feeling, an abstraction from the fully determinate unity of feelings constituting the alien subject, the "abstraction" is as particular as the subject from which it was abstracted. In the language of the previous example, the impact of the falling brick and the resulting painful reeling bear within themselves the concrete particularity of *this* falling of *this* brick. If a subjectively formed feeling lacks "this-ness," then physical feeling becomes merely feeling the vague presence of a faceless past and not feeling the feeling of a determinate and alien other. Under the former interpretation, the Whiteheadian system falls apart. To support the latter interpretation it is essential to reiterate that it is a subjectively formed *feeling* that is re-enacted in an emerging subject, not merely a complex pattern, and to elucidate *how* a feeling is more than its forms.

There is, in Peirce's language, a "secondness" about a feeling, an unintelligible aspect not expressible in terms of forms. This surd which eludes formal analysis is the "insistence" of the feeling, the dynamic stubbornness of a "this" whose brute individuality demands entry into the relevant future. If, as Whitehead maintains, "the fundamental example of the notion 'quality inhering in a particular substance' is afforded by 'subjective form inhering in feeling'" (PR 232), then what is this non-formal aspect of a feeling which gives the feeling both its haecceity and its insistence? What is it that the form forms? To give the question more classic expression: What is the principle of individuation?

Whitehead's general response—the creativity—is not particularly illuminating, because the creativity resembles the One of Plotinus, in that it is beyond predication, all predicates being instances of it. There is, however, another language Whitehead uses which, if adopted, sheds light on this foundational energy of the universe and suggests a philosophically interesting resolution to the above questions: the language of emotion. "Feeling," "satisfaction," "enjoyment," "eros," "appetite," "passion," "aversion," and the like are obvious instances of his curious use of psychological terms to express ontological phenomena. These instances are themselves specifications of the more general term "emotion" which, in several passages, Whitehead uses to denote the basal element in actuality:

> The basis of experience is emotional. . . . [T]he basic fact is the rise of an affective tone originating from things whose relevance is given [AI 176].

> The primitive form of physical experience is emotional—blind emotion, . . . sympathy, . . . feeling the feeling in another, and feeling conformally with another [PR 162].

> Life is the enjoyment of emotion [MT 229].

> The unity of emotion, which is the unity of the present occasion, is a patterned texture of values [MT 230].

> The more primitive mode of objectification is via emotional tone [PR 141].

> Feeling appropriates elements of the universe, which themselves are other than the subject; and absorbs these elements into the real internal constitution of its subject by synthesizing them into the unity of an emotional pattern expressive of its own subjectivity [PR 275].

The inescapable and deliberate ambiguity involved in the term "feeling" is rendered patently obvious in these extracts. A feeling is simultaneously a grasp (prehension) and an emotion. In the former sense, it "touches" the data; in the latter, it emotionally responds to them. Inasmuch as what are felt in the data are themselves feelings, the "touching" is at the same time a "being touched by." Conformation, re-enaction, repetition represent subjective passion "received as felt elsewhere in another occasion and conformally appropriated" (PR 162). Thus, a "flow of feelings" (PR 237), a current of emotion, binds the past into the present. Each feeling is a subjectively formed emotion, a determinate emotion belonging to the emotional complex of a determinate subject which is the final "unity of emotion" (MT 230) emerging from the intertwining of its feelings and pervading each feeling. Subjective forms are, therefore, patterns (a) rendering determinate and (b) individuated by the foundational dynamism of the universe: emotion.

The term itself is enormously pregnant with shades and aspects of meaning which do much to clarify what goes on at the interface between successive entities. In the first place, the very etymology of the word is both significant and revealing: *movere*, "to move," plus *e*, "out of." Emotion is a dynamism which by its very nature transcends the subject experiencing it. As Whitehead expresses it, "the notion of 'passing on' is more fundamental than that of a private individual fact" (PR 213). E-motion is the élan of the creativity "in the dictionary sense of the word *creare*, 'to bring forth, beget, produce'" (PR 213). Again, "the creativity of the world is the throbbing emotion of the past hurling itself into a new transcendent fact. It is the flying dart . . . hurled beyond the bounds of the world" (AI 177).

In the second place, emotion carries within it a connotation of "being affected by" as well as "effecting," of passion as well as action. Unless they are pathogenic, emotions have objects which provoke them; emotions are subjective reactions to the impress of objective facts, reactions that are internal to the subject, that are enjoyed in the incommunicable immediacy of subjective functioning.

In the language of time, an emotion is an interfusion of past and future at the present: an activity of the past reacted to in the immediacy of a present which by its own inner dynamism translates itself into action in and on the future. "An emotion transcends the present in two ways. It issues from, and it issues towards. It is received, it is enjoyed, and it is passed along, from moment to moment" (MT 229). A feeling felt is the flying dart imbedding itself in the texture of the present, to be absorbed in the present immediacy of an emotion which hurls it at the future.

Emotion can be taken, therefore, as Whitehead's alternative language for the creative energy which drives the universe. It is what is transmitted from occasion to occasion in a causal route, transmitted as formed, as subjectively formed, and as subjectively formed causal activity. The transmission of the energy is continuous (because of the continuity of subjective form in the energy route) yet epochal (since it is enjoyed under quantum conditions). The interface at which the transmission occurs appears from the side of the emerging subject (the effect) as a conformation—re-enaction of emotional energy subjectively formed in and received from the past, coupled with the absorption of that alien energy into the subjective immediacy of an emerging subject through the arising of mental functioning. To view the interface from the side of the completed subject (the cause), I must shift to the analytic perspective of the two final stages of an actual entity.

The Actual Entity as Self-Caused Creature: The Stage of "Satisfaction"

A subject has satisfied the creative urge dominating its becoming when it has reached the unity of one fully determinate feeling which expresses that subject's way of housing, experiencing, and enjoying all facts. "Something" has become, that something involving "repetition transformed into [the] novel immediacy" (PR 136–37) in which the entity achieves "satisfaction": the moment of closure, of absolute self-enjoyment, which is "the ultimate fact, individual to the entity" (PR 84).

> In the conception of an actual entity in its phase of satisfaction, the entity has attained its individual separation from other things; it has absorbed the datum, and it has not yet lost itself in the swing back to the "decision" whereby its appetition [toward the physical realization of what it conceptually grasps] becomes an element in the data of other entities superseding it. Time has stood still—if only it could [PR 154].

That Whitehead expresses the "standing still" of time as a velleity rather than as a fact is prima facie evidence that any consideration of the satisfaction in and for itself is a high-order abstraction. The stage of satisfaction examines "the 'entity as concrete' abstracted from the 'process of concrescence,' . . . the outcome separated from the process, thereby losing the actuality of the atomic entity, which is both process and outcome" (PR 84). This abstraction can be imaged as the point in the accompanying figure at which the vectors from the past mutually intersect, through which they pass to become vectors for the future.

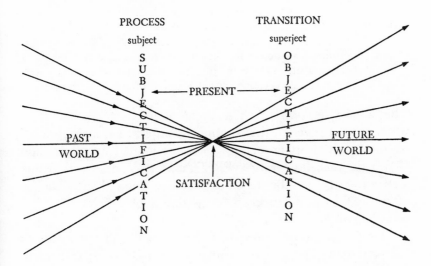

As abstracted from the self-creative process, it "never really is"; as immersed in the process, it is the interface between subject and superject, an interface with no temporal extensity and hence no existence.[7] If its abstract character be borne in mind, however, an examination of the stage of satisfaction can enrich the ongoing discussion of the cause–effect relation.

It has already been seen that a subject houses the actualities of its past by re-enacting a multiplicity of past feelings each of which transfers a past item into its present subjective immediacy. The important question to be asked is: Is it *only* the past which is vivified in a subject's present? If so, then the life history of an enduring object—of a personally ordered thread of actual entities—has a discontinuity inherent in it. The present ruptures past from future rather than "futuring" the past. Whitehead's point is that the future has *objective* reality in the present (PR 214) because the goal aimed at in subjective process is, *not* the subject in its self-centered satisfaction, but rather that subject as alive in the future—which is to say, as objectively immortal, as functioning in future subjects. The present subject

> bears in its own essence the relationship [its feelings] it will have to the future. It thereby includes in its essence the necessities to which the future must conform. The future is there in the present, as a general fact belonging to the nature of things. It is also there with each general determination as it lies in the nature of the particular present to impose on the particular future which must succeed it. All this belongs to the essence of the present, and constitutes the future, as thus determined, an object for prehension in the subjective immediacy of the present. . . . Thus the future is to the present as an object for a subject. It has objective existence in the present [AI 194–95].

The subjective form of these prehensions (a subjective form which is interwoven in the emotional complex) is "anticipation," an aim "at intensity of feeling (a) in the immediate subject and (b) *in the relevant future*" (PR 27; emphasis added). This subjective form is the subject's emotional realization of the principle of relativity: that "it belongs to the nature of a 'being' that is a potential for every 'becoming' " (PR 22).

The key to the possibility of the immanence of the future in the present is the arising of mentality in subjective process. Physical feelings can feel only the fully determinate entities of the past, can relate only to achieved actuality; whereas it is of the essence of mentality that it relate to the partially indeterminate, to forms,[8] to the possible ways in which the multiplicity of physically felt facts could be structured into subjective unity.[9]

Mental functioning does not originate *in vacuo*, but arises from physical functioning. In a metaphysical as well as an epistemic sense, *nihil est in intellectu quod non prius fuerit in sensu*. A physical feeling is inevitably followed by a feeling grasping (registering) and evaluating the subjective form structuring the received causality.[10] The registered form is grasped as a possible, i.e., as a form whose actualization in the received causality does not exhaust its possibility for further actualization. Thus pure physical feeling (the re-enaction of one of the cause's feelings) becomes hybrid physical feeling (the grasp of the formal structure of the feeling as the formal structure of *that* feeling), which passes over into pure conceptual feeling (the feeling of the structuring form as a possibility for realization in the present and in the relevant future). With mentality, appetite enters the universe—a subject's response to the lure of the forms, which thereby entice (rather than compel) their realization. "Whether or not there be conceptual novelty, the subjective forms of the conceptual prehensions constitute the drive of the universe [its emotional energy], whereby each occasion precipitates itself into the future" (AI 194). Mental functioning provides the "principle of unrest" (PR 32) in terms of which realized fact inexorably transcends its immediate realization toward future realizations of what "is not but may be" (PR 32). "The point to remember is that the fact that each individual occasion is transcended by the creative urge, belongs to the essential constitution of each such occasion" (AI 193). The future trajectory of the received vector is immanent in and decided by the present occasion.

This "drive of the universe," this "principle of unrest," this private appetite for public immortality is what negates all possibility of the endurance of the satisfaction, of its *esse* being anything other than *sentiri*. In its full determinateness, it obstructs, lies in the way of, and prevents the realization of itself in the future. Hence its fully determinate unity perishes so that the subject can become the flying dart, "stubborn and with unavoidable consequences" (PR 219). Immediacy of self-enjoyment must yield to objective agency. The perishing of immediacy is precisely the entity's "assumption of a new metaphysical function in the creative advance of the universe" (AI 204). Thus, perishing is not so much a tragedy an entity falls passive victim to as its self-initiated shift to a new mode of activity. It is a beginning, not an end; an existential culmination, not an existential frustration. It marks the subject's entrance into objective immortality as a functioning agent.

The Actual Entity as Cause: The Stage of "Decision"

As a result of the perishing of a subject's satisfaction, the subjects beyond it can appropriate its achievements, can affirm "it is mine." "But the possession imposes conformation" (PR 82) to decisions made in the immediacy of the perished subject, which decisions throw the flying darts of vector feelings at the future and constitute the thrower as *super*-ject as well as *sub*-ject.

It is the thesis of the ensuing pages that the superject cannot be interpreted as dead, as static, as inert. My position, succinctly stated, is that "superject" is both a noun *and* an active verb. Therefore, the "throw" (or decision) which forms part of the determinateness of the perished subject *is* the emotional energy conformed to and re-enacted by the emerging subject. However, the language of "throw" has implications suggesting a linear sequence of throw and catch—which implications I disavow. The idea central to my interpretation of Whitehead at this point (an idea which will have to be elaborated and defended) is that the throw and the catch are the same essential dynamism viewed from two different perspectives—the perspectives of the subjects involved in the transaction. As I have said earlier, it is impossible to take a third, privileged perspective which would subsume the two, thereby allowing us to speak impartially about the intersubjective relation, because the universe can be viewed *only* from *within* the perspective of an actual entity.

From the analytic perspective taken in this section, the superject is the public unity of its throws, dated and located in a particular quantum of space–time, with its own particular identity and definiteness. It is a public datum thrown forward to superseding entities. This thrown character is the *terminus ad quem* of the subjective process, the self-realized fact aimed at and hence immanent in and conditioning each phase of subjective process. Whitehead is insistent that subject and superject cannot be torn apart save in high-order abstraction. In the concrete, each is what the other makes it to be; hence neither has any reality in abstraction from the other. The interfusion of both gives the actual entity its self-functioning (formal reality) and its causal functioning in the future (objective reality).

The link inseparably joining the two modes of functioning is to be found in the mental functioning of the subject–superject. It has already been alluded to that conceptual feelings initiate an appetite for the physical realization of what is conceptually grasped. This appetite takes the form of anticipation, with "this decisive result, that the entity arises as an effect facing its past and ends as a cause facing its future" (AI 193–94). Future entities that experience the future-facing cause experience it as anticipating (i.e., as seizing in advance) its re-enaction. In this sense, the anticipation is self-fulfilling prophecy, for the anticipation "causes" the re-enaction to take place by laying upon superseding subjects the obligation to take it into account. Viewed from the standpoint of the datum stage, this anticipation takes the form of the stubbornness with which the data of experience present themselves. The question relevant to the standpoint assumed in the stage of decision has to do with the relation between the objective functioning anticipated and the self-creative process.

Since subjective process is a growing together of feelings (a concresence), it is only in terms of those feelings that the objective career of a subject is carried on. Hence the immanent decisions involved in a subject's selective objectification of its past are at the same time decisions *for* the transcendent future. As the subjective forms of the initial feelings develop beyond their initial character as subjective re-enactments of objective personalities, they progressively acquire an emotional tone expressive of their future orientation. The alien feelings, originally felt as anticipating their own future realization, become realized feelings in a new subject, feelings which themselves bear the appetite for transcendent embodiment, an anticipation which lays the re-enactment obligation on the future. "Feelings pass into appetition, which is the feeling of determinate relevance to a world about to be" (PR 163).

A further decision is involved, therefore, a decision which specifies that relevance and hence qualifies the obligation. The decision resulting in selective objectification is a decision based on relevance received; hence it is a decision ratifying that received relevance. In a very real sense, this decision is not so much made *by* the emerging subject as made *for* it by each fact it feels in its actual world. The focus of this section must be the decision transmitted and the character of that decision such that (1) it is relevant to superseding occasions (i.e., is coordinated with a nexus of other decisions likewise made for the entities of the future); and (2) it lays an obligation on the superseding entities (i.e., functions causally within them).

The coordination of decisions made by subjects each immersed in the privacy of its subjective process is easily groundable in the partial (yet mutual) immanence of their actual worlds and the consequently shared order in the background from which they arise. It is the second aspect of the transcendent decision which is central to the present discussion. The relevant question is: What is the ground of obligation?[11] The answer developed in response to this question will lead directly into the terminal focus of this essay: the nature of that transfer of energy called efficient causality.

It has already been shown that the immanent decision is the selection of a past feeling to be re-enacted in the present. The transcendent decision is, not an additional decision, but a decisive modification or series of modifications of the immanent decision, modifications which turn the immanent decision away from the past and toward the future. As is the case with all future-oriented activity, it is mental rather than physical functioning which assumes dominance—in this instance, the type termed "valuation." The subjectively formed emotions re-enacted in the physical feelings are evaluated with respect to their relative importance in the subjectivity of the immediate present and the relevant future. (The element normative of these evaluations is the determinate subjective identity sought in the subjectification process—the "subjective aim.") The net result of the evaluations is the grading of the dative feelings in degrees of importance, some being "valued up," i.e., admitted as significant elements in the identity of the subject (which significance itself is graded), others being "valued down," i.e., admitted in varying degrees of triviality, or positively eliminated as irrelevant. "Thus, the conceptual feeling with its valuation has primarily the character of a purpose, since it is the agent whereby the decision is made as to the causal efficacy of its subject in its objectifications beyond itself" (PR 254). Mental functioning, in deciding the importance of its objective data *for* the subject and *in* the subject, ensures that that data will be transmitted *beyond* the subject with a stamp of importance obliging its re-enaction.

It must be pointed out, however, that obligation is moral necessity and not brute force, and that subsequent to the obligatory re-enactment of transmitted valuations in superseding subjects, re-enactions which admit the valued data into those subjects with the same degree of importance with which they were clothed in the past subjects, those valuations are revalued from the new subjective perspectives, wherein the received valuations can undergo significant modifications or be rejected entirely. In this way, Whitehead can safeguard the autonomous creativity of the present and thereby avoid a "block universe," without at the same time cutting that creativity off from the creative accomplishments of the past and thereby creating a neo-Leibnizean monad.

Conclusion:
Whitehead's Doctrine of Causal Efficacy

If anything has emerged from the complexity of the foregoing pages, it is that the key element involved in developing a theory of genuine efficient causation from the Whiteheadian corpus is the physical feeling. The analyses have been complex out of a necessity imposed by the kind of relativism unique to the philosophy of organism, a relativism which asserts that no item in the universe is "simply located," i.e., capable of being or being examined in isolation from the rest of the universe. Although Whitehead carefully escapes the Bradleyan position that therefore to know anything one must know everything, nevertheless, if the Whiteheadian system is to be self-referential, then no *single* account of a phenomenon can be taken as complete. I have therefore been compelled to mount a four-pronged investigation of physical feeling, seeing those aspects of it revealed when it is considered as the datum for subjective feeling, those aspects it displays when it is considered as a subjective re-enaction of that datum, those aspects revealed when its functioning in the completed subject is under scrutiny, and those aspects which appear only when it is viewed in its transcendent functioning.

When these four aspects are "thought together," when these four perspectives are reunited, it is possible to interpret a physical feeling as an interface between successive subjects, between past and present—as a locus of transition which is as much an element in the past as it is an element in the present, as much an activity of a past subject as it is of a present subject. It can be seen as an "overlap" where past and present can interfuse without each losing its identity and autonomy. In other words, as a result of the preceding analyses, I have established the *theoretical* grounds for the attribution of a doctrine of efficient causality to Whitehead. What remains is to determine if Whitehead's writings give any evidence testifying that he actually DID hold such a doctrine.

That he considers causality a factual relation rather than a logical category is obvious from the texts. "All agency is confined to actuality. . . . The very meaning of existence is 'to be a factor in agency'" (AI 197). "No element in fact is ineffectual" (PR 517). The ontological principle restricts the exercise of causality to actual entities: "to search for a reason is to search for an actual entity" (PR 24). Each actual entity "arises as an effect facing its past and ends as a cause facing its future" (AI 193–94). Furthermore, by "to cause" he clearly means "to condition," not "to be a condition." (The latter sense reduces causality to material implication.) He clearly uses the term as a verb, not as a noun. "One occasion . . . *conditions* the formation of a successor" (MT 225). An occasion of experience "conditions the creativity," "lays an obligation on the future," etc. Finally, the conditioning activity spoken of is to be interpreted as the immanence of the cause in the effect, not as the transference of a quality from cause to effect.

> The mere notion of transferring a quality is unintelligible. Suppose two occurrences may in fact be detached so that one of them is comprehensible without reference to the other. Then all notions of causation between them, or of conditioning, become unintelligible. There is . . . no reason why the possession of any quality by one of them should in any way influence the possession of that quality, or of any other quality, by the other. . . . The only intelligible doctrine of causation is founded on the doctrine of immanence [MT 225–26].

This immanence is, moreover, an active immanence, not the immanence of one entity merely lodged in another. An actual entity *houses* its world; it does not take in lodgers.

This immanence of a cause in its effect, though complete to the point of partial identification (PR 237), is such as to preserve the subjectivity of both. To think this identity in diversity is difficult without the right sort of illustrative model. Whitehead himself provides such models: one drawn from the experience of perception (PR 81), the other borrowed from Hume and used to criticize Hume's reduction of causality from an existential relation to a subjective habit of anticipation (PR 147ff.). An examination of these models proves beyond a reasonable doubt that Whitehead overtly holds the classic conception of the causal relation.

The first illustration is situated in the context of Whitehead's presentation of his theory of perception. The details of the theory are irrelevant to our purposes. What is relevant is his insistence on three distinct yet interrelated modes: perception in the mode of causal efficacy, perception in the mode of presentational immediacy, and perception in the mode of symbolic reference. The presentational mode is Humean perception: the vivid display of the contemporary environment, a display accomplished by sensa contributed by bodily functioning in the immediate past. This mode reveals nothing about the world save its geometry. On the other hand, perception in the causal mode yields a vague sense of controlling presences, a vague awareness of derivation from the past, a vague experience of causal influence.[12]

Maintaining that the causal mode is the most primitive (probably shared differentially by all life forms), he characterizes the experience in the following images:

> In the dark, there are vague presences, doubtfully feared; in the silence, the irresistible causal efficacy of nature presses itself upon us; in the vagueness of the low hum of insects in an August woodland, the inflow into ourselves of feelings from enveloping nature overwhelms us; in the dim consciousness of half-sleep, the presentations of sense fade away and we are left with the vague feelings of influences from vague things around us [PR 176].

Causality and perception in this mode are two faces of the same coin: causation, the streaming of vaguely differentiated influences from vaguely differentiated, alien others into the subjective present; perception, the vague but active illumination of those influences in and as the conscious present. The experience is dim, heavy with emotion, easily pushed into the background of awareness by the vivid displays of the presentational mode of perception; nevertheless they are a component in the perceptual experience. The clearest manifestation of this experience of influence can be found with respect to the more proximate causal influences brought to bear on the conscious perceiver by the activities of his own body in the immediate past, influences vaguely perceived as productive of present experience. This "feeling the body as functioning" (PR 81), this "feeling of derived feeling" (PR 81), is the perceiver's awareness of derivation from his body. In more concrete language, it is the perceiver's full awareness of the fact that he sees *with* his eyes and *because of* his eyes. It is his consciousness of the fact that the causality of the eyes is, not an item in a dead past merely remembered, but the active functioning of the past in the immediacy of the present. The eyes are experienced as *acting in* the present, compelling the perceiver to see and to see these sights: i.e., compelling a re-enaction of a past actuality under an aspect of itself (in this case, the sensa produced by the eye and stubbornly given) which transfers the eye as cause into the present, where it causes. Whitehead's own example, if taken seriously, testifies to the fact that he intends us to construe re-enaction, not as "instant replay," but as the "acting again" of a cause in its effect: its *causing*.

Whitehead's second example of causal functioning as experienced in the causal mode of perception reveals not only that component of perceptual experience contributed by the functioning of the end organ, but also the received causality which the end organ subjectively appropriates and transmits. Just as perception is not merely perception of the functioning of the end organ, so an account of the causal situation cannot be described in terms of a single cause and its proximate effect. The concrete, causal situation is describable only in terms of chains of causal transmission in the past, chains which culminate in the present effect and press beyond it into the future. The illustrative model Whitehead uses is that of a man reacting to a blinding flash of light via the reflex action of closing his eyes. The flash is the dominant element in one "drop of perception"; the eye closure, in the next. In a still later moment, the subject instinctively expresses this succession of experiences as "the flash *made* me blink" (see PR 175). He testifies to the character of the blinking episode as a *compulsion*, an irresistible activity of one event in a subsequent event. The flash, though no longer existent in the immediacy of its self-functioning, is objectively immortal in the compulsion producing the blink. Furthermore, the man expressing the flash–blink sequence feels within himself an analogous compulsion: to report the experience as it actually happened and not to say "I blinked because I felt like it" or "I blinked because a camel flew into my eye." The impulse to "tell the truth," although a moral compulsion, is nevertheless a *com*-pulsion: an experience of simultaneous undergoing and doing linked as cause and effect, an awareness of the "immanence of the past *energizing* in the present" (AI 188; emphasis added). On the basis of his own examples, that Whitehead holds to the classic conception of causality is patently obvious.

His interpretation of that conception is cast in the framework of the doctrine of feelings elaborated earlier. The act of causation is the simple physical feeling. "The actual entity which is the initial datum is the 'cause,' the simple physical feeling is the 'effect,' and the subject entertaining the simple physical feeling is the actual entity conditioned by the effect" (PR 236). The actual entity which is the initial datum is related to the physical feeling as cause to effect (1) insofar as the feeling felt is an element in the constitution of that initial datum (one of its anticipatory feelings, its feeling of its future action in its subsequent effects); and (2) insofar as the present feeling which is compelled to re-enact that anticipatory feeling is thereby effected by it, given form by that which compels it to take form. The interface, the overlap between successive entities, is the identity of a feeling in the "now" of the cause—its decisive grasp of its future functioning—with a feeling in the "now" of subject conditioned by that decision—one of its initial physical feelings. The reading this essay gives Whitehead's doctrine is that these feelings are "two" only in appearance, that *in fine* they are the same dynamic relational fact viewed from within the perspective of each of the involved subjects. Thus, what goes on at this interface is a genuine transaction between past environment and present organism, between present organism and future environment. The simple physical feeling is the mechanism through which creative transaction initiates, energizes, and finds future immortality. It is this emotion, this "moving out of," which, as conformally re-enacted, decisively subjectified, and causally superjected, grounds the dynamic, cumulative, organic character of temporal transition, and in so doing provides the metaphysical basis for the ongoing interaction between organism and environment which is the central theme of American philosophy.

NOTES

1. Or perhaps *because* he was British by birth and hence heir to the same philosophical traditions transplanted to these shores by the early colonists, where those traditions took root, adapted to a pioneer environment, and brought forth an American fruit.

2. Those works of Whitehead's which will be cited are:

AI   *Adventures of Ideas* (New York: Free Press, 1967)
MT   *Modes of Thought* (New York: Capricorn, 1958)
PR   *Process and Reality*, corr. ed., edd. David Ray Griffin and Donald W. Sherburne (New York: Free Press, 1978)
SMW   *Science and the Modern World* (New York: Free Press, 1967).

3. Those who argue for the inertia of the given do so for very good reasons. They seek to affirm and safeguard the autonomy of the self-creative process of an actual entity. But they achieve their goal by rendering impotent the very entity which emerges from that process as a new "one" added to the environing "many."

4. Just as Whitehead is inconsistent with respect to the number of perspectives from which an actual entity can be "genetically divided" (i.e., analyzed with respect to its becoming), he is likewise inconsistent with respect to his use of the language of "stage" and "phase." To avoid unnecessary confusion, this essay will use "stage" in the sense of major analytical perspective, and "phase" in the sense of sub-stage.

5. The language of "bond" or "relation" is as misleading as it is unavoidable, because English is incapable of coping with internal relatedness. "Relation" inevitably connotes two autonomous relata and a bond joining them. For Whitehead, however, a relation is the immanence of one entity functioning in the constitution of another.

6. These five factors are "(i) the 'subject' which feels, (ii) the 'initial data' which are felt, (iii) the 'elimination' in virtue of negative prehensions, (iv) the 'objective datum' which is felt, (v) the 'subjective form' which is *how* that subject feels that objective datum" (PR 221).

7. The quantum of time actualized by an actual entity is the subject-superject, not the satisfaction.

8. Whose essence is the possibility for further determination.

9. To speak of "mental" or "conceptual" functioning is in no way to imply that the entity involved in such functioning is conscious. Mental functioning is to be construed as the more general activity of grasping or admitting forms as structuring principles.

10. In a low-grade entity, the registration and ratification of received forms and valuations constitute the totality of mental functioning. Hence such entities merely transmit what they receive as they receive it. But as more complex environments permit more elaborate mental functioning, the door opened by primitive mentality widens to encompass all types of conceptual activity, from simple physical purposes to the complexities of conscious judgment.

11. In using the language of obligation, I do not wish to imply that *first* the obligation is established and *then* it is obeyed: i.e., that activities are involved which are separate (*a*) in the sense of being temporally successive, or (*b*) in the sense of being numerically two. The thesis being developed

here is that the transcendent decision of one actuality and the immanent decision of an immediately superseding actuality are the same decision, the same activity of "cutting off," the same dynamic transition, viewed from alternate sides.

12. Symbolic reference, the normal mode of human perception, is the synthesis of these two modes, with one being related to the other as symbol to object.